DATE DUE

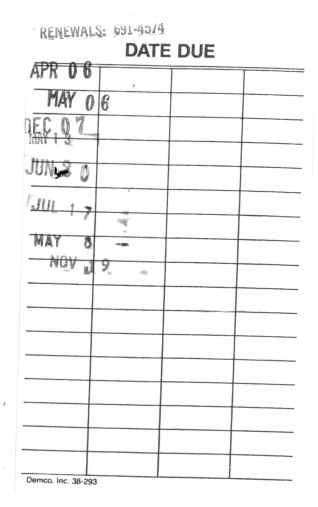

APR 0 6			
MAY 0 6			
DEC 07			
JUN 2 0			
JUL 1 7			
MAY 8			
NOV 1 9			

The Transfer of International Technology

The Transfer of International Technology

Europe, Japan and the USA
in the Twentieth Century

Edited by

David J. Jeremy
Manchester Polytechnic

Edward Elgar

Published by
Edward Elgar Publishing Limited
Gower House
Croft Road
Aldershot
Hants GU11 3HR
England

Edward Elgar Publishing Limited
Distributed in the United States by
Ashgate Publishing Company
Old Post Road
Brookfield
Vermont 05036
USA

A CIP catalogue record for this book
is available from the British Library

Library of Congress Cataloguing-in-Publication Data

The Transfer of international technology: Europe, Japan, and the USA
   in the twentieth century / edited by David J. Jeremy.
        p. cm.
    Includes index.
    ISBN 1-85278-453-9
    1. Technology transfer.   I. Jeremy, David J.
  T174.3.T669   1992
  338.9'26–dc20   91–32715
                                             CIP

ISBN 1 85278 453 9

Printed in Great Britain by
Billing & Sons Ltd, Worcester

Contents

PART II   TRANSFERS FROM JAPAN

PART III   TRANSFERS OF MANAGEMENT

Figures

Tables

Contributors

Tetsuo Abo, Professor, Institute of Social Science, University of Tokyo, Japan

John Hassan, Senior Lecturer, Economics and Economic History Department, Manchester Polytechnic

David J. Jeremy, Senior Lecturer, Economics and Economic History Department, Manchester Polytechnic

Akira Kudo, Professor, Department of Social and International Relations, University of Tokyo, Japan

Tetsuya Kuwahara, Professor, Department of Business Administration, Kyoto Sangyo University, Japan

Wayne Lewchuk, Assistant Professor, Labour Studies Programme, McMaster University, Hamilton, Ontario, Canada

Peter J.T. Morris, Senior Curator in Experimental Chemistry, Science Museum, London

Jennifer Tann, Professor of Innovation Studies, School of Continuing Studies, Birmingham University

Geoffrey Tweedale, Research Fellow, Department of History, Sheffield University

Acknowledgements

These essays continue into the twentieth century the themes explored for the pre-1914 period in *International Technology Transfer* (1990).

Professor Takeshi Yuzawa kindly made contacts with Japanese colleagues to participate in this collective endeavour. As with the earlier volume, I have been much assisted by Dr Geoff Tweedale in some editorial matters, and by my younger daughter Rebecca who retyped some of the chapters. Photocopying and postal resources have been supplied by the Faculty of Management and Business, Manchester Polytechnic. The inspiration for my work has remained the same: Theresa my wife, now dearly remembered.

DAVID J. JEREMY
Whaley Bridge

1. Introduction: New and Old Problems in the Transfer of Technology

David J. Jeremy

Even the most cursory examination of the spectacular world economic growth achieved over the last century shows that the contribution of technology absolutely dwarfs the input from a rising but qualitatively unchanging supply of capital and labour factors. Not surprisingly, therefore, in recent years technological change has come to absorb an increasing amount of attention from economists, economic and business historians and sociologists. Yet many of the questions surrounding this extremely rapid rate of technological change remain unanswered: in particular, why do some firms, industries, regions and countries show an apparently greater willingness and aptitude for technological innovation than do other firms, industries, regions and countries? The question may be given a further historical dimension if we seek to explain movements of technology and innovative activity from one country (or firm, industry, region) to another at different points in time. In any explanation, our understanding of the mechanism of technology transfer is crucial.

In the first part of this two-volume study, case-studies documented the years before 1914. This was an era dominated by those great engines of change – iron and steel, railroad, textile, shipping, telegraph and chemical technologies – that moulded the Industrial Revolution. Britain was then the world's leading technological nation and the era was characterized by the attempts of less advanced nations, particularly European countries and the USA, to close the technology gap. In the twentieth century the international transfer of technology has become more dynamic, involves more countries and has become immeasurably faster. It also involves 'new' technologies – automobiles, offshore oil production, synthetic rubber and chemicals, and computers – which have gone some way towards supplanting the 'old' industries of the Industrial Revolution. The complexity, internationalization and burgeoning of new technologies are reflected in this book.

In considering technology transfer, each author was invited to write a case-study, incorporating the latest research, of a key industry or episode in the movement of technology. Methodologies, chronological periods and

1

conclusions therefore differ: however, authors were asked to address a number of common questions:

1.   What kind of inhibiting factors in the originating economy slowed down (or accelerated) the transfer of technology?
2.   What does the case-study demonstrate about the following: vehicles of transfer; networks of access to the originating economy; information goals of acquirers; and methods of information collection?
3.   What factors influenced the adoption of the imported technology in the receptor economy/society? What was the rate of adoption; what networks of distribution were utilized; and what obstacles faced importers of the new technology?
4.   Was the imported technology modified in any way? If so, was this because of economic, social or environmental factors?
5.   Can any reverse flows of technology be identified? In other words, did modifications to the transferred technology prove appropriate for the originating economy and were they adopted successfully?

The answers to these questions might appear to be of purely academic interest. So ubiquitous has technical change become and so dramatic its impact (indeed it is often stated that we live in a global 'village' and are in the midst of a second Industrial Revolution – one dominated by computers and information systems) that technology transfer would seem to be easily realizable. These case-studies would appear to support such a view. When all the technical, social and political factors mesh perfectly even the most advanced technologies can be transferred in a staggeringly brief period, seemingly without hindrance. In computing technology, advances in the development of the digital computer ricocheted back and forth across the Atlantic between Britain and America during the 1950s and 1960s, to the mutual benefit of each. The result was the birth of the data-processing industry and the advent of the information age. Similarly the highly innovative offshore oil industry rapidly exploited the British sector of the North Sea in the 1970s. Technology transfer in the oil industry appeared to be as fluid as the product itself and the world-wide diffusion of offshore technology proceeded so rapidly that discussion of counterflows becomes almost meaningless. In these industries there were few inhibiting factors in the transfer of technology and diffusion was characterized by its speed and rapid adaptation to economic, political and environmental circumstances.

Yet other evidence suggests that matters are not so simple. The Brandt Commission on International Development Issues in 1980 identified difficulties in technology acquisition as central to the problems of the developing world. The fact that a substantial proportion (at least 20 per cent) of the world's population continues to live in poverty and hunger begs an urgent answer to the question as to how the benefits of technology can be more effectively disseminated.

Some of the problems associated with technology transfer are highlighted in this volume. Factors that contributed to the success of some industrial transfers were precisely those that hindered the assimilation of technologies by similarly endowed societies. Nothing could be simpler, it would appear, than to transfer American Fordist mass production innovations in the motor industry to other countries sharing similar outlooks, beliefs and consumer tastes. Yet British Fordism, although it was transmitted with relative ease through the technical press and by personal visits, never worked quite as efficiently as the American model owing to the unwillingness of British managers to follow Fordism's originators. Different British social and political characteristics modified the technology at least as much as did the smaller British market. Ironically, it was again social and political characteristics within the receptor economy – in this case the American – which blunted Japan's attempt to transfer its competitive advantage in motor vehicle manufacturing abroad.

Elsewhere, of course, the Japanese were more successful, both at absorbing foreign influences and at exporting technology to their neighbours and to the West. They effectively transferred their production know-how in cotton spinning to China in the early twentieth century, with a blend of shrewd management of local labour, careful attention to detail and sheer hard work. These qualities proved successful despite the unpromising situation in China for foreign cotton spinning firms. In heavy chemical ammonia synthesis Japanese engineers are shown ambitiously and successfully absorbing Western technologies, though even here there are lessons to be learned since some firms proved more expert at this than others. Interestingly, a slavish imitation of Japanese methods is not always recommended: the transatlantic transfer of synthetic rubber technology is said to show that America should study its own past successes and not imitate countries with different social, economic and historical backgrounds.

The Japanese chapters in this book will be of particular interest in the light of the Japanese economic 'miracle'. So too will the discussions of those twentieth-century factors which have changed the conditions under which technology may be effected: the rise of science, the globalization of big business, the spread of information technologies and of management techniques. The authors reveal the subject of technology transfer in all its complexity: at times so easily effected, at others so difficult to achieve in even the most advanced settings. Their case-studies will thus provide a surer historical perspective and better understanding of the way modern technology transfer has come about.

PART I

Twentieth-century Transfers Originating in the West

2. Fordist Technology and Britain: The Diffusion of Labour Speed-up

Wayne Lewchuk

Wedded to the machine heart and soul, Ford went so far as to declare in this 59th year that mankind had discovered a new deity. Mass production, he asserted, had become a 'new Messiah'.[1]

INTRODUCTION

The term Fordism today stands for a system of production which has come to symbolize factory technology in the twentieth century. It is usually associated with unskilled labour and mechanical innovations such as the moving assembly line, well suited to producing large numbers of standardized commodities. However Fordism also had important social implications. It involved a major reordering of authority relations on the shop floor and an increase in managerial control of production decisions including how hard labour would work.[2] This chapter will examine the rise of Fordism in the USA and its diffusion to the British motor vehicle industry. It will suggest that diffusion was incomplete because British management was unwilling, as distinct from unable, to reorder authority relations on the American model, making other aspects of Fordism less attractive.

Attempts to explain the diffusion of Fordism have focused on relative factor prices, the supply of skilled labour, the size of product markets in the host country and the structure of firm ownership.[3] It has been argued that European markets were too small and that skilled labour was too abundant and cheap to make the new system of production cost-effective. We do not wish to suggest that these factors were unimportant. However, given the magnitude of the productivity increases associated with the shift to Fordism, often in the vicinity of 100 per cent, it seems that more than an adjustment to relative factor prices or scale economies was behind the new system of production. Such a conclusion is reinforced by our analysis that changes in authority patterns and the resulting speed-up of the work pace were key components of the new technology.

7

This chapter will look at the way differences in institutions, customs, beliefs and attitudes, the legacy of an economy's past, influenced the diffusion of technology.[4] The suggestion that diffusion is path-dependent, in the sense that an economy's past shapes the context in which technology is examined and adopted, is in keeping with recent trends in economic thought criticizing mainstream post-war economic analysis and the project of placing economics on a scientific footing. Solow, one of the champions of mainstream economic analysis, recently voiced his suspicion that 'the attempt to construct economics as an axiomatically based hard science is doomed to fail'.[5] He went on to suggest that the reason for this was that 'all narrowly economic activity is entangled in a web of social institutions, customs, beliefs and attitudes'.[6]

There have been a number of attempts by economists to model technical change as more than an economic process.[7] However, the non-economics literature provides a richer source of guidance on the way sociopolitical factors influence technical change. Contemporary social critics stressed the links between Fordism's success in the USA and the sociopolitical context. Gramsci, in his classic essays on 'Americanism and Fordism', pointed to the absence of a large non-productive class which distorted consumption patterns in Europe away from mass-produced goods. He also pointed to unique American social characteristics, including the early rise of consumerism, the strengthening of the nuclear family and new views on sexual behaviour and the consumption of alcohol.[8] To Kate Richards O'Hare, Fordism was viewed not only as an efficient way of producing cars, but also as a means of spreading middle-class American values to unskilled and immigrant workers who needed to be 'Americanized'. To O'Hare, efficiency meant 'plenty of grub ... plenty of hot water and a bathtub ... and a contented, happy wife at home'.[9]

Burrage has provided a particularly illuminating thesis of the way sociopolitical factors influenced trends in American and British work organization. He argued that early reforms of American productive organizations were justified, not on the basis of their efficiency, but rather on moral grounds and their consistency with democratic principles. He wrote:

> Americans did not respond to Jackson's reforms [of the civil service] as to a useful, labor-saving administrative reorganization; on the contrary, they were emphatically, vociferously moral about them. It was believed that they would make America more democratic, and they were defended on the grounds that they were consistent with American democratic ideals.[10]

Burrage extended his analysis of work patterns in the civil service to other organizational features of the British and American economies. Of critical importance to his thesis were the different attitudes of the British and the Americans to the role of individuals and groups in society. In Britain, loyalty to groups remained an important feature of social and economic life, a response to the limited shifts towards democracy in the nineteenth century and reinforced by the persistence of social stratification and the class organization of society. It was argued that, in such a social context, individual behaviour would be influenced by internally generated group norms enforced by the individual's desire to maintain his/her standing in the group and not to offend its members.[11] In Britain, craft unions, the civil service, lawyers and doctors all relied on internally generated group norms and self-regulation. In the USA, on the other hand, eighteenth-century political reforms created the appearance, if not the reality, of a more democratic society, while less rigid social stratification blurred class distinctions and weakened individual adherence and loyalty to groups. American employers were forced to contend with a more individualistic ethos, hence closing the door to self-regulation based on group norms. In its place was substituted governance by rules enforced by a central authority, the model of power which would ultimately be captured by the Fordist system.[12]

Burrage used this model to suggest why both British workers and employers might resist American organizational methods.

> Why have the Americans legitimated more rational, individualistic, and bureaucratic work relationships than the British? The only plausible answer to this question at the present time is the one suggested by Tocqueville: the democratic ethic of the Americans ... The British have tended to explain their relatively inefficient industry as resulting from complacency, amateurism, and conservatism. However, any attempt to change existing work arrangements would threaten obligations and loyalties – to one's fellows, obviously, but also to one's predecessors and successors; in other words, there are moral grounds for British industrial conservatism ... The weaker group loyalties characteristic of American organizations appear to permit them to innovate at a faster rate than the British.[13]

An alternative, but complementary, approach to the question of Fordist technology and the role of sociopolitical factors can be found in the work of the French regulationist school.[14] Here, Fordism is analysed as both a physical system of production and a mode of regulation; that is, a set of rules and social procedures which guide individual behaviour.[15] While the regulationists see the willingness of American workers, particularly immigrants, to accept the deal of higher wages for higher effort as important, they also stress the ability of employers to enforce this deal where labour was reluctant. According to Aglietta, 'The norms that the immigrants had to internalize to accomplish their cultural assimilation were individualism, stable family life, and monetary gain as the mark of social success and the spur to labour discipline.'[16]

Social and labour historians have shown that, when the promised improvement in living standards failed to materialize in the 1890s, the immigrants rebelled. However the form the rebellion took was shaped by the unique American sociopolitical context. To Aglietta, it was the fact that America was a more democratic society than Europe, while Gerber and Haydu have focused on the disparity in power between organized American capital and labour.[17] The end result was a rebellion focusing less on political reform and more on the winning of improved standards of living. Economism became the central focus of the emerging American trade unions, a shift which was particularly well suited to Fordism and its promise of delivering the goods–lots of them.[18]

In Europe, the late nineteenth–century labour rebellions took more of a political tone and demands for greater worker control were heard alongside demands for improved standards of living. Numerous contemporary commentators suggested that the British state had been too soft on labour in the first decades of the century and that the working class had developed the idea that labour was the only source of wealth and hence labour should have a greater, if not dominant, say in how that wealth was to be produced and allocated.[19] As will be shown below, Fordism was especially ill suited to satisfying these political demands. Fordist labour regulation was moving in the opposite direction of giving labour less say over shop-floor decisions.

The above suggests that American and British economic agents did have different histories and that sociopolitical factors were extremely important to the evolution of American technology and, we will argue, to its diffusion to Britain. In the USA, the broader opportunities available to nineteenth-century workers, unique political institutions, the relative power of capital and labour, and the process by which immigrants acquired 'American' values were critical. American technology exploited this unique sociopolitical context. It was a very different story in Britain. In the remainder of this chapter we will examine in detail the different experiences of Fordism in the USA and Britain.

THE BIRTH OF FORDISM IN THE USA[20]

We have argued so far that major shifts in technology are a product of both economic and sociopolitical factors. In this section we will focus on the way in which Fordism was shaped by the American context. Our objective is to show that Fordism represented more than a response to relative factor prices or scale economies. In the final section we will look at the reasons why this American technology was ill suited to British conditions.

Hounshell has argued that Fordism was the first true system of mass production. It brought together the technology of interchangeable production perfected in the American armouries and cycle industry and the organizational advances pioneered by F.W.Taylor.[21] Ford failed twice before successfully establishing the Ford Motor Company in 1903. Following the strategy pioneered by Olds, he initially depended on outside suppliers such as Dodge to undertake the more complex and capital-intensive aspects of the production process. This was a strategy open to American producers who were well served by a network of job shops and who seemed less concerned about fitting standard components to their vehicles than was the case in Britain, where early firms insisted on making the entire vehicle in their works.

At first, Ford kept close to European practices. Assembly was done mainly by hand at stationary assembly benches by skilled workers. A paternalistic labour strategy was adopted to encourage the independent skilled workers to produce at levels acceptable to management. Ford visited the shops regularly and knew most of the 100 or so workers by name. The workers knew Ford as Henry or Hank.[22]

Of all the factors influencing the process of innovation at Fords between 1906 and early 1913, one alone seems to stand out: the need to coordinate thousands of workers and the need to transport the thousands of components used to produce a motor vehicle. Stationary assembly and the functional organization of machine departments, which grouped similar machines in the same area of the plant, required the extensive movement of components throughout the shops. Initial attempts to ease these transportation problems included the shift to moving teams of specialized assemblers and the sequential organization of machinery according to the component being produced. Table 2.1 traces the level of output and the level of employment at each stage in the innovation process at the Ford Motor Company.[23] It shows that many of the changes in production methods and organization took place at output levels numbering in the tens of thousands.

Although transportation problems stimulated the search for a new production system, the social implications of these changes soon became the dominating factor shaping further technical change. As long as Ford operated a small shop, employing mainly skilled labour, there appeared to be neither the need nor the potential for managerial control of labour effort. As output and the size of the workforce expanded, and as more expensive machinery was adopted, control of the pace of work became a greater managerial concern. Between 1906 and 1913, Ford groped for a new managerial system of labour control. The initial strategy was to allocate labour supervision and the enforcement of effort standards to low-level supervisors who were given responsibility for hiring, firing and setting wage rates in their departments. In 1907, as an aid to these supervisors, crude time studies were performed. Wollering described the system at Ford in 1907 as follows:

Table 2.1   Chronology of Ford Innovations

Year	Output	Employment	Assets per Worker ($)	Innovation
1903/4	1 700	100	1 460	Paternalistic labour relations, skilled labour, stationary assembly
1904/5	1 745	–	–	Functional organization of machines, general purpose machines
1905/6	1 599	–	–	
1906/7	8 423	700	700	Beginnings of shift to jig and fixture production, introduction of production on an interchangeable basis, enhanced authority for foremen, crude time and motion studies, first labour spy recorded
1907/8	6 398	575	2 436	First gravity slides, sequential lay-out of machinery, Model T launched, average task duration 514 minutes
1908/9	10 607	450	–	First reports of experiments in line assembly, assembly by specialized teams, profit sharing
1909/10	18 664	1 655	1 732	Highland Park plant opens, introduction of single purpose and special purpose machines, 54 per cent of work force skilled.
1910/11	34 528	2 773	1 909	
1911/12	78 440	3 976	3 361	
1912/13	168 304	6 867	2 975	Average task duration before first line 2.3 minutes, first moving assembly lines, profit sharing abandoned, transfer of authority to hire and fire to employment office, new pay system reduces discretion of foremen over wages, 26 per cent of work force skilled
1913/14	248 307	14 366	2 439	First mechanized moving assembly lines, Five Dollar Day, Ford Sociology Department

Sources: A. Nevins, *Ford: The Times, the Man, the Company*, (New York, 1954). See
references in text for innovations.

I had studies made on the various manufacturing operations ... We would get a man whom we had confidence in and who knew what he was doing as to whether it was a lathe or a screw machine or a grinder. He knew the fundamentals of it and he would take a stopwatch and operate the machine himself to get a fair idea of what could be done.[24]

In 1906, Ford hired the first of his infamous labour spies whose report left little doubt as to the limitations of managerial authority on the shop floor.[25] In 1908, profit sharing was introduced to overcome the growing social tension between labour and management.[26] Throughout this period, Ford was substituting less-skilled labour for skilled labour. This shift was not simply a move from more costly to less costly labour. It was also a shift to a type of worker who was vulnerable to the centralized regime of labour control Ford was moving towards.

These early changes created as many problems as they solved. The continued pressure for more output clashed with the growing labour disenchantment generated by the new working conditions. The deskilling of labour generalized labour skills and, when combined with the tight Detroit labour market, gave Ford workers a significant degree of mobility. Annual labour turnover of 200 per cent was common in Detroit. At Fords this figure approached 400 per cent in 1913, while daily absenteeism reached 10 per cent. The situation was aggravated by the extreme division of labour and autocratic foremen, which gave workers new reasons to move. In the words of one contemporary spokesperson, 'They [labour] are conducting a continuous, unorganized strike.'[27] Under these conditions the objective of the final elements of the Fordist system introduced in 1913/14 was not to substitute less expensive for expensive labour, but rather to increase managerial control of labour time.[28]

The final stage in the transition to Fordism began in mid-1913, when responsibility for hiring, firing and setting wage rates was centralized under the control of a new employment office directed by J.R. Lee. Evidence suggests that this eroded the ability of low-level supervisors to enforce labour effort norms. According to Meyer, productivity growth was falling at the same time that managerial responsibilities were being reorganized. In 1911, productivity rose 41 per cent; in 1912, it rose 15 per cent; while, in 1913, it rose only 4.7 per cent.[29]

The moving assembly line resolved many of the remaining technical and social constraints facing Ford. The first Ford line was introduced in late 1913, some months after the responsibilities of the supervisors had been reorganized. It was unmechanized, 150 feet long and employed 140 assemblers.[30] Mechanization followed in 1914. As late as 1922, the entire capital outlay in the chassis department was less than $40 000.[31] The new system was more efficient as components could now be delivered to a single station.

Equally important, the line held great potential as a mechanism of labour control. It was argued by a contemporary Ford manager that:

> If the idea is good for one thing, it takes a lot of people that want to be paced ... You take the slant that we are trying to make you do things with a mechanical pace setter; that is my own version of this thing. I never thought that would take too kindly with the average working man. He didn't like to be put on a tread mill, you know, that was the idea.[32]

Another contemporary observer argued, 'Speed up the electric motors a notch and presto! Ford production has increased another hundred cars per day without the necessity of hiring a single workman.'[33] Within months of the adoption of the assembly line, the labour time needed to produce a Model T chassis fell from 134 to 67 hours and the time needed to produce an engine fell from 36.6 to 23.07 hours.[34]

The role of foremen in converting labour time into effort was not completely eliminated. Foremen remained the front-line supervisors and hence higher-level management was reluctant to undermine their authority by overruling their decisions. While foremen had lost direct control of hiring and firing, making it somewhat more difficult to run their shops as personal empires, they still had significant influence over employment. In an era when seniority had little bearing, shop-floor foremen could still influence who was laid off, the allocation of the 'good' jobs within their department and the allocation of minor tasks, and the perks associated with them, such as crew chief, set-up man, lead man, pusher, gang boss and straw boss. The ability of Ford foremen to find workers willing to break solidarity with their mates and to act as pushers and straw bosses is another element in the American sociopolitical context.[35]

The simplicity of the early assembly lines is of significant importance to our interpretation of Fordism's success in Detroit and its diffusion to Britain. The lack of major new investment associated with line production and the ease with which a plant could be converted to the new principle led contemporary observers to argue that the mere reorganization of assembly tasks allowed one to double productivity.[36] Ford officials would later write, 'Costs fell two-thirds in a single period of six months, with the same machines, the same tools, the same men – seemingly nothing done to decrease costs.'[37] Of course something drastic had changed; management had taken direct control over the setting of effort norms and was using machine pacing to speed up the work pace.

In order to realize the potential of Fordism and direct labour control to convert labour time into effort, labour still had to be brought on side.[38] This was done by a dramatic doubling of wages in 1914, which caused a riot outside the Ford gates, and the introduction of the Ford Sociology Department to guide workers towards a new style of life. The latter not only shifted social values and labour's shop-floor efficiency, as Gramsci argued, but also encouraged changes in consumption patterns such as home ownership and the elimination of alternative sources of income such as boarders, all of which made Ford workers more dependent on Ford employment and the high wages offered.

The ability of Ford to implement this package of high wages in return for high effort should be viewed as one of the critical components of the entire system. It marked the final chapter in the reform of time discipline which had begun in Britain in the late eighteenth century with the rise of the first factories.[39] Under Fordism, the frontier of control shifted dramatically in management's favour. Increasingly the terrain of conflict between labour and management shifted, from how to use time to how much time to use. Here more than anywhere else the role of history and the sociopolitical context loom large. The balance of power between capital and labour, attitudes towards mechanization and centralization of authority, labour's acceptance of economism and the willingness to trade off control for higher wages, Ford's ability to spread middle-class consumer values amongst his workers and the ability to break work-group cohesion were central to the success of the new regime.

What little we know of production methods at other American firms suggests that news of the advances made at Fords spread rapidly through the engineering press and that most other American producers adopted elements of the Ford system.[40] According to Hounshell, even firms producing 1 000 or 2 000 vehicles adopted moving assembly lines.[41] However the degree to which management was able to control labour effort norms seems to have varied. Neither Chrysler nor Studebaker appear to have been as successful as Ford in centralizing managerial control.[42] Most American producers also resisted the shift to high fixed day wages, although there was a general movement towards less individualized payment systems such as the group bonus schemes with bonus rates of between 5 and 20 per cent.[43] The less than complete diffusion of Fordism to other American vehicle producers suggests that Ford's decision to supply the low end of the American market, a niche which Ford virtually monopolized until the 1920s, contributed to the final shape of Fordism.

THE DIFFUSION OF FORDISM TO BRITAIN

As was the case in Detroit, the period prior to the First World War was one of rapid technical change in the British motor vehicle industry.[44] In the British case, the arrival of cheap American imports acted as a spur to innovation.

However it would be untrue to argue that this was the only factor leading to change. British firms were also looking in the pre-war period for new production techniques to allow them to produce better vehicles and new systems of organization to manage their relatively large workforces in a period of heightened social unrest.

Ford's early models did not sell well in Britain and the Model N's sales of 102 in 1907 marked a pre-Model T high point. The introduction of the Model T in November of 1908 dramatically shifted the fortunes of Ford. Improvements in machine techniques, such as grinding, meant that American firms could now manufacture to within a 1/1000 of an inch, allowing product quality to match or exceed that of the skilled craft worker. The Model T sold well in 1913 and 1914, capturing one-quarter of the British market.[45] British producers responded quickly to the American challenge by introducing their own small cars, beginning in 1912 when Singer and Standard offered new models, followed by the Morris Oxford in 1913. These cars were priced at between £165 and £195, compared with £135 for the Model T.[46]

By 1910, the growing sales of the Model T convinced Ford's Detroit management to begin assembly in Britain. Ford's British operations were completely owned by the parent firm, a situation which would persist until the 1930s. Product design was dictated by the parent firm, an arrangement which worked poorly. American management also played a major role in dictating production methods. Visits by American managers such as Couzens in 1907 and 1909 and Ford in 1912 helped transfer Fordist practices.[47]

British-born Percival Perry was hired as managing director and the Ford Manchester plant began operations in November of 1911. Initially, knocked-down kits were shipped from Detroit and reassembled in Manchester. The difficulty of shipping bulky components such as bodies, mufflers and petrol tanks led Ford to begin manufacturing them in Britain in 1912. It was proposed to manufacture these components under conditions similar to those found in plants in Detroit. New employees were hired as handymen and were expected to perform any task which management felt to be necessary. Descriptions of the plant in 1915 confirm that many of the jobs had been made suitable for unskilled labour.

> All parts are machine cut to templates and jigs, and little indeed is left to be done by hand, except actual putting together. The processes in the department of this factory are almost automatic, little being left for hand work beyond the insertion of screws.[48]

The attempt to reorganize the workplace along American lines resulted in numerous small strikes during early 1912. Towards the end of the year, the United Kingdom Society of Coachmakers shut down the body plant for 22 weeks. The union claimed to be striking against the pernicious 'American

System' which they argued ignored the rights of unions.[49] This strike received only the moral support of the other unions in Manchester. Chassis assembly continued during the strike, using bodies imported from Detroit. The reluctance of the other workers to support the body shop reflected the vulnerability of less-skilled workers, even in the more highly organized British context, and Ford's policy of allowing wages to rise during the strike.

When Perry first came to Manchester, he considered the existing hourly wage of four and one-half pence per hour a starvation wage. Before the strike began the minimum hourly rate was still only five pence per hour, rising to six pence when the strike began and, over the next few months, drifting up to ten pence per hour. These increases all took place before Ford introduced the Five Dollar Day in Detroit, after which a further five pence per hour profit-sharing bonus was added to the Manchester wage.[50] Perry was also allowed to depart from American practice by offering elements of a more paternalistic employment relationship through the Ford Sports Club and the Ford Employees' Pension and Benefit Scheme.[51] The Coachmakers strike ended in defeat for the union and for the next 30 years Ford operated as a non-union shop. Having eliminated union resistance, Ford installed the first British mechanized assembly line in September of 1914, less than a year after it was adopted in Detroit. Initial capacity was between 50 and 150 per day.

Reminiscences of former workers and the lack of organized labour agitation in the Ford plants for 30 years suggest that shop-floor British labour was at least sympathetic to the high wage/high effort deal which Ford offered. This was certainly true of their leaders. During national negotiations in 1925, union officials noted that, while British labour initially resisted the Ford system, they had come to accept it.[52] The strong criticism of British-style management by labour leaders and their support of American techniques further suggest that the primary obstacle to the diffusion of Fordism was not labour. In 1919, Brownlie, the leader of the Amalgamated Society of Engineers, the strongest union in the vehicle industry at the time, advocated the modernization of British industry on the American model. He argued, 'The individual or the organization that stands in the way of utilizing the improvement of the machine tool, or the improvements brought into being by the application of science to industry, is standing in its own light.'[53] In 1921, the Trades Union Congress condemned British factory organization and pointed to American factories as a model.[54]

Although Ford succeeded in Americanizing the production process in Manchester and transferring control over effort norms to management, all was not well. Ford's British management showed some preference for granting workers minor privileges, such as smoking, and was reluctant to exercise draconian hiring and firing practices in the face of irregular British output.[55] More serious, however, was Ford's reluctance to introduce new models tailored to the British market. Post-World War I Ford cars were too expensive, too heavily taxed to compete against products from Morris and Austin and until 1923 still had left-hand drive. The inappropriateness of the Ford model design created serious problems for Ford's new plant in Dagenham, which opened in 1931 with a capacity of 200 000 vehicles. In 1929, Ford sold fewer than 8 000 cars, which represented less than 5 per cent of the British market.[56] The imbalance between model design, sales and plant capacity would only begin to be resolved with the introduction of the Model Y in 1932. Ford captured 22 per cent of Big Six sales in 1937, but by 1939 had slipped back to 15 per cent and it was only after 1945 that Ford returned to the dominating position the firm held in 1914.[57] Despite these difficulties, there is little evidence of a retreat from American-style management techniques. A Ford line worker of the 1930s recalled, 'Discipline was very strong ... if you didn't do your job properly and, for example, keep up with the line as they used to say, you would obviously lose the job.'[58]

Ford was the only American producer to undertake large-scale British manufacture prior to the late 1920s. General Motors had done some assembly in Britain in the early 1920s and decided to enter the market in a more serious way in 1925.[59] Attempts first to invest in and then to purchase Austin failed and instead they purchased Vauxhall.[60] Vauxhall had set up their first assembly line earlier that year and weekly output was about 30 chassis. The new American management set about reorganizing the Vauxhall works, raising output to 130 per week and increasing managerial control of shop-floor decisions. Hancock, the works manager, was sent to Detroit for a crash course in American methods and on his return oversaw the introduction of flow production techniques, machine pacing and a shift from individual piece work to a group bonus system. Bonus rates averaged about 25 per cent, half of the recognized rate and perhaps one-quarter of the actual rate in many British vehicle shops. Model policy was also changed and soon General Motors products were coming off the lines. This was not a successful strategy. Again the American cars were too expensive and heavily taxed to compete with British models. It was not until the mid-1930s that this policy changed with the introduction of new smaller models in 1933 and 1937.[61]

General Motors stopped well short of completely Americanizing Vauxhall's labour relations. Fearing a nationalistic backlash against American domination, the board of directors remained relatively independent of Detroit and retained its British character until the 1950s. This allowed Charles Bartlett, who became the managing director in the 1930s, to practise a form of paternalism in an attempt to create loyalty. Profit sharing, group bonus payment systems, a grievance system, even attempts to ease lay-offs during the seasonal swings in the industry were instituted. The intention was to get workers to practise a form of loyalty to the firm and to regulate their activities themselves. One worker recalled that, during the Bartlett years, workers helped each other out when they got behind and, no doubt motivated by the incentive structure of group bonus payment systems, disciplined fellow workers who did not pull their weight or spent too much time on breaks or in the toilet. However, it is clear that a different labour culture was nurtured on the shop floor at Vauxhall. The workers felt that Bartlett was trying to create an environment where everybody should cooperate.[62] He was described as a manager who 'never lost his simple and sturdily democratic approach to industrial management ... he seemed to have an innate respect for physical toil and a complementary lack of appreciation for the brain worker.'[63] These deviations from American practice were tolerated until the 1950s, when the plant was placed on straight day work and management took greater direct control of operations and effort norms.

FORDISM AND THE BRITISH MOTOR VEHICLE PRODUCERS

Amongst the independent British firms, the diffusion of Fordism was even less complete;[64] instead a distinctly different system of production emerged. By 1914, many of the machine advances adopted in Detroit were in use by leading British producers. British producers had been exposed to the advances of the American system of production as early as 1851 at the Crystal Palace Exhibition, which led directly to Colt producing guns in London with American methods and the purchase of a set of American machines for the armoury at Enfield. American firms such as Singer were also using best American practice in their British branch plants.[65] The wide availability of American machines from specialist suppliers and the fact that the advances in metal working machine techniques after 1850 depended less on fundamental advances in machine technology and more on incremental improvements to existing machine types also eased their diffusion.[66]

An important mode of diffusion of American technology was via extensive descriptions of the new methods in various trade journals and numerous visits to Detroit by British managers. Not only did American firms bring their own British managers to Detroit, they also welcomed other British managers to inspect their plants. One has the sense that American industrialists such as Ford viewed their workplaces as monuments to their success and something to be displayed to the entire world. The Institute of Automobile Engineers organized a tour of Detroit and Cleveland, including a visit to the Ford works, in 1913.[67] Morris visited Detroit twice in 1914, searching for a firm willing to supply him with components and at the same time examining local production techniques. Hans Landstad, who accompanied Morris to Detroit, remained for six months, watching over Morris's order and observing American practice before returning to take up a position with Morris in December of 1914.[68] The secretary and business manager of Associated Equipment Company visited the USA in 1916.[69] In 1922, Austin and one of his top managers, Ernest Payton, visited Detroit and the Ford and General Motors plants. Austin was sufficiently impressed with Ford to have an autographed photo of Henry hung on the stark walls of his Longbridge office.[70] Engelbach, the works director at Austin, visited Detroit in 1927, before reorganizing the Austin shops. He suggested to the board that they should follow a regular practice of sending someone to Detroit every other year.[71]

The link between the British cycle trade and the motor vehicle trade also encouraged the diffusion of modern machine technology. The cycle trade had been slow to adopt the repetition methods pioneered by the American firms in the 1880s, but the 1890s witnessed a rapid conversion.[72] The cycle trade's experience was quickly absorbed by the young motor vehicle industry. As early as 1897, reports suggest that, in the Midlands, the area in which many vehicle makers were located, employers had made rapid progress in the use of new machine techniques and the employment of unskilled labour.[73] Reports of the first Daimler factory indicate that careful attention was paid to machine organization so as to minimize transportation and that a large stock of American machines had been installed. By 1899, additions to the machine stock included self-sequencing lathes, multiple-head boring machines and milling machines. The latter are of interest as they became the workhorses in many repetition machine shops, replacing lathes.[74] Similar advances in machine technology could be found at Humber, Belsize and at Hozier, where it was claimed in 1903 that the extensive use of jigs, fixtures and limit gauges had provided complete interchangeability and had eliminated the 'personal element'.[75]

By 1911, Legros, the president of the Institute of Automobile Engineers, noted that 'the tendency in the bigger factories is to diminish the amount of responsibility left to the individual worker in respect to the employment of ... shop knowledge'.[76] In 1914, a management consultant argued that 'In the motor trade ... a large portion of the workers were either turret hands who do not do much more than pull certain handles, or milling machine hands who only put work in a fixture and let it go, having the speed and feed set for them, and jig drillers.'[77] These changes in machine practice were taking place in part because the high-speed/high-compression automobile engine required a degree of precision fit which only new types of machines could deliver.[78] This explains why, at firms such as Daimler, engine production was on an interchangeable basis by 1907, while the chassis department was still dependent on the skilled fitter and the file.[79] Even firms such as Vauxhall and Rolls-Royce made extensive use of potentially deskilling machine techniques on their luxury chassis and engines.[80]

Despite the advances in machine techniques and a substantial reduction in the demand for skilled labour, the critical labour control methods employed by Ford did not receive widespread support in Britain.[81] Pullinger, manager of the Arrol Johnston plant, which was built in 1913 and modelled on Packard, argued against American labour practices and rigid managerial control and in favour of 'kindly and sympathetic' treatment of labour.[82] A.W. Reeves from Crossley argued:

> An important factor to the author's mind, and one which appears to be entirely ignored in the wonderful systems on the other side of the Atlantic, and among many idealists on this side, is that of the personal or human element. Anyone with any knowledge of the independent and, it must be confessed, awkward spirit, characterising the workers of say the Northern Midlands, would hesitate before applying the extreme methods of the latest American Scientific Management, well knowing the futility of the task.[83]

Bayley, before the British Institute of Automobile Engineers, argued:

> In America, I understand, the labour available is much more amenable to systematised working. In England there is difficulty in getting a man to do exactly what he is told, because he is apt to think a great deal more for himself than do his fellows in America. Therefore, a system in this country has to be more elastic and less precise than many American systems are said to be.[84]

Perry Keene from Austin had the following observation on American labour management methods:

> In America you have to employ methods which a crowd can carry out, but the British individual will not have that ... the Britisher will not have 'herd' methods. He has the individualistic tendency, and it is a British tendency that you have to allow for.[85]

Having rejected direct control of labour on the model of Henry Ford, largely owing to perceived differences in the sociopolitical context, British management still needed a strategy to convert labour time into effort. Many British employers were sympathetic to welfarism, paternalism or copartnership as a means of winning labour's confidence and increasing productivity.[86] Central to the British post-war labour control strategy in the motor vehicle industry was the spread of incentive payment systems with much larger bonus rates than in the pre-war period. Much as the decision by Ford to take direct control of effort norms encouraged further investment of capital whose productivity could now be assured, the British preference for indirect control of labour effort norms through incentive payment systems made capital investment a riskier strategy, slowed the rate at which the managerial function evolved in Britain, and slowed the rate of growth of wages which was critical to the expansion of the market for mass-produced goods.[87]

After the First World War, the Coventry employers resisted labour's demand to move to fixed day rates on the grounds that they could neither depend on labour to produce voluntarily at a given level nor directly enforce the desired level of effort.[88] Negotiations between the unions and the Employers Association resulted in the Humber Agreement, which was particularly important in the motor vehicle trade. The workers agreed to continue working on systems of payment by results, with the understanding that the recognized bonus level would be 50 per cent of base wages. These higher bonus rates tied labour earnings even more directly to effort and, in this way, the Coventry employers could control effort norms indirectly. Similar strategies were used in many American firms; however the extent to which British management relied on British labour to coordinate shop-floor activity under incentive payment systems seems extraordinary.[89]

The justification for making incentive payment systems such an important component of post-war managerial strategies was based in part on managerial perceptions of the British sociopolitical context. Howe, chairman of the Higher Productivity Council, wrote in 1919, 'The whole point is that workmen now say that they want a share of the control of business and this scheme [payment by results] gives them the share that they want.'[90] A similar argument can be found in an editorial in the British journal, *Machinery*: 'Employers and the heads of departments are inclined to suggest that our industrial troubles would at any rate be considerably reduced if we could have a general payment-by-results scheme, and that confidence would thereby be established between employers and men.'[91] In an extensive examination of 'What the British Worker Is Thinking', another author argued that the Fordist system of direct control was incompatible with trends in labour thinking. 'He [labour] wants to be admitted into the management of industry … What he is really resenting therein is the exercise of almost unbridled power which modern industry associates with management.'[92]

It would be false to suggest that similar pressures were not exerted by labour in the USA during this period. However, it seems safe to conclude that the weakly organized American workers were unable to make their case forcefully, while American managers appear to have been better organized. Work by Harris and Tomlins suggests that powerful American employers intervened in the political process to make sure that a set of labour institutions emerged after the depression which would ensure capital's authority at the workplace.[93]

While undoubtedly the size of the British market produced an environment which did not force British producers to alter their strategy, our reading of changes at Fords and the statements of contemporary British observers suggest that market size was not the critical factor shaping decisions on technology in Britain. During Austin's visit to Detroit in 1927, he marvelled at the size of the Ford works and the impossibility of achieving such a level of output in Britain. However, he also reported that an output of around 15 000 per year allowed a good return on investment under the American system and at 50 000 per year most economies of scale were exhausted.[94] Another observer argued that, following the First World War, there would need to be some increase in scale from pre-war levels, 'but not by any means to an amount numbing to the intelligence, and certainly not beyond the capacity of the markets of the British Empire'.[95]

This suggests that the average cost curve of the Fordist system of production fell rapidly initially and that many of the scale economies were exhausted at surprisingly low levels of output. Further expansion did lead to minor cost reductions, but Fordism's great advantage in the American context was that average costs remained at this relatively low level of output until very large levels of production were reached. Fordism was capable of supplying massive markets. Whether massive markets were necessary for Fordism seems doubtful. The same arguments cannot be made for the post-1945 era. The introduction of automatic transfer machines dramatically increased minimum efficient scale, leading to the eventual decline of the British motor vehicle industry in the 1970s.

Although we have argued that, in the 1920s, British workers escaped direct managerial control of effort norms and hence the extreme forms of labour speed-up practised in Detroit, it is not at all clear that by the 1960s the workload per hour worked was still lighter in Britain. In the USA, the rise of industrial unionism had checked some of the power of management to speed up the work pace. In Britain, the combination of self-discipline via incentive payment systems and the failure of British firms to invest in new technology created an atmosphere where labour had to work very hard to maintain pay levels and ensure the survival of their jobs. While stoppages due to both managerial incompetence and sectional labour strikes reduced the number of working hours it is less clear that hours worked were less intense in Britain than in the USA.[96]

Of all the British firms, the entry of Morris Motors was most directly a response to Ford's success in the British market. From the start Morris intended to build a limited range of vehicles and to appeal to the same segment of the market as Ford. The first Morris product, the Oxford, was placed on the market in 1913.[97] Morris closely followed the policy of buying as many components as possible from job shops, reserving for himself the task of design and assembly. Frustration with the conservatism of British job shops led him to seek supplies in Detroit in 1914 and eventually led to Morris buying many British suppliers to ensure the scale of output he desired.

After the war Morris adopted a crude assembly line when output levels were still only a few thousand. The reliance on a hand-powered line remained until 1934, by which time output exceeded 60 000. Frank Woollard, production manager at Morris Motors, was known to be a strong supporter of incentive payment systems and doubtful of British management's ability to coordinate shop-floor activity on fixed wage systems.[98] Evidence is limited about the distribution of authority on the shop floor at Morris or the ability of labour to influence effort norms, although the failure to mechanize the assembly line suggests that Morris workers did have more input into effort decisions than did Ford workers.

Experiments in automation at Morris Engines suggest that, in this particular area, Morris actually led the Americans. In the early 1920s, Morris introduced the hand transfer machine for producing cylinder blocks and this was followed by fully automated machines for manufacturing flywheels and gearboxes. This experiment in automatic transfer technology failed in part because of imperfections in hydraulic clamping devices.[99] It was not until the 1930s that clamping devices were perfected and really only in the 1950s that automated techniques became widespread.[100]

The influence of sociopolitical variables on the choice of technique is clearly evident in the post-war strategy of the Austin Motor Company. The firm's output reached 9 500 in 1924, rose to 25 000 in 1926 and exceeded 40 000 after this date.[101] Austin's strategy was influenced by the Fordist system which he observed during visits to the USA. What impressed Austin about the Ford factories was not the sophistication of the machinery used, but rather the amount of labour effort forthcoming from the workforce. He was impressed that 'everybody in the establishment seemed to be trying to do their best'.[102] This led him to argue that, if Britain was to compete with the USA, it needed an improved spirit amongst labour, not new machine methods. During the 1920s, Austin made changes in the production process and moved the firm some way towards flow production.[103] Assembly lines were installed after 1924, but they remained relatively simple and unmechanized until the late 1920s. More important, Austin's system of labour control was vastly different from Ford's. The Austin workers were placed on piece work and allowed to earn bonuses often exceeding 100 per cent.

The shaping of the Austin strategy was influenced by managerial perceptions of relations between British labour and management in the early 1920s. P. Keene, the head of the costing department, argued that 'the obvious difficulty at the moment is the lack of confidence as between employer and employed'.[104] This lack of confidence was to be resolved not by direct managerial control or machine pacing, but rather through a novel payment system called 'Bonus on Time', under which prices were set in units of work time earned rather than money earned. P. Keene suggested that the system worked because

> [with] such a basis, many economic problems become common to both employers and employed, and interests flow in one direction ... The reason why the system of control became really efficient was that they inculcated into the whole staff a maximum idea of personal responsibility to the firm itself whereby they and the firm were likely to prosper.[105]

To Keene, the efficiency of the payment system was obvious. 'The remuneration he [the worker] is able to obtain through savings is a sufficient incentive to the worker to make large output effective with the minimum of supervision.'[106]

Statements by Austin managers indicate that they saw their system as an alternative to the Ford system. They argued:

> There are still a few employers who object to piecework on principle. Their stand-point is that an efficient management ought to be able to get the same results at an agreed rate of wage without having to pay more money to encourage the men to work harder ... The daily task system at fixed wages may, perhaps, be workable in American, or even Continental factories, but the necessary ... driving works policy would not be acceptable either to English Labour or Management.[107]

Those British managers who did show greater sympathy for direct managerial control of effort norms and the high wage policy of Fordism were severely criticized by other British managers. Captain Wilks from Rover had expressed interest in the Fordist system. Cole from the Employers Federation argued that:

> Captain Wilks, to my mind is suffering from some rather ill-digested views with regard to Capital and Labour. He is a great admirer of Mr. Ford and American methods. His idea is that everybody should receive a high day rate and then be compelled to work as hard as possible and if they do not they are to be fired out.[108]

The extent to which many British employers had become dependent upon labour self-regulation rather than direct managerial control is revealed in their attitude towards the experiments at Associated Equipment (AEC) in the late 1920s. AEC was the first British vehicle maker to adopt a mechanized moving assembly line, in 1915, and by the 1920s had adopted a system which looked very similar to Fordism, including the payment of high wages on a fixed day rate scheme. The London Engineering Employers Federation threatened to expel the firm from the Association unless they changed their wage policy. They argued that 'The essential difference between his Southall scheme, and schemes in operation at Walthamstow and at other federation firms was a payment in anticipation (of output), whereas the scheme approved by the Association were payments made after the results had been assured.'[109] Management at AEC claimed that they controlled effort norms and hence it was reasonable to set wages in anticipation of certain performance standards. Their critics doubted that this was possible in the British context, and went as far as diagnosing Fordist sympathizers as suffering from a new disease, 'Forditis'. The inability of British management to enhance its authority in the shops at the expense of labour between 1900 and 1950 was evident to the 66 teams who examined American practice after the Second World War as part of the Anglo-American Council on Productivity. In their report they claimed, '[In America] the function, scope and authority of management are more widely recognized and asserted to inside the firm.'[110]

CONCLUSIONS

Our study of the rise of Fordism in Detroit and its diffusion to Britain suggests that history and sociopolitical factors play an important role in shaping new technology and limiting its spread. The standard focus on relative factor prices and scale economies at best tells only part of the story. While the smaller market in Britain made the transition to Fordism less urgent, the evidence suggests that most elements of the new technology were applicable at the levels of output British firms had attained by the 1920s. The basic Fordist innovations were relatively simple and information regarding them was easily transmitted in professional journals and through personal visits to Detroit.

We have argued that the decision by American employers such as Ford to strengthen management's authority and rely on direct control of effort norms, while British employers in general failed to increase their authority and instead relied on indirect control of effort norms through incentive payment systems, can best be explained by looking at differences in British and American sociopolitical characteristics. The relative power of capital and labour, the role of group norms and group loyalty, attitudes towards consumerism, the legacy of previous economic periods such as the size of nonproductive classes, whom Gramsci so vividly referred to as 'economic pensioners', all played as important a role in managerial decisions as the relative price of skilled and unskilled labour or the size of markets.

In the case of Fordism it seems that tension between external demands for more democratic economic decision making and Fordism's tendency to centralize that power in the hands of management was important. For a variety of reasons, Ford was able to effect such a change in Detroit and it seems was relatively successful in transferring that system to Manchester. British managers were decidedly unenthusiastic about American labour control practices and adopted different strategies based on their perceptions of labour attitudes in Britain even though, as we have suggested, these perceptions may have been mistaken. The British system of labour control relied on internally generated group effort norms formed in the context of incentive payment systems offering high bonus rates. Our analysis of Fordism's experience in Britain supports Burrage's thesis that social variables such as loyalty to groups had an important impact on the evolution of industrial technology. History did matter in this case.

NOTES

1.   K. Sward, *The Legend of Henry Ford* (New York, 1968), p. 42.
2.   This perspective of technical change in the motor vehicle industry has been the theme of some of my previous work, including W. Lewchuk, *American Technology and the British Vehicle Industry* (Cambridge, 1987). For a similar approach to this question, which focuses on the American industry, see D. Gartman, *Auto Slavery: The Labor Process in the American Automobile Industry, 1897–1950* (New Brunswick, 1986). The relationship between authority, technical change and effort norms has been explored in a series of papers by Clark. See G. Clark, 'Authority and Efficiency: The Labor Market and the Managerial Revolution of the Late Nineteenth Century', *Journal of Economic History*, **44**, (1984), pp. 1069–83; G. Clark, 'Why Isn't the Whole World Developed? Lessons from the Cotton Mills', *Journal of Economic History*, **47**, (1987), pp. 141–73; G. Clark, 'Productivity Growth without Technical Change in European Agriculture before 1850', *Journal of Economic History*, **47**, (1987), pp. 419–32. For a discussion of technical change and authority in the American canning industry, see M. Brown and P. Philips, 'Craft Labor and Mechanization in Nineteenth-Century American Canning', *Journal of Economic History*, **46**, (1986), pp. 743–56.
3.   See H.J. Habakkuk, *American and British Technology in the Nineteenth Century* (Cambridge, 1967); J. Foreman-Peck, 'The American Challenge of the Twenties: Multinationals and the European Motor Industry', *Journal of Economic History*, **42**, (1982), pp. 865–81. See also S. Tolliday, 'Management and Labour in Britain, 1896–1939', in S. Tolliday and J. Zeitlin (eds), *The Automobile Industry and its Workers* (Oxford, 1986), pp. 29–56; R. Church, 'Family Firms and Managerial Capitalism: The Case of the International Motor Industry', *Business History*, **28**, (1986), pp. 165–80.
4.   For studies which touch on some of these themes, see D.C. Coleman and C. MacLeod, 'Attitudes to New Techniques: British Businessmen, 1800–1950', *Economic History Review*, 2nd ser., **39**, (1986), pp. 588–611; D.F. Davis, 'The Price of Conspicuous Production: The Detroit Elite and the Automobile Industry, 1900–1933', *Journal of Social History*, **16**, (1982), pp. 21–46. For attempts to explain the diffusion of major production systems, see T. Veblen, *Imperial Germany and the Industrial Revolution* (Ann Arbor, 1968); P. O'Brien and C. Keyder, *Economic Growth in Britain and France, 1780–1914* (London, 1978); D. Jeremy, *Transatlantic Industrial Revolution: The Diffusion of Textile Technologies between Britain and America, 1790–1830* (Oxford, 1981); G. Tweedale, *Sheffield Steel and America: A Century of Commercial and Technological Interdependence, 1830–1930* (Cambridge, 1987).

5. R.E. Solow, 'Economics: Is Something Missing?' in W.N. Parker (ed.), *Economic History and the Modern Economist* (Oxford, 1986), p. 21.

6. Solow, 'Economics', p. 22; On the role of institutional and structural variables on economic development, see B. Elbaum and W. Lazonick (eds), *The Decline of the British Economy* (Oxford, 1986). On path-dependent economic analysis, see P.A. David, 'The Future of Path-Dependent Equilibrium Economics: From the Economics of Technology to the Economics of Almost Everything?', (unpublished paper, 1988).

7. See J.E. Sawyer, 'The Social Basis of the American System of Manufacturing', *Journal of Economic History*, **14**, (1954); E.S. Ferguson, 'The American-ness of American Technology', *Technology and Culture*, **20**, (1979).

8. A. Gramsci, *Selections from the Prison Notebooks of Antonio Gramsci* (London, 1971), pp. 304–5.

9. D. Roediger, 'Americanism and Fordism–American Style', *Labor History*, **29**, (1988), pp. 247–8.

10. M. Burrage, 'Democracy and the Mystery of the Crafts: Observations on Work Relationships in America and Britain', *Daedalus*, **101**, (1972), p. 155. On the related question of the evolution of British unions and the role of democratic impulses, see C. Behagg, 'The Democracy of Work, 1820–1850', in J. Rule (ed.), *British Trade Unionism, 1750–1850* (London, 1988), pp. 162–77.

11. On a similar theme, see S. Jones, *The Economics of Conformism* (Oxford, 1984).

12. Burrage, 'Democracy', pp. 144–5.

13. Burrage, 'Democracy', p. 156.

14. See M. Aglietta, *A Theory of Capitalist Regulation: The US Experience* (London, 1979); A. Lipietz, *Mirages and Miracles: The Crisis of Global Fordism* (London, 1987); C. Palloix, 'The Labour Process: From Fordism to Neo-Fordism', C.S.E. Pamphlet 1 – The Labour Process and Class Strategies.

15. Lipietz, *Mirages and Miracles*, p. 15.

16. Aglietta, *Theory of Capitalist Regulation*, p. 83.

17. Aglietta, *Theory of Capitalist Regulation*, p. 83; L.G. Gerber, 'Corporatism in Comparative Perspective: The Impact of the First World War on American and British Labor Relations', *Business History Review* **62**, (1988), pp. 93–127; J. Haydu, *Between Craft and Class: Skilled Workers and Factory Politics in the United States and Britain, 1890–1922* (Berkeley, California, 1988).

18. See D.T. Rodgers, *The Work Ethic in Industrial America, 1850–1920* (Chicago, 1974), p. 35; Merrit Roe Smith, *Harpers Ferry and the New Technologies: The Challenge of Change* (Ithaca, 1977); D. Montgomery, *Workers Control in America: Studies in the History of Work, Technology and Labour Struggles* (Cambridge, 1979).

19. As an example, see 'Labour Problems and Methods of Production', *Engineering and Industrial Management*, (6 March 1919), pp. 101–2.

20. On the history of Fordism in Detroit, see S. Meyer, *The Five Dollar Day* (Albany, 1981); A. Nevins, *Ford: The Times, the Man, the Company* (New York, 1954); D. Hounshell, *From the American System to Mass Production, 1800–1932* (Baltimore, 1984); J. Russell, 'The Coming of the Line: The Ford Highland Park Plant, 1910–1914', *Radical America*, **12**, (1978), pp. 29–45; Gartman, *Auto Slavery*.

21. Hounshell, *American System*, p. 215.

22. Nevins, *Ford*, pp. 211–13 and 271; O.E. Barthel, Biography, Detroit Public Library, Automotive History Collection, p. 30; Rockelman, Ford Archives, Reminiscences, pp. 9–11; Wandersee, Ford Archives, Reminiscences, p. 9; W.J. Abernathy, *The Productivity Dilemma* (Baltimore, 1978), p. 89.

23. On Ford production methods, see F.L. Faurote, 'Ford Methods', *The Engineer*, (May–Aug. 1914); Abernathy, *Productivity*, pp. 89 and 158; Dickett, Ford Archives, Reminiscences, pp. 11-14; Wollering, Ford Archives, Reminiscences, pp. 6–13; Wibel, Ford Archives, Reminiscences, p. 58; Rockelman, Ford Archives, Reminiscences, p. 9; S. Meyer, 'The Persistence of Fordism: Workers and Technology in the American Automobile Industry, 1900–1960', in N. Lichtenstein and S. Meyer (eds), *On the Line: Essays in the History of Auto Work* (Urbana, 1989), pp. 72–99.

24. Wollering, Ford Archives, Reminiscences, p. 26.

25. Gartman, *Auto Slavery*, p. 33.

26. G. Heliker, *Detroit Labor: 1900–1916*, (Ford Archives), p. 25.

27. Meyer, *Five Dollar Day*, pp. 82–5.

28. Gartman, *Auto Slavery*, examines this point in detail, p. 55.

29. Meyer, *Five Dollar Day*, p. 72 and ch. 5.

30. Litogot, Ford Archives, Reminiscences, p. 7; H.L. Arnold and F.L. Faurote, 'Ford Methods and Ford Shops', *The Engineering Magazine*, (1915), p. 673.

31. Department Appraisals 1919, Ford Archives, Acc. 73; Plant Accounts, Highland Park, Ford Archives, Acc. 571.

32. Wibel, Ford Archives, Reminiscences, p. 18.

33. H.W. Slauson, cited in Meyer, *Five Dollar Day*, pp. 60–1.

34. Ford Archives, Acc. 125, Model T Cost Books.

35. For a detailed study of the automobile foreman, see N. Lichtenstein, '"The Man in the Middle": A Social History of Automobile Industry Foremen', in Lichtenstein and Meyer (eds), *On the Line*, pp. 153–89.

36. 'The Manufacturer Much to be Admired', *Automobile Topics*, **45**, (24 Feb. 1917).

37. Ford Publicity Flyer, Ford Methods and Ford Shops, Detroit Public Library, Company Publications, pre-1950.

38. D.M.G. Raff, 'Wage Determination Theory and the Five-Dollar Day at Ford', *Journal of Economic History*, **48**, (1988), pp. 387–400, has argued that labour peace was the direct motivation behind the five-dollar day which was only indirectly related to effort norms.

39. The classic article on this subject is E.P. Thompson, 'Time, Work-discipline and Industrial Capitalism', *Past and Present*, **38**, (1967), pp. 56–97. This topic has recently been re-examined by R. Whipp, in 'A Time to Every Purpose: An Essay on Time and Work', in P. Joyce (ed.), *The Historical Meanings of Work* (Cambridge, 1987), pp. 210–36.

40. See 'Factory Transportation', *Machinery*, (1 Nov. 1917), pp. 117–19 and *Machinery*, (27 Dec. 1917), p. 347; *Automobile Engineer*, (Oct. 1917), p. 299; 'Motor Car Assembly at Hudson Plant', *Iron Age* (29 April 1920); 'Assembly of Cars in Packard Plant', *Iron Age*, (14 Oct. 1915); 'Shop Methods at the Packard Motor Company', *Automobile Engineer*, (Jan. 1916), p. 13.

41. Hounshell, *American System*, p. 261.

42. See S. Amberg, 'The Triumph of Industrial Orthodoxy: The Collapse of Studebaker–Packard', in Lichtenstein and Meyer (eds), *On the Line*, pp. 190–218. See also S. Jefferys, *Management and Managed: Fifty Years of Crisis at Chrysler* (Cambridge, 1986).

43. See K. Wennerlund, 'The Group-Bonus Wage-Incentive Plan', *Journal of the Society of Automobile Engineers*, (Nov. 1922); H.G. Perkins, 'The Group Wage-Payment Plan', *J.S.A.E.*, (Nov. 1924); J. Lanner, 'How the Group Bonus Operates', *J.S.A.E.*, (Feb. 1926).

44. On the history of the British motor vehicle industry, see G. Maxcy and A. Silberston, *The Motor Industry* (London, 1959); S. Saul, 'The Motor Industry in Britain to 1914', *Business History*, **5**, (1962); R. Church, *Herbert Austin: The British Motor Car Industry to 1941* (London, 1979); D. Lyddon, 'Workplace Organisation in the British Car Industry: A Critique of J. Zeitlin', *History Workshop Journal*, **15**, (1983), and J. Zeitlin, 'Workplace Militancy: A Rejoinder', *History Workshop Journal*, **16**, (1983); Tolliday, 'Management and Labour'; S. Tolliday, 'Government, Employers and Shop Floor Organisation in the British Motor Industry', in S. Tolliday and J. Zeitlin (eds), *Shop Floor Bargaining and the State: Historical and Comparative Perspectives* (Cambridge, 1985); Lewchuk, *American Technology*.

45. M. Wilkins and F.E. Hill, *American Business Abroad: Ford on Six Continents* (Detroit, 1964), pp. 9–25, 51.

46. W.C. Bersey, *The Motor Car Red Book* (London, n.d.).

47. Wilkins and Hill, *American Business*, pp. 31, 39, 48–9.

48. *Automobile Engineer*, (1915), p. 189. Ford Motor Company, Historical Notes, 1912, (Ford Archives, Warley).

49. *UKS Quarterly Journal*, (July 1913).
50. Wage rates supplied by the Ford Motor Company, Dagenham. See also Special Edition of the *Ford Times*, (1914) and the *Automobile Engineer* (1915).
51. E.N. Duffield, *Ford through European Eye Glasses* (Chelmsford, 1947), pp. 38–9.
52. EEF Archives, Special Conference, 1 May 1925. On British labour attitude towards the Ford operation, see *Manchester Evening News*, June 1978.
53. EEF Archives, Conference EEF and ASE, 24 July 1919, p. 29.
54. TUC Archives, Comments on the Present Economic Position of the Engineering and Allied Industries, pp. 23–4. See also 'Payment by Results', *Machinery*, (11 March 1926); 'The Correlation between Wages and Profits', *Engineering and Industrial Management*, (4 Sept. 1919), p. 2.
55. See Tolliday, 'Management and Labour', p. 35.
56. G. Maxcy, 'The Motor Industry', in P.L. Cook and R. Cohen (eds), *The Effects of Mergers* (London, 1958), p. 367.
57. See R. Church and M. Miller, 'The Big Three: Competition, Management, and Marketing in the British Motor Industry, 1922–1939', in B. Supple (ed.), *Essays in British Business History* (Oxford, 1977), pp. 163–86.
58. BBC Interviews, Fred Harrop, p. 3.
59. On Vauxhall, see E.W. Hancock, 'The Trend of Modern Production Methods', *Proceedings Institute of Production Engineers*, 7, (1928), pp. 69–83; 'The Works of Vauxhall Motors', *Automobile Engineer*, (Aug. 1930), p. 384; L. Holden, 'Think of Me Simply as the Skipper: Industrial Relations at Vauxhalls, 1920–1950', *Oral History*, 9, (1981).
60. Minute Books, Austin Motor Car Company, 17 Feb. 1920.
61. A.P. Sloan, Jr., *My Years with General Motors* (London, 1965), p. 328.
62. Holden, 'Think of Me', p. 62.
63. J. Wood, *Wheels of Fortune* (London, 1988), pp. 67–8.
64. See P. Fridenson, 'The Coming of the Assembly Line to Europe', in Krohn, Layton and Weingart (eds), *The Dynamics of Science and Technology* (Dordrecht, 1978), pp. 159–75.
65. See E. Ames and N. Rosenberg, 'The Enfield Arsenal in Theory and History', *Economic Journal*, 78, (1968); D.L. Burn, 'The Genesis of American Engineering Competition: 1850–1870', *Economic History Review*, 2, (1931); H.L. Blackmore, 'Colt's London Armoury', reprinted in S.B. Saul (ed.), *Technological Change: The United States and Britain in the Nineteenth Century* (London, 1970); Hounshell, *American System*, pp . 93–6 .
66. On the evolution of machinery, see B. Carlsson, 'The Development and Use of Machine Tools in Historical Perspective', *Journal of Economic Behavior and Organization*, 5, (1984), pp. 91–114.
67. *Proceedings of the Institute of Automobile Engineers* (1912/13).
68. R. Jackson, *The Nuffield Story* (London, 1964), pp. 59–65.
69. Minute Books, Associated Equipment Company, 9 March 1916.
70. Church, *Herbert Austin*, p. 70.
71. Minutes, Austin Board of Directors, 25 May 1927.
72. *The Engineer*, (18 June 1897), p. 620; J. Newton, 'Looking Backward', *Rudge Record*, (1909); 'Repetition Bicycle Plant', *The Cycle Referee*, (16 Feb. 1899, supplement); 'The Firms You Do Business With', *The Cycle and Motor Trades Review*, (7 June 1906), p. 541.
73. 'The Engineering Strike', *The Engineer*, (27 Aug. 1897), p. 207.
74. Simms Papers, University of London, 16/33; 'The English Motor Industry: Description of the Plant and Practice of the Daimler Company Works', *The Cycle Referee*, (19 Jan. 1899).
75. 'Direct Assembly', *The Autocar*, (4 July 1903), p. 24; 'The Humber Works (Beeston)', *The Engineer*, (4 Sept. 1903); *Motor Trader*, (8 Oct. 1913), p. 101, (7 Sept. 1910), p. 1036, (7 Aug. 1912 and 10 Dec. 1911).
76. L.A. Legros, 'Influence of Detail in the Development of the Automobile', *Proceedings Institute of Automobile Engineers*, (11 Oct. 1911).

77. Owen Linley, 'Manufacturing on a Medium Scale', *Motor Trader*, (8 July 1914); A.A. Remington, 'Some Possible Effects of the War on the Automobile Industry', Presidential Address, *Proceedings Institute of Automobile Engineers*, (1918), p. 7.
78. See Gartman, *Auto Slavery*, p. 41, on development of Norton Grinders. See Hounshell, *American System*, on accuracy of new machine techniques. R. Lumley, 'The American System of Manufactures in Birmingham: Production Methods at the Birmingham Small Arms Co. in the Nineteenth Century', *Business History*, **31**, (1989), pp. 29–43 argues that new machine techniques were adopted because they provided more accurate finish than hand techniques.
79. 'Erecting Shop Methods', *The Automobile Engineer*, (1912), p. 216.
80. 'Quality Production', *Engineering Production*, (Aug. 1923); 'The Works of Rolls Royce', *The Automobile Review*, (Feb. 1927); 'An Interesting Visit', *Engineering Production*, (4 Jan. 1923); *Engineering Production*, (8 June 1922); *Automobile Engineer*, (June 1920); 'The Works of Vauxhall', *Automobile Engineer*, (Oct. 1925).
81. For a recent study of scientific management in Britain, see M. Rowlinson, 'The Early Application of Scientific Management by Cadbury', *Business History*, **30**, (1988), pp. 377–95.
82. T.C. Pullinger, 'Opening Address', *Proceedings Institute of Automobile Engineers*, (1917/1918), p. 432. For a generally unfavourable review of scientific management, see H. Briggs, 'Repetition Work in the Engineering Industry', *Proceedings Institute of Production Engineers*, (1922), pp. 377–89. Other criticisms of American practice can be found in 'Mass Production', *Machinery*, (27 Nov. 1919); 'Robert Hadfield's Toast to the London Association of Foremen', *Managing Engineer*, (May 1916), p. 7; 'Applied Time Studies', *Automobile Engineer*, (Dec. 1920), p. 502.
83. A.W. Reeves and C. Kimber, 'Works Organisation', *Proceedings Institute of Automobile Engineers*, (1916/1917), p. 375.
84. Comments on a paper titled, 'Works Organisation', *Proceedings Institute of Automobile Engineers*, **11**, (1916/17), p. 396.
85. A. Perry Keene, 'Production – A Dream Come True', *Journal of the Institute of Production Engineers*, **7**, (1928), p. 31.
86. 'Labour Problems and Methods of Production', *Engineering and Industrial Management*, (6 March 1919), pp. 101–2.
87. On the long-run effects of this strategy, see Lewchuk, *American Technology*, especially ch. 9, 'The Collapse of the British System of Mass Production, 1930–1984'.
88. EEF Archives, P(5)27, Local Conference, CDEEA and CEJC, 6 March 1919 and 13 March 1919; ASE Coventry, Minute Books, 14 Dec. 1918, 21 Jan. 1919; EEF Archives, P(5)27, Local Conference, 18 Dec. 1918; EEF Archives, Letter CDEEA to EEF, 11 Feb. 1919 and 30 March 1919; EEF Archives, M(17)6, Fifty Per Cent Agreement, 26 June 1919.
89. On incentive payment systems in the American electrical industry, see R.W. Schatz, *The Electrical Workers: A History of Labor at General Electric and Westinghouse, 1923–60* (Urbana, 1983).
90. EEF Archives, P(13)5, Letter from Howe to EEF, 29 Oct. 1919.
91. 'Payment by Results', *Machinery*, (11 March 1926), p. 768.
92. C.H. Northcott, 'What the British Worker Is Thinking', *Industrial Management*, (Aug. 1920), p. 96.
93. See H.J. Harris, *The Right to Manage: Industrial Relations Policies of American Business in the 1940s* (Madison, 1982); C.L. Tomlins, *The State and the Unions: Labor Relations, Law, and the Organized Labor Movement in America, 1880–1960* (Cambridge, 1985).
94. 'Visit of the Chairman and Mr. E.L. Payton to the U.S.A.', Austin Archive, Modern Records Centre, MSS 226/AU/1/1/1.ii, p. 5 and 14.
95. A.H.C., 'Economy in Relation to Efficiency in the British Automobile Industry', *Automobile Engineer*, (Aug. 1915), p. 231; A.H.C., 'Notes Regarding American Production Methods', *Automobile Engineer*, (Oct. 1915), p. 305. See also F. Woollard, *The Principles of Flow Production* (London, 1954).

96. For a detailed and critical reappraisal of the many studies which have tried to claim that British labour effort norms are lacking compared with other countries, see Theo Nichols, *The British Worker Question: A New Look at Workers and Productivity in Manufacturing* (London, 1986).

97. For details on the history of Morris, see R.J. Overy, *William Morris: Viscount Nuffield* (London, 1976); P.W.S. Andrews and E. Brunner, *The Life of Lord Nuffield* (Oxford, 1955); R. Jackson, *The Nuffield Story* (London, 1964).

98. On Woollard's management philosophy, see F.W. Woollard, 'Some Notes on British Methods of Continuous Production', *Proceedings of the Institute of Automobile Engineers*, (1924); Woollard, *Principles*.

99. Woollard, *Principles*, p. 30.

100. See Gartman, *Auto Slavery*, pp. 109–14, on the spread of automation in the USA.

101. Church, *Herbert Austin*, p. 84.

102. Third Annual Meeting IAE, as reported in *Proceedings Institute of Automobile Engineers*, (1924/25), p. 7.

103. C.R.F. Engelbach, 'Some Notes on Re-Organisation of a Works to Increase Production', *Proceedings Institute of Automobile Engineers*, (1928).

104. For statements by Engelbach and Keene, see Ward Papers, MRG1, Organisation Section, W/8/29-34/13/476, pp. 2-14, housed at the Business History Unit, London School of Economics.

105. Ibid.

106. Ward Papers, W/8/29-34/476, P. Keene to MRG 1, 2 Dec. 1930.

107. EEF Archives, W(3)129, Piece Work in the Toolroom, 1 Feb. 1934, pp. 26–8.

108. EEF Archives, P(20)5, Cole Memo, 10 Sept. 1930; EEF Archives, Membership Files AEC., W.L. Bayley to A.C. Bayley, 18 March 1927.

109. EEF Archives, Membership Files AEC., Failure to Obey Rules, p. 4.

110. G. Hutton, *We Too Can Prosper: The Promise of Productivity* (London, 1953).

3.   Japanese Technology Absorption of the Haber-Bosch Method: The Case of the Taki Fertilizer Works

Akira Kudo

INTRODUCTION

The Haber-Bosch method for ammonia synthesis was of epoch-making importance to the modern history of the chemical industry since it resulted in the production of pure hydrogen and nitrogen gases, allowed for the industrial control of high-temperature, high-pressure reactions, and subsequently developed an effective industrial catalyst. The world-wide diffusion of this method was largely occasioned by the requisition of the process patented by the allied countries belligerent to Germany during the First World War. Following this, development of similar manufacturing methods took place in a number of countries, including France, Italy and the USA.[1] The first case of actual licensing was that made to the Japanese joint stock company Taki Fertilizer Works, leaving aside the case of the politically forced licensing by the German chemical firm Badische Anilin und Soda Fabrik (BASF), which held the patent, to a French firm in Toulouse during the chaotic, immediate post-war years, and also excepting the case of licensing in 1927 by IG Farben to the Norwegian subsidiary Norsk Hydro-Elektrisk Kvaelstof.[2]

In 1935, Taki Fertilizer was a phosphate fertilizer manufacturer with a paid-up capital of 3.5 million yen (approximately one million US dollars); it had approximately 800 employees in 1938.[3] It was ranked as number 159 among the largest 200 Japanese firms in 1930 as regards assets.[4] However, while it was not a small firm, it could not be regarded as representative of the large-size firm of this period. Also the calcium superphosphate sector is an area of the chemical industry which is not especially sophisticated. The very fact that such a firm should enter into a contract at this early date for technology transfer with IG Farben, the world's largest chemical firm at the time, and that it should undertake the challenge presented by the high technical standards of ammonia synthesis, is of considerable interest. In this chap-

33

ter, I shall investigate the ambitious attempt at achieving the technology transfer of the Haber-Bosch method by Taki Fertilizer Works. My analysis will concentrate on developments from construction of the plant to the beginning of operations. If one takes all of the activities involved in this process, from the initial contact between the technology supplier and the receiving party, on to contract negotiation and agreement, construction and actual operation, to be covered by the term 'technology transfer', then the most vital steps in this process from the technological viewpoint are those from construction to opening of operations. I wish to emphasize the technology receiving end as the main structural constituent in these steps, and will refer to these particular steps of transfer as the process of technology absorption. In other words, the process of technology absorption constitutes the central steps which are involved in a transfer of technology.

During the process of technology absorption frequent technical problems arose, and these in turn often resulted in conflicts. In the case of Taki Fertilizer Works, what were the particular technological problems? Also, how did both IG Farben and Taki Works undertake to overcome these problems? Further, what disputes developed between the two parties during this process? In this connection, our attention will obviously be directed towards the business strategies and organization of Taki Works. This case-study provides very good documentation for a better understanding of the reception in Japan of the advanced chemical industry, which initially developed in the West. In the course of the chapter I frequently refer to Taki Fertilizer Works (*Taki Seihisho* in Japanese) and IG Farben in the abbreviated forms of Taki and IG respectively.

DIFFUSION OF THE HABER-BOSCH METHOD IN JAPAN

Change in IG Farben's Strategy

Japan is no exception to the process of global diffusion of the Haber-Bosch method which took place through the development of similar methods in various countries, and chiefly in France, Italy and the USA. Development and commercialization of the Tokyo Industrial Institute method was carried out in Japan. After the introduction of the Casale method in 1923 by Nippon Chisso Hiryo (Nippon Nitrogenous Fertilizers) a succession of various methods for ammonia synthesis, including the Claude, Fauser, Mount Cenis (Uhde) and NEC methods were introduced into Japan. Regarding this situation one cannot help but feel a strong sense of agreement with the following remark made by the IG engineer stationed in Japan: 'The Japanese mentality is always in search of something new. However, it does not seem necessarily important whether the novelty be superior to what precedes it.'[5] The development of the Japanese ammonium sulphate industry in the 1920s was supported technologically by this kind of energetic introduction of technology.

The patent for the Haber-Bosch method in Japan had already been requisitioned by the Japanese government during the First World War and the exclusive rights had been sold off to Toyo Chisso Kumiai (Eastern Nitrogen Agency), which had been set up by the main *zaibatsus* or financial combines. However Japanese firms, including those of the *zaibatsus*, did not possess the expertise needed to commercialize this method. Further there were firms which made approaches to BASF to acquire the expertise for the Haber-Bosch method in the aftermath of the war, but these were forced to give up the idea in view of the excessive fees demanded.[6]

The reason why only the Haber-Bosch method had not been introduced along with the numerous other methods for ammonia synthesis is to be found, above all, through an analysis of IG Farben's strategy. IG did its utmost to refrain from employing alternative strategies of licensing or direct investment where expansion of exports was at all possible. This position was not only adopted *vis-à-vis* Japan but was employed world-wide. However by the mid-1930s, IG had decided to change its strategy in the case of Japan and had started to consider licensing. The background to this change was the fact that the Japanese market was already almost completely covered by Japanese firms and expectations for an export expansion seemed small. A second equipment investment boom in the ammonium sulphate industry in Japan, following on that of the early 1920s, was experienced in the period from the end of the 1920s to the early 1930s. This exactly coincided with a period of worsening global overproduction as the world depression deepened. For IG, the equipment investment boom in the Japanese ammonium sulphate industry meant the loss of the Japanese market and posed a threat to the Chinese market. The policy adopted by IG in response was to establish individual agreements with Japanese firms. This was done against the context of the international cartel (the Convention Internationale de l'Azote, CIA) established with firms in continental Europe, Great Britain and Chile. Following on a number of tentative endeavours over several years, three agreements were signed between 1934 and 1935. IG was successful in limiting Japanese exports through these but, in return, was forced to limit its own exports to Japan. Consequently, as an alternative to exports, IG began to consider licensing.

Moreover the increasing activation of the market situation for Japanese ammonium sulphate in the early 1930s had resulted in a succession of new entrants and expansion plans aimed at ensuring a share of the high profit rate. A number of these firms sounded out IG as to the possibility of the introduction of the Haber-Bosch method. Also IG was offered extremely favourable conditions, because of the strong desire for introduction, and the high expectations regarding the plant export were also attractive. This situation promoted the change in IG's strategy.

At this time, IG was considering the change in strategy not only as regards Japan, but also Finland, Egypt and Spain. IG was also considering a plan for direct investment via a joint venture to be set up with the Mitsubishi zaibatsu. However IG's choice of licensing seems quite natural in view of the rapid development of the Japanese market. Also the Haber-Bosch method was to play the role of technological support for the third wave of equipment investment which took place in the last half of the 1930s.[7]

Five Cases of Haber-Bosch Method Introduction

As can be seen from Table 3.1, five Japanese firms were involved in the importing of the Haber-Bosch method at this time. These were Taki Works, Yahagi Kogyo, Nippon Tar Kogyo, Dai Nihon Tokkyo Hiryo and Dai Nihon Seito. Of these, only Dai Nihon Seito, besides Taki, is listed among the 200 largest firms for 1930, being rated in eighth position, though Nippon Tar Kogyo was not yet formed in 1930.[8]

An analysis of these five cases, covering the steps involved from the initial approaches, signing of technology transfer agreements up to the operation, while showing a number of particularities in individual cases, reveals a number of more or less common points.[9] For example, one common point evident is the positive effort made on the Japanese side for the realization of the contract. Moreover the Japanese firms competed with each other in efforts to realize contracts. This would seem to be a kind of bandwagon effect. A second point was that the question of plant supply became the main point of dispute in negotiation. IG wanted to ensure a commission in the form of the export of German equipment, but Japanese firms desired supply to be carried out domestically, wherever possible. However, and this is the third common point, the actual contract drawn up stated that equipment supply was to be largely from Germany. Furthermore responsibility for activities from planning, equipment installation and test runs on to operations was to be taken by the IG engineers and foremen dispatched to the site. Fourthly, in many cases technical problems developed, and these gave rise to disputes between IG and the Japanese parties. These disputes were largely caused by the reluctance of the Japanese parties to entrust operations completely to IG, including those of a technological nature, and the desire of the Japanese to participate actively. It is fair to highlight a difference between this arrangement and the full turnkey basis generally adopted currently in technology transfer to developing countries. Finally, despite the various

Table 3.1 The introduction of the Haber-Bosch method in Japan[1]

Company name	Current name	Location	Intermediary	Contract signed	Start of operations[4]	Scale (ammonium sulphate tons, per year)	Hydrogen production method	Payment (yen)
Taki Seihisho	Sumitomo Precision Chemicals	Befu Hyogo Prefecture	Mitsubishi Shoji Co.	1935	1938	50 000	Aqueous	2 579 000
Yahagi Kogyo	Toa Gosei Kagaku Kogyo	Nagoya	Mitsubishi Shoji Co.	1935	1938	50 000	Winkler	2 390 000
Nippon Tar Kogyo	Mitsubishi Kasei Kogyo	Kurosaki, Fukuoka Prefecture	Mitsubishi Shoji Co.	1936	1939	80 000	Winkler	4 109 395
Dai Nihon Tokkyo Hiryo	Nitto Kagaku Kogyo	Yokohama	Mitsubishi Shoji Co.	1937	1939	50 000	Aqueous	unknown
Dai Nihon Seito[2]	Nitto Kagaku Kogyo	Hachinohe	Mitsubishi Shoji Co.[3]	1937	1940	50 000	Aqueous	unknown

Notes

[1] In Japanese records another name is given as the Manchurian Ammonium Sulphate, which was planned to produce 200,000 tons of ammonium sulphate using the Haber-Bosch method. However the start of Soviet–German hostilities made the import of machinery impossible and the plant was never realized. Refer to Sumitomo Kagaku Kogyo Co., *Company History of Sumitomo Kagaku Kogyo* (Osaka, 1981), p. 73. Since documents concerning the Manchurian Ammonium Sulphate are not to be found in the BASF archives, it is presumed that the contract was not finalized. Besides this case it is possible that there were other contracts which were not actually carried through to completion.

[2] In actual fact Nitto Kagaku Kogyo, a subsidiary of Dai Nihon Seito.

[3] Assumed.

[4] The date indicated in the contract for the start of operations (that is, indicating the date when IG turned over equipment to the Japanese party). Concerning Nippon Tar Kogyo, this is why Japanese data indicate 1939 instead of 1937. For Dai Nihon Tokkyo Hiryo and Dai Nihon Seito, since documents were not found in the contract files relating to these, the entries here are as indicated in the documents of the Japanese parties.

Source: Mainly from the records in the archives of the BASF, supplemented by Japanese Association of Ammonium Sulphate Industry (ed.), *History of Japanese Ammonium Sulphate Industry* (Tokyo, 1968), pp. 136–7, 148–9, 152–7; Tokuji Watanabe (ed.), *History of Modern Japanese Industrial Development*, vol. 13 (Tokyo, 1968), p. 311. Records concerning the introduction of the Haber-Bosch method by Yahagi Kogyo were not included in the latter source.

problems, a number of Japanese firms went on to draw up expansion plans with greater equipment scale.

Of the five cases, Taki Works and Nippon Tar Kogyo stand out, particularly with regard to the above points. These two firms were the most energetic. Moreover both persisted on the issue of domestic equipment supply and this either caused negotiation difficulties with IG when insisting on exports (Taki), or resulted in disputes after negotiations (Nippon Tar Kogyo). Also a number of serious technical problems developed in both cases in the period of operational start-up. These caused conflicts with IG and delays in planned deadlines for the equipment transfer from IG. Despite these events, both companies were already planning the second phase during the first phase, while plant construction was still in progress.

However there are also some differences between the two cases. First, whereas Taki entered into direct contact with IG, a trading company, Mitsubishi Shoji, played an important intermediary role for Nippon Tar. Nippon Tar also dispatched a technical team to observe plant and conduct tests on raw material coal. Taki does not seem to have done this. Nippon Tar also had access to the raw material coal of Mitsubishi zaibatsu, and introduced the Winkler method of hydrogen production, the most advanced method at this time. In contrast, Taki introduced the aqueous method. Moreover, whereas the managerial staff of Nippon Tar took IG as their model for a comprehensive chemical firm and aimed at creating an 'Eastern IG', Taki does not seem to have had any such managerial idea.

These differences are probably related to the question of whether the firm was or was not affiliated with a zaibatsu. Taki was a family concern, but its undertakings were not diversified enough to constitute a zaibatsu, while Nippon Tar in effect functioned as the chemical arm of Mitsubishi zaibatsu and consequently enjoyed a number of advantages.[10] In the analysis of the process of technology transfer of the Haber-Bosch method by Taki, I shall endeavour to point out any contrasts existing with the case of Nippon Tar.[11]

TECHNOLOGICAL ABSORPTION BY TAKI WORKS OF THE HABER-BOSCH METHOD

Employment of Technical Staff and General Workers

The first task which Taki undertook after the signing of the contract with IG on 28 May 1935 was the recruitment of technical staff and workers. Kitsushiro Kikuchi entered the company as chief engineer on the reference of Suzuki & Co., where he had worked before his engagement at Mitsui Mining Co. He began duties at the end of March 1936. As he was the sole engineer with experience of ammonium synthesis, he was put in charge of construction.[12] As engineer staff there were five new employees with university or technical school education, who entered the company in the spring of 1936. An unusually large number of university and technical school graduates was recruited in this year for posts including those of an administrative nature. This was part of the preparation for the entry into the ammonium sulphate sector to be achieved with the introduction of the Haber-Bosch method.[13]

Before entry into the ammonium sulphate sector, personnel in May 1934 had numbered 44, of whom seven were graduates of technical subjects of either university or technical college (university graduates, four; technical college, three). In December 1938, after entering the ammonium sulphate sector, the number of personnel had increased to 62, which represents an approximate increase of 50 per cent over this four-year period.[14] Further the seven graduates of university or technical college represented 16 per cent of the total 44 personnel in May 1934. By 1943, with regard to the ammonium sulphate plant only, there was a total technical staff of eight (one university graduate and seven technical college graduates) which accounted for 35 per cent of the total staff. An absolute and relative increase in the number of personnel, especially of technical staff, accompanied the entry into the ammonium sulphate field.[15] Further, as can be seen from Tables 3.2 and 3.3, employment of graduates from university agricultural faculties (agrochemical departments) was arrested and instead the number of graduates recruited from applied chemistry departments was augmented. The employment of graduates from electrical departments was also begun. Regionally the main source of employees shifted from the Kansai region to the Hokuriku and Chubu areas, so that recruitment was expanded.

Since the post of plant manager was an administrative one, matters concerning plant construction were left almost entirely untouched by him, and also by Minato Tsuji, the consultant who had been introduced to the firm by Suzuki & Co.; Buichi Yokoyama, the plant manager of Showa Denko (Showa Electric Industries) Kawasaki Plant, provided advice of a technical nature on an entirely personal basis, but only actually visited the plant two or three times.[16] The technical team at Taki actually responsible for plant construction consisted of a number of the newly recruited engineers taken on about the time of the decision to enter the ammonium sulphate field, and these were under the direction of the newly recruited Kikuchi.

The workforce of the ammonium sulphate plant was partly made up of workers transferred from the main factory, but largely comprised new recruits. Of these 40 were skilled workers involved in the finishing processes, and some 30 were naval petty officers experienced in the operation of machinery. Altogether a workforce of 100 workers was assembled at the ammonium sulphate plant.[17] The organization and numbers of the general

Table 3.2   College graduate personnel, May 1934

| | Technical | | | | Administrative | Total |
	Mechanical engineering	*Chemistry*	*Agriculture*	*Sub-total*		
University						
Hokkaido		1	1	2		2
Kyoto			1	1		1
Kansai					1	1
Kyushu			1	1		1
Technical college						
Nagoya Technical High	1			1		1
Kobe Technical High	1			1		1
Hiroshima Technical High		1		1		1
Total	2	2	3	7	1	8

Source: 'Report on Personnel Ages and Life Histories', Taki Kagaku Co., 'Work Regulations: Personnel List' (unpublished).

Table 3.3   College graduate personnel, ammonium sulphate plant only, 1943

	Technical					Administrative	Total
	Mechanical engineering	Chemistry	Electronics	Agriculture	Sub-total		
University				1	1	1	2
Kyoto				1	1		1
Keio						1	1
Technical college	1	5	1		7		7
Nagaoka Technical High		1			1		1
Kanazawa Technical High		2			2		2
Hamamatsu Technical High		2			2		2
Nagoya Technical High	1				1		1
Kobe Technical High			1		1		1
Total	1	5	1	1	8	1	9

Source: 'Personnel List for Ammonium Sulphate Plant', Taki Kagaku Co., 'Work Regulations: Personnel List' (unpublished).

staff and operative workforce after the commencement of operations are as
shown in Table 3.4.

*Table 3.4   Organization of general and operative personnel, 31 December
1938*

	Annexe plant	Main plant	Total
General staff	31	31 (2)[1]	62 (2)[1]
Administration	10	19 (2)[1]	29 (2)[1]
Technical	21	12	33
Operatives	387	352	739
Fertilizer production[2]	135	167	302
Sulphuric acid production	83	73	156
Lead production	7	6	13
Gasoline engine	8	12	20
Electrical engineering	26	11	37
Lathe work	2	3	5
Iron processing	15	25	40
Wood processing	1	14	15
Tin plating	0	2	2
Ammonium sulphate production	95	0	95
Miscellaneous processing	15	39	54
Total	418	383	801

Notes
[1] Figures in brackets indicate the number of female employees.
[2] Engaged in the production of phosphate fertilizers.
Besides the above, an additional 48 male and 12 female workers were employed, presumably
engaged in material handling.

Source: Taki Kagaku, 'Tables for Plant Report from 1933 to 1947' (unpublished).

Arrival of Plans and Machinery

In accordance with the contract the plant plans began to arrive from Germany.
The young engineer, Genzo Ema, who had only entered the firm in the
spring of 1936, recalled the situation as follows:

> As the plans from Germany started arriving one after the other, the first task was
> to organise and file these and then to make any necessary tracings. Next, calcu-
> lations and the designing of necessary items had to be done, but it was impossible
> for me, lacking any experience, to envisage what the plant was going to turn out
> like. For example, Mr Kikuchi would give an offhanded order such as, 'Calculate
> the pressure loss of the synthetic plant', but it was impossible to foresee what the

pipe lengths were going to be. Even if I managed to get some idea after searching through the plans for a long time, it was still impossible to tell what the resistance inside each of the particular towers was going to be. I was in the dark as to the structure of the synthesis towers. If I was seen hesitating Kikuchi would start reprimanding, 'Well, what are you doing then?' I became nervous. I would timidly confess, 'I'm afraid there is a point I'm not certain about.' He would throw some basic reference book in my direction with a brusque, 'Look it up then.' In the end, after considerable searching, I would usually come up with some hint or clue. When I went to make my report after a certain lapse of time the reply was either 'OK' or 'You infernal ass.'[18]

The immediate entrusting of such tasks as the interpretation and calculation of the plans sent from IG and of the design work based on these activities to the newly recruited technical staff caused considerable difficulties. Taki frequently consulted H. Ahrens Co. concerning difficult questions or uncertainties which arose over the plans. Ahrens replied at one point:

Your reiterated enquiry with regard to the matter to which, heretofore, a reply on our part has already been addressed, would seem, with all due respect, to stem in our opinion from a less than sufficient comprehension of the technical clarifications previously indicated in our correspondence and the plans attached therein ... We are of the opinion that you should perhaps entertain the idea of employing an engineer with the competence to satisfactorily undertake a translation and provide clarifications of the technical terminology used in the correspondence and plans sent to you.[19]

This is the first letter from H. Ahrens Co. which points out the deficiencies of Taki's technical staff. This was to become a central issue between Taki and H. Ahrens.

After the plans, machinery started to arrive. The machinery loaded on ship at Hamburg, Antwerp and Rotterdam was transferred to barges after arrival at Kobe docks and sent on to Befu. By the end of 1936, the total dispatch had been received.[20] The details and manufacturers were as follows: high-pressure compressors, gas circulating pumps – Borsig; water gas plant, conversion plant – Bamag Meguin; high-pressure apparatus, pipe lines and fittings, measuring instruments – IG; high-pressure centrifugal pumps – Hydraulik; NH_3 water pressing pumps – Balke; free jet turbines – Escher Wyss; transformer for electric heater – Siemens Schuckert; centrifuges – Gebr. Heine; saturators – Schütze A. G.; synchron motors – A.E.G.[21] With regard to the storage of the machinery let me again quote Ema's recollections:

Eventually the machinery from Germany began to arrive, and I was ordered to look after the reception; to check items against the inventory list, to sort out equipment by workshop destination, choose storage areas and draw up handling precautions. I did my best to fulfil these duties, but looking back afterwards I'm afraid these efforts were not adequate. When one of the German engineers would come asking for such and such a machine part, I was sometimes unable to reply and had a lot of trouble searching it out. As the machinery and other steel items, including pieces weighing over 1,000 tons, were without a warehouse, I had difficulty in providing protective and waterproof storage ... I had been ordered to undertake storage of the received machinery ... I had spent all my time inspecting, removing rust, coating machinery with paint or grease, etc. ... Three workmen were newly employed and placed under my direction but this was only some time after the machinery had been received.[22]

Arrival of the German Engineers and Foremen

In accordance with the contract with IG, German engineers and foremen were sent out to Japan. The first group to arrive, a five-member team, arrived at Befu in the summer of 1936. This team, which was to spend a relatively long period on site, consisted of Walter Brennecke, a mechanical engineer, entrusted with overall supervision; J. Grafe, a mechanical engineer sent from Bamag, in charge of the gas generator furnace; foreman Karl Grässle; Werner Lück, a foreman from Borsig, in charge of compressors; and foreman J. König, in charge of ammonium sulphate production.

As can be seen from Table 3.5, the number of German engineers and foremen gradually increased following the arrival of the first team and reached a peak in August 1937, with a total of 12 members. Three of these held doctorate degrees. In addition, Otto Ruhl, the chief engineer, dispatched from H. Ahrens Co., occasionally made inspection visits from Tokyo, and H. Steenbuck and G.R. Schmidt of the same company also made visits.[23]

In a large number of cases of technology transfer to Japan which occurred during the inter-war years, a similar dispatch of technical teams on a relatively large scale is to be observed. These teams were responsible for tasks involved from plant construction to the beginning of operations. Other firms introducing the Haber-Bosch method at this time, and also receiving technical direction from a German team dispatched for that purpose, were Yahagi (two engineers and three foremen) and Nippon Tar Kogyo (three engineers and four foremen).[24] In contrast to the so-called 'employed foreigners' recruited by the Japanese government in the early Meiji period, these German engineers and foremen were dispatched on a firm-to-firm basis and formed into teams to supervise the on-site construction of plants. These little-known foreigners in Japanese employ formed the advanced guard of a process of organizational teaching.

Up to this point, the site selected for the ammonium sulphate plant was to be on the land reclaimed from the sea in the vicinity of the annexe plant. It was therefore to take the form of an extension of the annexe plant site. After reclamation, the first official approval for use of the site accorded in December 1937 was for 88 000 square metres. After this, a second area approval

Table 3.5 Numbers of German engineers and foremen

		Mechanical engineers	Chemist[1]	Foremen	Others	Total
1936	Dec.	2	0	2	0	4
1937	Jan.	2	0	3	0	5
	May	2	0	3	0	5
	June	2	1	6	0	9
	July	2	2	7	0	11
	Aug.	2	2	8	0	12
	Sept.	2	2	6	0	10
	Oct.	3	2[2]	3	1[3]	9
	Nov.	3	1	4	1	9
	Dec.	2	1	5	1	9
1938	Jan.	3	1	6	1	11
	Feb.	2	1	5	1	9
	March	2	1	5	1	9
	April	1[4]	1	5	1	8
	May	0	1[5]	1	0	2
	Aug.–Dec.	0	0	1[6]	0	1

Notes

[1] Listed as chemical engineer.

[2] W. Scharlibbe (present from October to November 1937 and in January 1938) was the engineer in charge of compressors. He also had duties in Yahagi Kogyo and Nippon Tar Kogyo. H. Ahrens to Taki Works, 21 September 1937. Taki Kagaku, 'Ammonium Sulphate Plant'.

[3] Kurt Mau (October 1937 to April 1938) was chemical assistant. The salary for engineers and chemists was 1 000 to 2 000 yen, with an allowance of 800 yen. The salary of a foreman was 800 yen, with an allowance of 600 yen. However, Kurt Mau's salary was 600 yen, with no allowances. He had been taken prisoner during the First World War at Tiantsin, China, and after the war had gained teaching experience at the Dai Ichi High School and elsewhere in Japan.

[4] Chief engineer Brennecke returned to Germany.

[5] The chemist, Ernst Münzing.

[6] Foreman Grässle.

Source: 'Monthly bill for salaries owing sent from H. Ahrens to Taki Works', Taki Kagaku, 'Ammonium Sulphate Plant: H. Ahrens' (unpublished).

was given for an area of 37 000 square metres adjoining the first area.[25] Takenaka was the original contractor and undertook the work directly. Posts were driven in, to act as reinforcements, as the site was on reclaimed land.[26]

Once the site had been prepared, the construction and the installation of machinery began right away, since plans and machinery had already been received from Germany. As can be seen from Table 3.5 a chemist was present at the plant in June 1937 and a full-fledged installation of the plant would presumably have been under way then.

The German–Japanese Interface

The establishment of a cooperative network between the German and Taki teams followed closely upon the arrival of German engineers and foremen. The lower-class Japanese engineers were chosen for direct liaison activities with the Germans. Many of these were high school graduates who had only been in the firm a short time. Organization of the interface was built up around them, with the synthesis section handled by Grässle and Ema, the gas section by Grafe and Suzuki, the ammonium sulphate section by König and Wada, the compressor section by Lück and Usui. The chief engineer, Brennecke, was in overall command, and his orders were passed down through the German engineers to the lower-class Japanese engineers. All orders and instructions therefore passed via these lower-class Japanese engineers. There were sometimes disagreements with the Germans concerning the division of tasks among the workers or the drawing up of schedules and decisions on these matters were implemented on the responsibility of the lower-level Japanese engineers.

Around the time of the arrival of the German team, the work tasks for the Japanese foremen were divided up. This was necessitated by the division of the teams into groups of 10 to 15. The chief engineer, Kikuchi, chose those new operative employees who were efficient and had potential leadership to be foremen. The management of the workforce was neither by an internal nor by a foreman contractual system, but was by direct employment. The control over the workforce was basically in the managerial network.[27]

In this way, the flow of command at the construction site was from the German chief engineer to the German engineers and foremen, to the lower-class Japanese engineers, on to the Japanese foremen and then to the operatives. The key position was held by the young, lower-class Japanese engineers, as they received the instructions of the Germans directly and transmitted these orders to operatives via their foremen, and were in charge of establishing work tasks and the drawing up of schedules. They became the intermediaries between the Japanese operatives and the German team and so constituted the vital link in the chain of command.

These young Japanese engineers showed great eagerness in absorbing the technology passed on to them via the interface link with the German team. This is clear in the following recollection:

It was a great help that the foreign engineers spoke in very clear, simple English ... It was inconvenient that the foremen only spoke German but during the work it was possible to get by, just using a few German words, and this actually worked well enough and the work proceeded ... Our education by the German engineers began with basic science, and they would test our knowledge of physics and chemistry. While occasionally praised we were frequently caught out. For example, they would not accept the use of a certain formula for the solution of a given problem unless one gave a proof of the formula itself, which caused us difficulties. When this happened they would call us makeshift engineers. During training they would severely reprimand us on the position chosen for directing work if it didn't provide a vantage point for supervising all operatives and subordinates. We were given daily lectures on 'duty' and 'responsibility'.[28]

The Japanese engineers gained specialist expertise and supervisory practice and also absorbed theoretical knowledge and a certain technico-managerial philosophy with uniform humility. Their training was perfected through on-the-job training as described above. Ema recollects:

There was no educational training per se such as exists now, when we first entered the Taki Works ... Until the construction of the ammonia plant was begun I was temporarily superintendent of the calcium superphosphate plant ... Once some progress had been made with the construction of the buildings I was ordered to take charge of synthesis ... Some thirty operatives were allocated to us and with difficulty arrangements for operations with the Germans were pushed ahead.[29]

Their expertise increased rapidly through such superintendent work.

The final phase of plant construction and equipment installation was started in October 1937. On hearing of Ema's conscription, Kikuchi, chief engineer, remarked, 'It was like losing my right arm.' The young engineers played a vital role as engineers and superintendents, and made rapid progress over the short period of 18 months.[30]

Through this process Kikuchi, who was the keystone of the technical team before the arrival of the German team, was put in an increasingly unstable position in the system of control. This reflected relations with the Germans and in particular with Brennecke. Of Kikuchi it is noted,

[he] was in fact quite an aggressive man with a marked self-confidence in professional matters. He refused to give ground, convinced he was in the right. The Germans were equally obstinate at times and this caused heated arguments, often with the Germans withdrawing half winners, half losers.[31]

Moreover Brennecke and Kikuchi were 'often in disagreement with regard to the construction, and would have intense discussions'. These disagreements 'seem to have arisen between the rationalistic stance of the Germans and the more easy going thinking of Kikuchi'. For example, if a purchase order for 30m angle or 50m pipe was brought in, Kikuchi would add another 0 and change the figure to 300m or 500m. Ema records that this was 'a product of his familiarity with the American, magnanimous way of doing things'.[32] Kikuchi was experienced in operating ammonia synthesis equipment in the Claude method in Hikoshima, and had gained observation experience in the USA. He was a top-level engineer with great self-confidence and pride. His attitude on the construction site often resulted in tense relations with the German engineers.

Technological Difficulties and Conflicts regarding Construction

Generally speaking, there are usually troubles and conflicts during the construction of plants. Taki was no exception. One cause of conflict was the differing interpretations of the contract. For example, transportation costs for the early construction phase were higher than anticipated. A conflict arose as to who should bear the burden of the difference.[33] Technological friction was even graver.

Taki seems to have tried to maximize savings on the building costs. Thus the sea sand dredged during reclamation was used for factory construction by Kikuchi. The Germans demanded that this be rectified, but Kikuchi ignored their orders.[34] A similar question concerning the quality of the synthesis equipment, bricks and operatives will be examined below. Yokoyama, providing technical cooperation from Showa Denko, remarked, 'It is perhaps true that Taki was good at buying materials and machinery for the new plant. It seems that construction costs were cheapest. But because of this the functioning of the equipment seems to have been hampered.' His view does not seem accurate if one compares actual figures with the amount stated in the contract to be paid to IG. Yahagi Kogyo, introducing the Haber-Bosch method immediately after Taki, paid a total of 2.5 million yen, including commission paid to Mitsubishi Shoji Co., which is almost the same as the 2.58 million yen paid by Taki.[35] However there are signs that the construction costs, which were not included in the contract, were met as cheaply as possible and, in this regard, the hypothesis seems verified.

On the German side, there was an awareness that this attempt by the Japanese to cut costs on materials and equipment would result in quality problems: 'There was little confidence in Japanese machinery and equipment. To give one example, inspection of each individual rivet to the steel frames was ordered.'[36] The Germans also repeatedly drew attention to the insufficiency of Taki's expenditure on experimental equipment and weaknesses in their technical staff. As a result H. Ahrens demanded a substantial strengthening of the level of experimentation quality and suggested the immediate employment of university- and technical school-level engineers.

They proposed the recruiting of a university graduate chemical engineer and three or four assistants.[37] Construction work dragged on beyond the planned deadlines. Since Yahagi Kogyo and Nippon Tar Kogyo had already begun construction, Taki was in competition with these and expressed dissatisfaction with the delays. Taki wrote asking whether the number of German engineers and foremen dispatched from H. Ahrens was not inferior to those of other firms. H. Ahrens immediately sent a strong denial.[38]

Conflicts regarding the Start of Operations

On 1 December 1937 the ammonium sulphate plant was at last completed. Test runs of equipment were begun. But, as recorded with frankness in the company history of Taki Chemicals, 'because of inexperience in running the technology, mistakes and unfamiliarity in handling and the breakdown of machinery, the actual operation was still unrealised for some time'.[39] Taki and H. Ahrens were in frequent disagreement as to the reasons for these problems. On 16 January 1938, H. Ahrens wrote, 'We are forced to stop every [sic] machinery ... the lack of about 60% of workmen ... there is no guarantee for the safety of run and machinery.'[40] Conflict intensified further. On 29 January, H. Ahrens wrote:

> We regret it the most [sic] that the production could not start last May or June, but you alone are responsible for the delay, as a great deal of the Japanese parts and delivery were not finished in time ... With regard to the workmen we would never have complained if actually 150 workmen had been available constantly. As, however, there is no proper supervision or discipline on [sic] your plant and every man can come and go as he pleases, the actual number of workmen has always been considerably smaller.[41]

Although obviously representing the view of one party in the conflict, the above observation does indicate the managerial situation inside the plant with regard to the workforce. Responsibility for the actual supervision of the workforce definitely lay with the management, which had shown itself to some extent loose. In particular, it seems there were difficulties in controlling the skilled workers. Taki, at the end of its patience because of the attitude of H. Ahrens and the grave technical problems which resulted in the complete halt of test runs, informed H. Ahrens on 4 May of a freeze on all salary and allowance payments to the German engineers and foremen until regular operations were made possible.[42] Shocked at this act, H. Ahrens continued to assert that the real cause of troubles was Taki's ill-placed skimping and poor technical quality. It took up the problems of the quality of the gas plant bricks and of operative expertise.[43] Further, on the basis of a report from Münzing, based in Befu, of an output of 165 tons in 24 hours, H.

Ahrens adopted a stronger tone and declared that it considered Article 9 of the contract as met and operations as formally under way.[44]

In this way an extremely critical phase of relations was experienced, but in the end a compromise was reached and a trial run was undertaken for the guaranteed production output of 4 110 tons of ammonium sulphate as guaranteed by Article 9 of the contract. The level of achievement was not very satisfactory. According to the 'Daily Report of the Ammonium Sulphate Plant', output around this time was 65 tons on 30 March, 67 tons on 31 March, 52 tons on 1 April and 47 tons on 2 April. Nevertheless on 1 April a telegram was sent to H. Ahrens informing the firm '... of our intention to take in charge the ammonium sulphate plant'. On the same day delivery out of the warehouse was begun and the 'Daily Report' for 1 April notes this fact.[45]

Thus, during the negotiations held on 21 April 1938, Taki declared that 'Taki considers the guaranteed output as having been proved according to Article 9 of the contract' and the equipment was transferred from IG to Taki's charge and the remainder of the equipment costs were paid.[46]

At the same time as the operations and warehouse dispatch of the ammonium sulphate on 1 April 1938, Taki joined the Union of Ammonium Sulphate Manufacturers, which had been established in accordance with the Important Fertilizer Control Law of May 1936. On 2 April the Ammonium Sulphate Production Increase and Distribution Control Law was passed and the Nippon Ammonium Sulphate Co. Ltd was established as the central distributor.[47] This is why Taki took over the equipment even though the output guaranteed by Article 9 of the contract had not been reached. Taki Works and Kumejiro Taki himself decided to take charge despite the technical uncertainties involved because of these developments in the ammonium sulphate control system.

After Initiation of Operations

The ammonium sulphate plant started operations on a two-shift system. However, as is frankly admitted in the company history, 'From the beginning of operations the productivity of equipment was quite far below the official capacity because of insufficient preparations and technical expertise.' Official capacity was 50 000 tons, while the performance record for 1938 and 1939 was 18 000 tons per year, which was further reduced after 1940.[48] There was a serious lack of engineers, especially of young engineers who had been conscripted or had left the company. Towards the close of 1941, after the departure of the last Germans, an explosion occurred as the result of a fault in a safety valve of the hydrogen generator, and this resulted in the death of three operatives.[49] The chief engineer, Kikuchi, left the firm around the time of this accident, for reasons which are unclear.[50]

While construction work was nearing termination, Kumejiro Taki set an expansion programme with a target of 100 000 tons and actually let H. Ahrens and Carl Illies & Co. have the use of a hydrogen production Winkler furnace for estimates purposes.[51] However imports of machinery became difficult owing to foreign currency factors on the outbreak of the Sino-Japanese war in 1937. Moreover, as the ammonium sulphate plant was already encountering the problems noted above, there was little possibility of realizing such a programme.

In March 1942 Kumejiro Taki died. Since he had been the main driving force behind Taki Works, his death, in addition to the unsatisfactory results due to technical problems, meant that the urge to continue the running of the ammonium sulphate plant was further eroded. Against this background, Taki Works took urgent steps to enter into contract with Sumitomo Chemicals, which had been involved in ammonia synthesis and ammonium sulphate production since 1931.

CONCLUSION

We have examined the case of Taki Works in connection with the ambitious absorption in Japan of the Haber-Bosch method, which was the most advanced technology available world-wide at the time. I wish above all to emphasize the important role which was given to the young cadre of Japanese engineers at the plant site in making them the vital link between the German specialist team and the Japanese workers. Moreover their enthusiasm in absorbing the advanced technology and the practical training their work gave them as supervisors is amply illustrated and can also be seen in the following extract:

> The synthesis plant was of a high pressure nature which intrinsically required a careful and accurate attention to each detail. For example, I was required to check each individual operation for the fitting of the pipe lining, regardless of size. The expertise involved to ensure that these were fitted, neither too tightly nor too loosely, and would not leak was very demanding, and so the work could not be entrusted to just anyone. The work was accomplished by a small number of particularly expert employees ... Once the piping for synthesis had been completed, a water pressure test for 450kg per sq. cm was conducted for all the high pressure sections on 20 October 1937. The total personnel were positioned and the water pressure was gradually raised to 450kg per sq. cm. No leakages or other malfunctions were observed. So the water pressure test was passed on the first trial. The German engineer came up and was praising us highly, saying, 'I've done work in various places, but this is the first time that a test run was passed first time so perfectly.' However, I felt naturally compelled to make a sign of grateful recognition to the assembled workers. The real triumph was due

to these workers who had almost forgotten food and sleep to put all of their energies into the construction work over the last few months, and who had shown an exemplary spirit of 'duty' and 'responsibility'.[52]

As can be seen from this, the absorption of technology was profound. The young engineers played the central role in the energetic absorption of the advanced technology and were vital to the bridging of the sharp technical discontinuities which existed between the technical supplying and receiving ends. However it must be admitted that there were deficiencies in the development of an organizational learning system which could fully respond to the organizational teaching carried out by the little-known foreigners in Japanese employ. The dissatisfaction of IG and H. Ahrens during the construction was directed towards the issues of equipment and material quality, endangered by Taki's cost-cutting endeavours, and towards the insufficiencies of the engineers available. On Taki's side there was no sign of an organizational reception and handling of such criticism. The insufficiency in the engineer staff was left unresolved to the end and there was no formation of a technical team under a chief engineer.

The direct cause of this lack in organizational learning was the technological difficulty involved in moving from the superphosphate sector into the ammonium sulphate sector. Kumejiro Taki, in the top managerial position as owner, seems to have shown insufficient understanding of such problems. However, more essentially, there does not seem to have been any professional managerial staff in a position to correct this misunderstanding. In connection with the impact of technology transfer and absorption the managerial organization was unable to make the necessary changes in order to develop a managerial hierarchy. Kumejiro Taki was a typically authoritarian type of leader, unable to discuss matters with inferiors and only capable of issuing orders. For the 60 or so years from foundation to 1942, no clear organizational layout plan had existed.[53]

In its managerial organization Taki Works contrasts with Nippon Tar Kogyo. The upper cadre engineers, lower cadre engineers and workers of Nippon Tar Kogyo were also lacking experience in ammonia synthesis. Consequently, despite the recruiting of German engineers and foremen to their site, technical troubles continued and these resulted in conflicts with IG.[54] However these technical troubles were due principally to energetic introduction of advanced technology such as the Winkler method and the Alkachit production method. Despite the conflicts, Nippon Tar Kogyo and IG were able to overcome the problem through organizational technical cooperation.[55] Employing the assistance of Mitsubishi Shoji, as stipulated in the contract, Nippon Tar Kogyo dispatched a technical commission and also received support from the veteran plant supervisors of Asahi Glass and engineers of Mitsubishi Mining.[56] Such support was only made possible with the back-up support of Mitsubishi zaibatsu. Nevertheless this was not the only reason for the contrast between the companies. Thanks to the determination of the Nippon Tar Kogyo managerial staff to establish the company as an 'Eastern IG', much was learned from IG in organizational aspects.[57] Such a spirit of organizational learning was not simply due to whether or not the company belonged to a zaibatsu. The two companies form a striking and illustrative contrast with regard to their managerial organizations. When finally Taki Works became aware of the need for organizational learning there was no longer either the appropriate context or the required managerial power to accomplish it. Taki embarked on a programme of organizational learning with the cooperation of the Sumitomo zaibatsu, but it was already too late.

NOTES

1. L.F. Haber, *The Chemical Industry, 1900–1930* (London, 1971), pp. 90–1,219.
2. English translation of the words addressed to Mr Taki by Dr Münzing on the occasion of the transference of the Haber-Bosch Ammonium Sulphate Plant to the Japanese management. Taki Chemical Co. Ltd. (descendant of Taki Seihisho), Historical Archives, File Box, Ammonium Sulphate Plant – H. Ahrens, referred to hereafter as Taki Kagaku, 'Ammonium Sulphate Plant – H. Ahrens'.
3. Taki Kagaku, *A Hundred Years of Taki Kagaku History* (Kakogawa, 1985), p. 83; also Taki Kagaku, Plant Report Tables from 1933 to 1947; refer to Table 4 cited later.
4. Tsunehiko Yui and Mark Fruin, 'The Largest 200 Japanese Firms in Japanese Business History', *Japanese Business History Review*, 18, no. 1, (1983), pp. 41–5.
5. Besprechung in Leuna uber Auslandsprojekte, 9 June 1939, BASF Archives, Nachlass Pier, 1 Japan 1936–45. Furthermore this engineer undertook the licensing in Japan of the IG method relating to synthetic oil. See Akira Kudo, 'IG Farben's Japan Strategy: The Case of Synthetic Oil', *Japanese Yearbook on Business History 1988*, (1989), pp. 94–5.
6. With reference to the activities for the Haber-Bosch method in Japan in the 1920s, refer to the following: Tokuji Watanabe (ed.), *History of Modern Japanese Industrial Development*, vol. 13 (Tokyo, 1968), pp. 312–18 (written by Takau Suzuki); Hidemasa Morikawa, *Studies in the Business History of the Zaibatsu* (Tokyo, 1980), pp. 168–75; Juro Hashimoto, 'The Establishment of the Ammonium Sulphate Monopoly', *Tokyo University Journal of Economics*, 45, no. 4, (1980), pp. 48–9. In connection with technology transfer and the investment boom in the 1920s, refer to Hashimoto, 'Establishment', pp. 49–55; Tsuneo Suzuki, *History of Japanese Ammonium Sulphate Industry* (Kurume, 1985), pp. 62–108.
7. For greater detail, see Akira Kudo, 'IG Farben's Japan Strategy: The Case of Nitrogen', *Tokyo University Journal of Social Science*, 39, no. 2, (1987), pp. 45–50. This paper is based largely on the document files of BASF Archives for historical documents relating to Japan. Further as the patent for the Haber-Bosch method became ineffective from the beginning of 1933, the provision of technology by IG after that date should, for accuracy, be described as technological assistance and not licensing. Actually there is no item in the contract between IG and Taki Works relating to the implementation of the patent rights. However the term licensing has been taken in the wider sense to include the provision of technology, whether with or without patent.

8.   Yui and Fruin, 'Largest 200 Japanese Firms', pp. 41–5.
9.   In detail, see Kudo, 'IG Farben's Japan Strategy: The Case of Nitrogen', pp. 51–76. This analysis makes use of the scheme proposed by Hoshimi Uchida for the analysis of technology transfer processes. See Hoshimi Uchida, 'Technology Transfer and Autonomous Development in the Chemical Industry in the Taisho and Early Showa Periods: Industrial Activities relating to International Technology Transfer Processes', *Japan Business History Review*, 7, no. 1, (1972), pp. 69–72.
10. This is based on the definition given of 'zaibatsu' by Hidemasa Morikawa: 'A diversified managerial body under the exclusive ownership and control of a rich clan or family'; see Morikawa, *Studies*, p. 4.
11. Fortunately, moreover, the situation regarding historical materials for the two companies is comparatively good. For Taki Works, in addition to the company history, there are a large number of in-company historical materials preserved. These are the only internal company data available relating to the theme of technology absorption of the Haber-Bosch method in Japan. Internal company historical data for Nihon Tar Kogyo has been lost, but reference was made to materials remaining in 'Thirty Years of History of Mitsubishi Kasei (Mitsubishi Chemicals): Foundation and Establishment' (manuscript), third manuscript no. 1 (1966). Historical internal company data do not exist for the other companies.
12. Kikuchi's life history up to the time of joining the firm is as follows. Born 1891, graduated from Tokyo Technical High School (now Tokyo Institute of Technology) in 1912. After working at the Taiwan Niitaka Sugar Refinery, he was employed by Suzuki & Co. in 1915, responsible for oil manufacturing, and in 1924 he was employed by the Claude Method Chisso Kogyo Co. This company was set up with the aim of manufacturing ammonium sulphate by Suzuki & Co., which had received a licence for the Claude method from L'Air Liquide Co., and a plant was constructed in Hikoshima, Yamaguchi Prefecture. From 1928 to 1929, for approximately six months, Kikuchi made an observation tour in Europe and the USA. In 1929, during this voyage, Suzuki & Co. went bankrupt and, as the managerial rights for the Claude Method Chisso Kogyo (later Dai Ichi Chisso Kogyo) went to Mitsui Mining, he became an employee of that company. From 1934 he worked at Toyo Koatsu Kogyo in Omuta City. (Taken from the curriculum vitae dated 16 June 1936, Taki Kagaku, 'Work Regulations: Personnel List'.) There were several business transactions relating to raw materials with Taki Works before the bankruptcy of Suzuki & Co. and Kumejiro Taki knew Naokichi Kaneko, the top manager of Suzuki. (The above data were collected in an interview of 1 February 1988 with the present Chairman of Taki Kagku, Rintaro Taki).
13. From an interview held on 2 February 1988 with the ex-managing director for the manufacturing department of Seitetsu Kagaku Co., Genzo Ema, 'Recollections of My First Company Days', *Befu Chemical Company Report*, no. 4 (1959), p. 7. Ema's career is briefly as follows. He graduated from the applied chemistry section of Hamamatsu Technical High School (now Shizuoka University, Technology Department). He entered the company in March 1936. He was conscripted just a little over one and a half years later, and this may explain the clarity with which he especially recalls the plant construction period. He returned to the company in autumn 1942.
14. From Taki Kagaku, 'Report on Personnel Ages and Life Histories', 'Work Regulations: Personnel List', 'Plant Report Tables from 1933 to 1947'.
15. From Taki Kagaku, 'Report on Personnel Ages and Life Histories', 'Work Regulations: Personnel List'; 'Table of Ammonium Sulphate Plant Personnel', 'Work Regulations: Personnel List'.
16. Taki, *Hundred Years*, p. 83; also in the interview with Taki and that with Ryotaro Minami, the present Managing Director of Personnel on 1 February 1988.
17. Interview with Ema.
18. Ema, 'Recollections', p. 7.
19. Letter of 26 February 1936 from H. Ahrens affiliate to Kumejiro Taki, Taki Kagaku, 'Ammonium Sulphate Plant – H. Ahrens'.
20. Committee for Biography of Kumejiro Taki, *Kumejiro Taki* (Kakogawa, 1958), p. 122.

21. H. Ahrens to Taki Seihisho, 11 September 1937, Taki Kagaku, 'Ammonium Sulphate Plant – H. Ahrens'.
22. Ema, 'Recollections', p. 8.
23. The monthly wage bills sent from H. Ahrens to Taki Works. Other data from Taki Kagaku, 'Ammonium Sulphate Plant – H. Ahrens'; Taki, *Taki*, p. 122; Taki, *Hundred Years*, p. 82; Ema, 'Recollections', p. 8. 'Finally the Germans started to arrive, and there were considerable fluctuations as to their number; at their most numerous they were around ten in all; the longest staying and most familiar were the three from IG, the employee from Borsig and the one from Bamag.' Incidentally, only Brennecke, the chief engineer, was accompanied by his wife, the others being single and staying in hotels. (Interview with Ema.)
24. H. Ahrens to Taki Works, 21 September 1937, Taki Kagaku, 'Ammonium Sulphate Plant–H. Ahrens'.
25. Taki, *Taki*, pp. 121–2, 286.
26. Interview with Ema.
27. Ibid.
28. Ema, 'Recollections', p. 8.
29. Ibid., pp. 7–9.
30. Ibid., p. 9.
31. Ibid., p. 8.
32. Letter from Ema, 9 February 1988.
33. H. Ahrens to Taki Works (Re. starting of your S/A Plant), 10 June 1937. Taki Kagaku, 'Ammonium Sulphate Plant – H. Ahrens'.
34. Interview with Ema.
35. Taki, *Taki*, p. 64; Kudo, 'IG Farben's Japan Strategy: The Case of Nitrogen', p. 62.
36. Ema, 'Recollections', p. 8.
37. H. Ahrens to Taki Works, 10 June 1937, Taki Kagaku, 'Ammonium Sulphate Plant – H. Ahrens'.
38. Ibid., 21 September 1937.
39. Taki, *Hundred Years*, p. 83.
40. H. Ahrens to Taki Seihisho, 16 January 1938, Taki Kagaku, 'Ammonium Sulphate Plant – H Ahrens'.
41. Ibid., 29 January, 1938.
42. The salary and allowance for German engineers was 1 800–2 000 yen, for foremen 1 400 yen. The salary for the Japanese engineers was 50 yen starting salary and 55 yen for employees starting in 1944, and 150 yen for chief engineers (interview with Ema, and 1944 personnel records). A rough calculation shows that the German engineers and chemists received 40 times the salary of the Japanese engineers newly recruited, and foremen 30 times. The grand total pay roll for March 1938 was 16 334 yen and, though the actual amount is small compared to the total payment to IG, the psychological burden for Taki may have been great.
43. H. Ahrens to Taki Seihisho, 7 March 1938, Taki Kagaku, 'Ammonium Sulphate Plant – H. Ahrens'. However Ema, responsible for the gas plant as of autumn 1942, gives a completely different reason: the chimney bricks at the aqueous gas generator would often fall out and interrupt plant operations. The reason was the oval-shaped chimney, resulting in a small exposed part of the brick. This shape was due to German rationalism since a saving could be made on pillar dimensions used in the gas plant. Ema rectified it by changing to a round shape and operations were smooth afterwards. Letter from Ema, 9 February 1988.
44. H. Ahrens to Taki Seihisho, 16 March 1938, Taki Kagaku, 'Ammonium Sulphate Plant – H. Ahrens'.
45. Daily Reports of Ammonium Sulphate Plant, Taki Kagaku, 'Ammonium Sulphate Plant – H. Ahrens' and Taki, *Hundred Years*, pp. 83–4.
46. H. Ahrens to Taki Seihisho, with Agreement, 22 April 1938, Taki Kagaku, 'Ammonium Sulphate Plant – H. Ahrens', Vertragsmappe 1940, BASF Archives.
47. Taki, *Taki*, p. 123.

48. Taki, *Hundred Years*, pp. 87, 96.

49. Interviews with Taki and Ema.

50. After quitting the company, Kikuchi entered the Union of Ammonium Sulphate Manufacturers. After the war, in 1951, he entered Befu Kagaku (which took over from Sumitomo Taki Kagaku, set up with joint capital from Taki Works and Sumitomo Kagaku) on a temporary basis and was posted to the Mining Centre in Tokushima Prefecture. After supervising the development of a sulphur mine, he died in 1953. (From a letter of 26 March 1951 from Kikuchi to Saburo Taki, the second President, and other data. Taki Kagaku, 'Work Regulations: Personnel List').

51. H. Ahrens to Taki Seihisho (Estimate for a Nitrogen Plant to Produce 100 000 tons per year S/A). Taki Kagaku, 'Ammonium Sulphate Plant – H. Ahrens'. Also low-temperature carbonization of coal was considered. An 11-page report bearing Kikuchi's name and dated 28 May 1941, entitled, 'Low-Temperature Carbonization of Coal in Connection with the Ammonia Synthesis Industry', is extant. Taki Kagaku, 'Sumitomo Taki Kagaku'.

52. Ema, 'Recollections', p. 9.

53. From an interview in Taki, *Hundred Years*, p. 261.

54. 'All of the section chiefs were without experience in fertilisers and the personnel posted below them were young engineers just graduated in 1935 and 1936 ... Moreover, the operatives actually handling the machinery who were under the section chiefs and supervisors were new to the work and this rapidly resulted in breakdowns, the only personnel with experience being the naval machinists ... Breakdowns occurred as early as the installation and attachment of machinery. Initially, the section with the largest number of breakdowns was the oxygen plant.' The installation of machinery was finished in October 1937 and operations began in November. On 26 December, 1.5 tons of the first manufactured batch of ammonium sulphate were produced. This was almost exactly the same timing as for Taki Works. However breakdowns once again developed. This was in the Winkler furnace, fourth section, and in the Alkachit refining section. 'Thirty Years' History of Mitsubishi Kase', p. 160.

55. Ibid., pp. 161–7. In 1938, it is noted, 'In any case nearly full operation was achieved for the beginning of September.'

56. Ibid., p. 160.

57. Ibid., p. 115.

4. Transatlantic Transfer of Buna S Synthetic Rubber Technology, 1932–45

Peter J. T. Morris

INTRODUCTION

We are living in the 'Polymer Age', and few polymers have been more important than synthetic rubber.[1] World production reached 900 000 tonnes as early as 1944; it is now just over ten million tonnes a year, about twice the output of natural rubber.[2] This scale of production made synthetic rubber a pioneer in the field of high-tonnage polymers. Synthetic rubber research stimulated the development of other polymers, notably polystyrene, acrylonitrile-butadiene-styrene (ABS) and acrylic fibres. The production of butadiene from petroleum during the Second World War accelerated the growth of petrochemicals in the USA.[3] Furthermore rubber has always been of strategic importance, particularly in wartime, producing a degree of state involvement in the development of synthetic rubber that was unusually high for the chemical industry.

Buna S synthetic rubber is the classic example of a technology that was innovated elsewhere, but was soon transferred to the USA, which has continued to dominate the industry to the present day. America produced 900 000t of Buna S type (SBR) synthetic rubber in 1988, about twice as much as Japan, and three times more than West Germany. It is striking how comparatively modest transfers of know-how to the USA were rapidly transformed into a large industry. As in so many other cases, a new technology achieved its full potential away from its birthplace.

At the outbreak of the First World War, the German organic chemical industry lacked any serious rivals.[4] The USA was rapidly consolidating its position in inorganic chemicals and even pharmaceuticals, but imported most of its organic chemicals. Three decades later, when the Second World War ended, the USA had overtaken Germany in organic chemicals, above all in the new petrochemicals industry, and the West Germans had to import

57

American technology to rebuild their chemical industry in the 1950s.[5] The transfer of synthetic rubber across the Atlantic produced a remarkable web of technology exchanges, usually from Germany to the USA, but also in the reverse direction (Figure 4.1). The technologies that were developed as a result of these transfers have since been diffused to many other countries.

The technology of synthetic rubber manufacture is complex, but I have sketched an outline in the Appendix and in a flow chart (Figure 4.3). While the history of synthetic rubber is inseparable from its technology, it is not necessary, fortunately, to grasp the finer points of synthetic rubber manufacture to follow my general historical arguments. The use of different raw materials in Germany (coal) and the USA (ethanol and petroleum) is not addressed in this study,[6] which focuses on the final product processed by the rubber industry.

THE ORIGINS OF BUNA S

At the beginning of the twentieth century there was a rising demand for rubber, in particular for pneumatic tyres in bicycles and the new-fangled motor-car.[7] The supplies of wild rubber from the Amazon basin were clearly inadequate and plantations sprang up in the Far East to meet the demand. Rubber trees take several years to mature, however, and the rubber price continued to spiral upwards. The all-time high of 12s 9d (64p) per pound was reached in 1910.[8] The plantations now came into production and the price slumped to less than 3s (15p) per pound in 1913. In the meantime these high prices stimulated synthetic rubber research in the USA and Germany.[9]

Two rubber companies carried out research on synthetic rubber in the USA: under Lucas Petrou Kyriakides (he later shortened his name to Kyrides) at the Hood Rubber Co. of Watertown, Massachusetts, and under David Spence at the Diamond Rubber Co. of Akron, Ohio, which was taken over by B. F. Goodrich & Co. in 1912.[10] Both research groups decided to polymerize methylisoprene, but the falling natural rubber prices after 1912 foreclosed further development by either company. Kyriakides' research was particularly noteworthy; he prepared pure isoprene and used the four-step process for butadiene which was later developed by IG Farben.

Superficially Germany was in an excellent position to develop synthetic rubber. It lacked a secure supply of natural rubber, but possessed abundant reserves of coal for organic synthesis. Between 1863 and 1914, the German dye industry had created formidable industrial research and development systems based on German excellence in organic chemistry. By 1914, the German dye firms had successfully developed synthetic analogues of the natural dyes alizarin and indigo, countless synthetic colours, and a growing

Figure 4.1   Transatlantic transfers in synthetic rubber technology

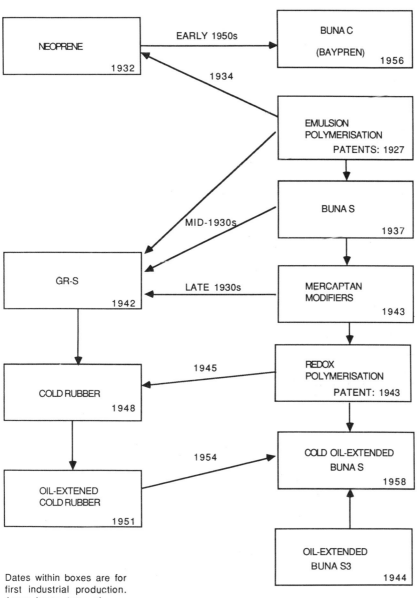

USA   GERMANY

NEOPRENE
1932

EARLY 1950s

BUNA C
(BAYPREN)
1956

1934

EMULSION
POLYMERISATION
PATENTS: 1927

BUNA S
1937

MID-1930s

GR-S
1942

LATE 1930s

MERCAPTAN
MODIFIERS
1943

1945

REDOX
POLYMERISATION
PATENT: 1943

COLD RUBBER
1948

1954

COLD OIL-EXTENDED
BUNA S
1958

OIL-EXTENDED
COLD RUBBER
1951

OIL-EXTENDED
BUNA S3
1944

Dates within boxes are for
first industrial production.
Approximate dates of
technology transfer are
shown on the arrows.

Figure 4.2   Synthesis of Buna S (GR-S) monomers

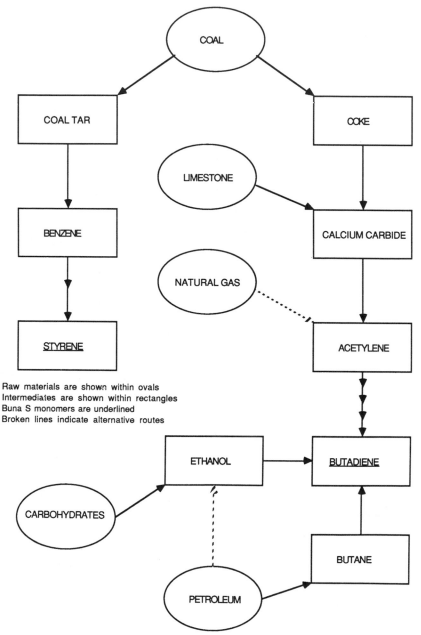

Raw materials are shown within ovals
Intermediates are shown within rectangles
Buna S monomers are underlined
Broken lines indicate alternative routes

number of therapeutic agents, including tuberculosis antitoxin, barbiturates, aspirin and Salvarsan. They had built up excellent sales organizations for dyes and pharmaceuticals. Furthermore German academic chemists were at the forefront of the new fields of physical and colloid chemistry and were in a strong position to develop the scientific study of polymers.[11]

Bayer was the first German company to tackle the synthesis of rubber. The impetus came from a surprising source, a speech made by (Sir) Wyndham Dunstan of the Imperial Institute to the Chemical Section of the British Association at its meeting at York in 1906, entitled 'Some Imperial Aspects of Applied Chemistry'. In the course of his discussion of rubber chemistry, Professor Dunstan remarked, 'it cannot be doubted that chemical science will sooner or later be able to take a definite step towards the production of rubber by artificial means'.[12] Fritz Hofmann, chief chemist in Bayer's Pharmaceutical Department, read a report of Dunstan's speech in *Chemiker-Zeitung*,[13] and immediately asked Carl Duisberg for funds to pursue this line of research. Duisberg provided a grant of 100 000 marks a year, and a small research group was set up.[14]

Hofmann initially concentrated on the synthesis of isoprene. He successfully produced polyisoprene in 1909, but his process was quite uneconomic, owing to the high cost of synthetic isoprene. Not long afterwards, Hofmann's assistants, Kurt Meisenburg and Curt Delbrück, prepared methylisoprene by dimerizing acetone with aluminium. Acetone was a relatively cheap product obtained from wood distillers, and it was manufactured from acetylene by Hoechst in 1916. Bayer adopted the seed polymerization noted by Ivan Kondakov. A small piece of polymer was added to a tank of methylisoprene, which was converted in a period of several weeks into a cauliflower-like rubber. This methyl rubber was first used (mixed with natural rubber) to make tyres in 1912, and was used as an *ersatz* material in the First World War. Bayer made over 2 000 tonnes of methyl rubber during the war, and BASF a much smaller amount using sodium polymerization. It was leathery, aged rapidly and was unsuitable as a tyre rubber; vehicles with methyl rubber tyres had to be jacked up overnight. As it was also three times more expensive than natural rubber, it is not surprising that the production of methyl rubber was abandoned at the war's end.

If the falling price of natural rubber, which declined by 76 per cent between February 1920 and March 1922, made synthetic rubber uneconomic, it also threatened to bankrupt the rubber plantations in British Malaya. In 1922, Winston Churchill, then Colonial Secretary, introduced a plan (the so-called Stevenson scheme) to restrict rubber exports from Malaya to force up the price and thereby protect the infant industry.[15] This produced predictable upheavals in the market and the rubber price suddenly accelerated to 4s 5d (22p) per pound in July 1925. To calm the situation, the British authorities raised the exportable percentage in November, but the damage was done. The major rubber consuming nations, enraged that they were at the mercy of the British government, encouraged research into synthetic rubber. The period between 1925 and 1932 saw the establishment of modest synthetic rubber production in the Soviet Union, Germany and the USA. Winston Churchill might thus be called the father of the modern synthetic rubber industry!

In 1925, the major German dyestuff companies, including BASF, Bayer and Hoechst, merged to form IG Farbenindustrie AG (usually shortened to IG Farben or IG).[16] The new concern decided, as a result of the rubber panic and with the encouragement of Germany's largest rubber company, Continental Gummiwerke AG (Conti), to resume research into synthetic rubber.[17] Initially attention was focused on the sodium polymerization of butadiene to produce polybutadiene or 'Buna' (a contraction of Butadien and Natrium, the German names for butadiene and sodium). While Buna rubber represented a significant improvement on methyl rubber, its tear and tensile strength, and its stickiness, were insufficient for use as a passable tyre rubber.

The former Bayer chemists in Leverkusen strove to replace sodium polymerization with emulsion polymerization. In emulsion polymerization, the hydrocarbon starting materials are suspended in an aqueous emulsion by soap, and the resulting polymer is in the form of small particles or 'crumbs' rather than a solid block. This allows a greater degree of control over the operating temperature and the final product is easier to handle. Buna S arose from an attempt by Claus Heuck, in Ludwigshafen, to 'lubricate' the unsatisfactory 'dry' and crumbly polymer produced by the emulsion polymerization of butadiene by adding drying oils, usually linseed oil, before the polymerization. Kurt Meisenburg – who was working on the polymerization of styrene in Leverkusen – then discovered that a small amount of styrene could produce a similar improvement. In June 1929, his colleague Walter Bock polymerized butadiene and styrene in a 2:1 ratio, to produce a copolymer with excellent wear resistance when compounded with carbon black. The key patent, perhaps the most important in the history of synthetic rubber, was filed on 21 July 1929.

By a remarkable coincidence, Herman Mark and Carl Wulff, in Ludwigshafen, patented a cheap route to styrene 19 days later. Now Buna S (S for Styrol, the German name for styrene) was not only better, but also cheaper than the sodium-based rubbers. Buna N, a copolymer of butadiene and the more expensive acrylonitrile (the N stands for Nitril), was patented by Leverkusen's Erich Konrad in April 1930. By this time, IG was concerned about the sharp fall in the price of natural rubber and the economic effects of the Depression. Six months later, before Buna S and Buna N had left the laboratory, the synthetic rubber research was practically suspended.

Fortunately tyre tests at the Nürburgring racecourse were permitted to continue and they revealed in December 1931 that Buna S was significantly more hard-wearing than natural rubber. It also became clear that it was impossible to process Buna S or Buna N on the machinery used by the rubber industry, because they were harder than natural rubber. In February 1932, IG decided to find an American rubber company to collaborate on experiments to overcome this problem, through its American ally Standard Oil of New Jersey. Negotiations with Goodrich were unsuccessful and, before a contract was signed with General Tire of Akron in June 1933, major technological and political changes had transformed the situation.

In November 1931, Du Pont announced that it was launching a new synthetic rubber, a polymer of 2-chlorobutadiene (chloroprene), made from acetylene.[18] It was originally called Duprene, but this was changed to neoprene in 1936 to avoid associating Du Pont with the finished products, which might be of poor quality. The effective marketing strategy of Ernest R. Bridgewater, the sales manager of the Rubber Chemicals Division, was the crucial factor in neoprene's commercial success. Faced with low natural rubber prices, he was convinced that neoprene had to be presented as a wholly new material with special properties, not just a new synthetic rubber. To persuade rubber manufacturers to use idle equipment to process neoprene, it had to be made comparable to natural rubber in processing characteristics. Du Pont kept in close contact with the rubber industry and publicized its new product widely, sending salesmen to large potential consumers and publishing material for smaller ones. As John K. Smith has remarked, Du Pont indirectly boosted demand for neoprene 'with this well-orchestrated sales campaign aimed at fabricators, engineers and consumers'.[19] This strategy enabled Du Pont to sell neoprene for 65 cents a pound in 1939, compared with a natural rubber price of 18 cents a pound.

The successful introduction of neoprene posed a major threat to the Buna copolymers, and IG Farben quickly appreciated the potential of a relatively cheap synthetic rubber that could command a premium price for its special properties, particularly its resistance to oil, solvents and aerial oxidation. That Buna S survived to become the most important synthetic rubber, at least in terms of volume, was the result of an equally dramatic upheaval in German and international politics.

BUNA S IN THE THIRD REICH

Hitler came to power at the end of January 1933, determined to increase Germany's economic self-sufficiency and military preparedness.[20] Synthetic rubber was one of the few fields in which autarky (self-sufficiency) was technologically feasible and would be vital in a motorized *blitzkrieg* if Britain imposed a naval blockade. It also complemented Hitler's interest in motor transport: his people's car (Volkswagen) would glide along the new autobahns on all-German tyres. Complex and energy-intensive, yet compact and clean, with an aura of high-technology, the desired Buna works were the ideal showpiece factories.

By contrast, IG Farben was sceptical about German self-sufficiency in rubber. In June 1933, IG's chief rubber chemist, Erich Konrad, wrote to Fritz ter Meer, the Vorstand member in charge of synthetic rubber, that 'synthetic rubber is simply unsuitable for an autarky experiment'.[21] IG's negative view of autarky was reinforced by its growing interest in the development of oil-resistant rubbers. Du Pont was demonstrating how it was possible to sell speciality rubbers at a premium, even during an economic depression. When Conti told Konrad in May 1933 that it was testing neoprene, he countered by offering Buna N, the oil-resistance of which had only recently been discovered by IG. IG began small-scale production of Buna N in 1934 and used Buna N, rather than Buna S, in the tests arranged with General Tire. The Akron firm experimented with Buna N in the spring of 1934, but complained that the synthetic rubber was destroying its machinery and was 'definitely inferior' to natural rubber.[22] At this stage, IG aimed to satisfy the government's demand for synthetic rubber with Buna N, and sell any excess production as an oil-resistant rubber in competition with neoprene.

After consolidating his power in the summer of 1934, Hitler stressed that he wanted the development of synthetic rubber to be pursued with 'an elemental force'.[23] When IG Farben failed to match his expectations, he goaded it into action by declaring at the 1935 Nuremburg rally that 'the erection of the first [synthetic rubber] factory in Germany ... will be started at once'.[24] As he later wrote in a secret memorandum, 'from now on there must be no talk of processes not being fully determined and other such excuses'.[25]

This pressure put IG in a quandary, as the company had not been able to obtain a licence for neoprene from Du Pont, nor was it ready to scale up the Buna S technology. Buna N had been found in the summer of 1934 to be unsuitable as a tyre rubber, because it could not be blended or repaired with natural rubber. In an attempt to secure a licence for neoprene, Fritz ter Meer travelled to Du Pont in Wilmington, Delaware, in October 1934, but the negotiations ended in deadlock.[26] Tests carried out in November 1935 showed that Buna S was possibly superior to neoprene as a tyre rubber, but the dual benefit of a general-purpose rubber that was also oil-resistant was so irresistible to IG that ter Meer continued to negotiate with Du Pont. The two companies eventually signed a modest agreement in September 1938. Du Pont gave IG a licence to use Du Pont technology to produce butadiene, which was not taken up by IG, but not to make neoprene. The Germans honoured this restriction and, while IG Farben prepared neoprene in experimental quantities during the war, it was never made on an industrial scale.

Under increasing pressure from Hitler, and lacking a neoprene licence from Du Pont, IG Farben was forced at the end of 1935 to choose Buna S as its main synthetic rubber.[27] This haste reduced the quality of Buna S and hindered the development of better synthetic rubbers. The firm attempted to meet the government's demands by building a pilot plant at Schkopau in March 1937, and a small, 24 000 tonnes a year plant in May 1938. The main works at Schkopau were completed in April 1939, and the second factory at Hüls, near Recklinghausen, started up in August 1940. After a long-running disagreement over the necessity of and the site for the third factory, IG agreed after the outbreak of war to build it at Rattwitz, near Breslau. The firm unilaterally abandoned the site in July 1940, after the French capitulation, but was forced to make provision for two factories a few months later when Britain failed to surrender. One was erected alongside the Ludwigshafen works, against the advice of the armed forces, on the condition that the fourth plant was located beyond the reach of British bombers. IG selected a site at Auschwitz, about seven kilometres from the concentration camp, but the factory never produced Buna S, despite the extensive use of forced labour. German production of Buna S increased from a mere 2 110 tonnes in 1937 to a wartime peak of 110 569 tonnes in 1943.

To overcome the processing problem, IG developed the thermal degradation (*thermisches Abbau*) process with the cooperation of Conti. This softened Buna S by heating it at a high temperature in air, breaking down the long polymer chains into more easily processed fragments, which also improved some of its physical properties. However it was also a time-consuming and technically tricky process, and the treated rubber had to be used within 24 hours.[28] The introduction of compounds into the polymerization recipe which 'moderate' the growth of the polymer chains and prevent them from becoming too long proved to be a better alternative. A range of moderators or 'modifiers' had been developed for sodium polymerization by the Ludwigshafen laboratory in 1929.[29] The first suitable modifier for Buna S, linoleic acid, was patented during the scaling-up research at Leverkusen in June 1936. Better modifiers, which contained sulphur, were discovered at Leverkusen by Kurt Meisenburg's group (diproxid or dixie) and Wilhelm Becker's group (long-chain mercaptans, later used in the USA) during 1937. IG preferred the original modifier until the growing shortage of linoleic acid impelled the introduction of sulphur-based modifiers in 1943 (Buna S3). However even Buna S3 required thermal degradation before processing.

AMERICAN ASSESSMENT OF GERMAN BUNA S

When American experts visited Germany in 1945, they were surprised at how little progress had been made in improving the quality of Buna S, which was no better than and probably not as good as the American equivalent.[30] The poorer quality of Buna S was partly a result of Hitler's impatience for synthetic rubber production, but also a consequence of the traditions and environment of the German organic chemical industry. The IG Farben predecessors shared a long tradition of successful research in organic chemistry. They had built up excellent sales organizations for dyes and pharmaceuticals. Rubber and the rubber industry stood outside this tradition. IG's success in organic chemistry and high-pressure chemistry had made its managers self-confident to the point of contempt for other companies. The firm was thus unwilling to concede that it could learn from the rubber companies, even the large and technologically advanced American corporations. Relations with the leading rubber companies, even Conti, were at best lukewarm. In 1938, the firm overturned a government plan for a joint venture between IG and the German rubber industry.[31]

The American investigators asked Erich Konrad why IG insisted on producing a tough rubber:

> The research man's answer ... was that the tough rubber was a better rubber, and that the synthetic manufacturer could not tell the tire company how to process Buna S. German tire technicians, on the other hand, stated that softer, better processing rubbers had been requested ... Apparently cooperation or understanding was quite lacking between the synthetic rubber maker and user.[32]

Furthermore physical chemistry was scarcely exploited. Buna S was developed by *Sparte II*, the organic chemicals division. After the war, Wilhelm Becker remarked that 'the Leverkusen approach to synthetic rubber has always been based largely on the cooperation between the straight organic chemist and the practical rubber technologist. Only small use has been made of the physical chemist.'[33] The investigation of the polymerization process and the structure of Buna S within IG lagged behind the concurrent American programme. In his history of polymer science, Herbert Morawetz comments that the principles of copolymerization were poorly understood by the IG researchers.[34] A review of the German research remarked:

> The team led by Dr. Marvel interviewed a number of prominent German chemists on their methods of studying the chemical structure of synthetic rubbers and ascertained that, although some attention had been given to chemical methods of determining polymer structure, little had been devoted to physicochemical methods.[35]

In any event, IG Farben's attitude towards the synthetic rubber programme was ambivalent. Never keen on the idea of complete autarky in rubber, it saw the programme as a means of underwriting its plans for the development of acetylene-based organic chemicals. IG's technical director, Fritz ter Meer, later commented that acetylene was 'a new chemical feedstock, useful in many types of chemical synthesis, and in a number of our laboratories we specially directed research in the acetylene field'.[36] Between 1928 and 1944, Walter Reppe of Ludwigshafen discovered entirely new acetylene reactions, which promised to make it the starting-point for numerous chemicals.[37] If the synthetic rubber programme assisted the development of acetylene chemistry by funding research and the construction of acetylene works, it also threatened to overwhelm it. As long as the relatively unprofitable production of Buna S continued, it drained IG's reserves of capital and scientific personnel, and crowded the other acetylene-based processes out of the new factories.[38]

Far from seeking success for Buna S, the available evidence suggests that the leaders of IG's rubber programme were nervous that it might become all too permanent. Hence IG concentrated on the development of new routes to butadiene, which had valuable spin-offs, rather than on the improvement of Buna S. IG's Byzantine relationship with the Third Reich not only hindered the development of synthetic rubber in Germany, but also affected the diffusion of Buna S technology to other countries, particularly the USA.

TRANSFER OF BUNA S TECHNOLOGY TO THE USA

The USA, like Germany, lacked significant colonies. The American rubber industry shared the German industry's concern about British attempts to push up the price of natural rubber and being cut off from the Far East in wartime. However the development of synthetic rubber in the USA followed a quite different path. Before the British naval blockade during the First World War forced the USA to manufacture dyes and organic chemicals hitherto imported from Germany, the Americans lacked a dyestuffs industry of any size. In terms of size, international influence and technological innovation, the petroleum corporations were the American equivalents of the German dye companies.[39] Indeed IG Farben was loosely modelled on the Standard Oil Trust, and Standard Oil of New Jersey was one of the few firms openly admired by the leaders of the German combine. Furthermore the American rubber companies were much larger and more innovative than their German counterparts.[40] Continental Gummiwerke was even partly owned by Goodrich between 1920 and 1929.[41] Du Pont was the only chemical corporation on an equal footing with the petroleum and rubber companies before Pearl Harbor.[42]

The importance of the American petroleum and rubber companies was a result of the early and rapid development of the American motor-car industry to a size unmatched anywhere else. In 1937, the USA had a population of 129 million, about twice the German population of 68 million, yet it manufactured nearly four million motor-cars, compared with only 269 000 in Germany; the USA had 23 private motor-cars registered for every one in Germany. Not surprisingly, the USA produced 60 million tonnes of motor spirit in 1937 and consumed 552 300 tonnes of natural rubber, exactly half of total world consumption. By contrast, Germany only produced 1.3 million tonnes of motor spirit (including some synthetic) and consumed about 80 000 tonnes of natural rubber.[43] Even Du Pont partly owed its rise to pre-eminence to its close, and profitable, relationship with General Motors. The big four rubber companies (Goodyear, Goodrich, Firestone and U.S. Rubber) dominated the development of synthetic rubber in America, with the marginal exception of Du Pont's neoprene. Naturally this ensured that far greater attention would be taken of the needs of the rubber processors and the final consumers, but, perhaps surprisingly, the Americans were quickly able to match IG in terms of chemical expertise. How did this come about and how was the necessary know-how transferred from Germany to the USA?

The giant oil company Standard Oil of New Jersey was an important go-between in the transatlantic transfer of synthetic rubber technology.[44] The early 1920s saw an upsurge of research on petroleum refining, especially the cracking of heavier oils into the gasoline used in motor-cars, based on the earlier research of William M. Burton at Standard Oil of Indiana, a smaller fragment of the former oil trust.[45] Standard Oil of New Jersey was not at the cutting edge of this technology and was also concerned about declining reserves in the traditional American oilfields. IG Farben was developing the Bergius process for converting coal into gasoline, which could be used for heavy oils or shale oil, but its development was expensive and IG was running out of funds.[46] With its long experience of petroleum refining, Jersey Standard could assist with the development of the Bergius process and also help to distribute the coal-based gasoline in Germany.

The first contact was made by BASF in 1925, just before the formation of IG, and the two sides reached a limited agreement in August 1927. In return for the rights to the oil-from-coal process in the USA and half of the royalties from third parties, Standard agreed to fund research into the process at its new Baton Rouge laboratories. Encouraged by its early results with the conversion of heavy oils, Jersey Standard then agreed, in November 1929, to form the Standard–IG Company (four-fifths of which was owned by the American firm) to hold all the rights to IG's oil-from-coal patents outside Germany. The German combine was compensated with 2 per cent of Standard's common stock. Standard also agreed in a further covenant to refrain from entering the chemical field, while IG undertook to keep out of petroleum refining. Any process patented by IG in the petroleum field would therefore be offered to Jersey Standard on reasonable terms, and vice-versa.

IG informed Jersey Standard that it was developing several processes, the most important of which involved synthetic rubber, that used petroleum or natural gas as a raw material. Standard's Frank Howard and IG's August von Knieriem reached an agreement in September 1930, whereby a new company, the Joint American Study Company (Jasco) – equally owned by the two corporations – was set up to develop and license any innovations made by either party in the 'oil-chemical' field.

There were two noteworthy innovations which arose out of this German–American collaboration: the arc process for acetylene and butyl rubber. In 1930, IG was already interested in the manufacture of acetylene from natural gas or by-product gas from the oil-from-coal process, using an electric arc. The process was studied by Jasco at Baton Rouge between 1932 and 1935, the resulting acetylene being converted into acetic acid and sold at a loss. By 1935, American and German chemists, working together, had brought the process to the industrial scale, but it had no future in the USA, not least because it interfered with IG's attempts to reach broad agreements in the acetylene field with Union Carbide.[47] The arc process was taken back to Germany and installed in the Buna factory at Hüls by Paul Baumann, who had worked at Baton Rouge. It is still used to make acetylene, but Hüls's synthetic rubber is now manufactured from petroleum.

In April 1932, IG told Jersey Standard about a polymer prepared from isobutylene at very low temperatures.[48] Standard initially used the process to make Vistanex, which increased the viscosity of motor oils. In 1937, however, two Jersey Standard chemists, William J. Sparks and Robert M. Thomas, had the idea of adding a small amount of butadiene to polyisobutylene, allowing it to be vulcanized like natural rubber. It was nicknamed 'bathtub butyl' because the first large-scale experiments were carried out with an ordinary washing machine, using liquid ethylene as the coolant. This butyl rubber was offered to IG under the Jasco agreement, and Standard was later attacked for giving an important American innovation away to the Nazis.[49] Ironically, IG never made butyl rubber, but manufactured a polyisobutylene plastic based on its own research. Despite a major development effort by Jersey Standard, butyl never became a major rubber, except for inner tyres.

While these innovations were not unimportant, Jersey Standard's role in the transfer of Buna S technology through its promotion of the Buna copolymers in the USA was ultimately of greater significance.[50] Goodrich and Goodyear, the two companies most interested in synthetic rubber, were willing to adopt IG's technology, given reasonable terms. Jersey Standard had approached Goodrich, on IG's behalf, in 1932 to seek help with the processing of the copolymers. The two companies were unable to reach agreement, and the contract for the testing was given to the smaller General Tire. Goodrich were still interested in the Buna rubbers and Waldo Semon, the leader of its synthetic rubber team, visited Germany in the summer of 1937, in a vain attempt to exchange Goodrich's superior plasticized PVC technology for IG's Buna know-how.

Goodyear was also contacted by Standard in 1933, and expressed an interest in developing the Buna copolymers. On the basis of the scanty information they obtained, the Goodyear chemists made significant advances with the polymerization process. Lorin Sebrell of Goodyear also made a pilgrimage to IG's Frankfurt headquarters in an attempt to reach an agreement with the German firm, but to no avail. IG Farben's experts could not accept that the American rubber companies were capable of making their own synthetic rubber, and even accused Goodyear of making its samples (including a complete tyre) from pirated German Buna S. Even Jersey Standard, IG's legal partner in the world-wide development of synthetic rubber, was able to learn little about the large-scale manufacture of Buna S and Buna N, in contrast to the free exchange of information in the oil-from-coal field.[51] The National Bureau of Standard fortuitously obtained some information about the Buna rubbers in 1938, when two of its rubber chemists, Lawrence A. Wood and Norman Bekkedahl, met Erich Konrad at an international conference and were invited to visit Leverkusen on the way home. To understand better what he had seen at Leverkusen, Wood carried out a thorough literature survey on synthetic rubber and published the result in 1940.

Irked by IG Farben's disdain, Goodrich and Goodyear independently pressed ahead with the development of their own copolymer rubbers. To circumvent IG's patents, they made a large number of experimental copolymers that did not use styrene or acrylonitrile; Goodrich called them non-infringing rubbers or 'nirubs'. To secure a cheap source of monomers, Goodrich formed the Hydrocarbon Chemical and Rubber (Hycar) Company with Phillips Petroleum in July 1940, and Goodyear collaborated with Dow Chemicals and Shell Oil.

Why did IG fail to respond favourably to Goodrich's and Goodyear's overtures? Most commentators have assumed that the German government (and IG) aimed to prevent the USA from developing Buna S.[52] Not surprisingly, there were German government restrictions on the dissemination of military-related technology. Many patent applications in the synthetic rubber field were kept secret by the Reich patent office and letters from the Reich Ministry of Economics were often marked 'Geheim' (secret). Having paid for much of the Buna research, the government not unnaturally felt it had the right to be consulted about its exploitation.

On the question of transfer of Buna technology to the USA, the Reich Ministry of Economics took a straightforward position, at least up to early 1939.[53] The ministry realized that IG Farben was likely to face commercial and technological competition from American companies if it did not license the Buna technology, and hoped that this transfer might reduce American hostility towards Nazi Germany. The ministry officials and the army high command (OKW) were therefore willing for IG to reach an agreement with the American firms. However there were two conditions: the final agreement would need the approval of the Reich Ministry of Economics (and indirectly OKW) and the work on the German Buna factories had to come first. It is also probable that the very latest technology would have been withheld, though a number of hitherto secret patent applications were released with the permission of OKW in October 1938. Of course there was no guarantee that the ministry would have granted permission, but it was willing to accept that Du Pont's neoprene and the two-step butadiene process based on Du Pont's technology could be superior to IG's technology, and would have been unlikely to object if IG had exchanged its processes for American know-how.

With its usual arrogance, however, the German firm believed that no other firm could develop a good copolymer without its cooperation. At the same time, IG feared the entry of other firms into the synthetic rubber field. It was thus reluctant to divulge its precious know-how without control over its use and substantial compensation. IG refused to give Buna know-how to the French Vichy government, and resisted attempts by the Italian synthetic rubber company to obtain the formula for Buna S3, despite the agreement of the German government to the transfer.[54] Du Pont, with its neoprene patents, was the one American firm that could offer IG technology of equal value and IG attempted to use its Buna patents to reach a wide-ranging agreement with Du Pont. The impetuous development of Buna copolymers, particularly the oil-resistant Buna N, by Jersey Standard and/or the rubber companies might have perturbed Du Pont and made an agreement less likely.

In any event, the outbreak of war in Europe in September 1939 made it difficult to continue the agreements between Jersey Standard and IG Farben. While the two companies did not expect war to break out between Germany and the USA, their cooperation posed problems for Standard's British and French associates; it was also becoming a political embarrassment for both sides.[55] IG Farben wanted to be free to sell the Buna technology to the Italians and Russians, countries within Jersey Standard's sphere under the original agreements, while Standard was eager to pursue the development of synthetic rubber in America even without IG's assistance. After three days of complex negotiations in The Hague, Frank Howard and IG's Fritz Ringer signed an agreement, on 25 September 1939, which dissolved the original arrangement and gave Jersey Standard the right to develop Buna S in the USA, the British Empire and the French Empire in return for giving up their joint rights elsewhere. IG did not lose much by this agreement. Jersey Standard (through Jasco) already controlled the US Buna patents and IG's ownership of the British and French rights was compromised by the outbreak of war. Furthermore IG Farben later declined to hand over the technical know-how on Buna S manufacture – in particular information about IG's full-scale production – to Jersey Standard to avoid a collision with the German government.

Nevertheless, armed with the full patent rights and the results of its own research, Jersey Standard suggested to the major rubber companies that they all cooperate to develop Buna S, by forming a joint company; a proposal not dissimilar to ter Meer's earlier plan. This was acceptable to Firestone and U.S. Rubber, who had not carried out much synthetic rubber research, but Goodrich and Goodyear declined the offer. In June 1940, Goodrich defied Standard's attempts to coordinate the development of synthetic rubber by launching Ameripol (American polymer), a copolymer of butadiene and methyl methacrylate. For a 30 per cent premium over the normal price, patriotic citizens and companies could buy Liberty tyres, made from a blend of natural rubber and Ameripol.

At this stage, however, the rubber companies and Jersey Standard were more interested in the highly profitable speciality rubbers, such as Buna N, rather than tyre rubbers. German Buna N was first exported to the USA in the third quarter of 1937.[56] It was able to gain a toehold in the American market after a major explosion in Du Pont's Deepwater, New Jersey, plant in January 1938 disrupted neoprene production for several months.[57] By June, IG's agent had gained orders for 20 tonnes of Buna N, which had been renamed Perbunan, apparently to circumvent a government export ban on Buna N. American stocks of Buna N soon ran out in the autumn of 1939, and the rubber companies were keen to make it themselves. By the end of 1940, Goodrich and Goodyear had independently erected small Buna N plants and sold it without a licence from Standard.

After waiting almost a year, Standard took the two rubber companies to court in October 1941 for alleged infringement of its patent rights. To protect itself, Goodrich had already carried out experiments to show that the Buna copolymers could not be prepared from the patents, as required by law. The legal problems and the divide between the three rival groups (Standard–Firestone–U.S. Rubber; Goodrich–Phillips; Goodyear–Shell–Dow) were overcome by the Japanese attack on Pearl Harbor in December 1941. Within a week of that event, Jersey Standard and the big four rubber companies had signed a patent- and information-sharing agreement under the auspices of the government-owned Rubber Reserve Co.

THE AMERICAN SYNTHETIC RUBBER PROGRAMME

After several changes of policy, and the appointment of a high-powered commission of inquiry (the Baruch Committee) by President Roosevelt, a joint production and research programme supervised by a Rubber Director was inaugurated in October 1942. The companies in the programme agreed upon a 'mutual' recipe for GR-S (government rubber-styrene), which was similar to the German recipe for Buna S. The crucial difference was the replacement of linoleic acid by one of the sulphur compounds patented by IG in 1937. This was usually called 'OEI': one essential ingredient. The Americans were enthusiastic about modifiers, because they produced an easily processible rubber which could be worked on existing machinery.

The expansion from an American synthetic rubber industry with an output of 231 tonnes of Buna S in 1941 to one that was producing 70 000 tonnes a month of GR-S in the spring of 1945 was a remarkable achievement. As with other American wartime industries, the reserve capacity of the US economy and the sheer scale of production were astounding. There were four striking differences from IG's operations: the polymerization plants were physically separate from the monomer plants; they were operated by the rubber industry; there was a large number of plants scattered across the country; and the major monomer, butadiene, was made from grain alcohol or petroleum, not coal-based acetylene.

A total of 15 polymer plants were planned; all were operating by December 1943. The butadiene-from-alcohol plants started up in the first half of 1943, and were soon producing at up to twice their rated capacity. The butadiene-from-petroleum plants were slow to come on stream, for a number of reasons, and the alcohol-based plants carried the burden for most of 1944. By 1945, however, as the petroleum-based plants came into full operation, GR-S production surged ahead of demand. Total GR-S production in 1945 was 730 000 tonnes, six and a half times German Buna S output at its peak. Smaller amounts of speciality rubbers – Buna N (GR-A), neoprene (GR-C), butyl rubber (GR-I) and Thiokol (GR-P) – were also produced during the war. The new Du Pont neoprene factory at Louisville, Kentucky expanded production from 10 000 to 60 000 tonnes a year with government help, and was bought back by Du Pont in 1949.[58]

From the outset the programme's leaders realized that a research and development programme would be necessary to solve the existing and potential problems surrounding GR-S manufacture. For instance, OEI rapidly disappeared during the polymerization process, thereby producing an unsatisfactory rubber. R. R. Williams of Bell Telephone Laboratories (BTL) was commissioned to set up and supervise this programme, which was centred on the rubber industry, the National Bureau of Standards, BTL and the major universities.[59] Williams drew on his experience with rubber and other polymers at BTL when he laid down the guidelines for the research programme at the end of 1942. The chemists at BTL believed that the quality of a polymer was crucial to its performance, and the study of a polymer's structure was the key to quality improvement. The problem of supervising numerous research groups, whose work often overlapped, was solved by adopting a 'hands-off' approach which allowed the groups largely to direct their own research. This liberal philosophy – shared by IG Farben, which had faced similar research management problems – reduced conflict between the central administration and the groups, but the trade-off was increased duplication between different research laboratories and the loss of a strong sense of direction.

The first year of the research and development programme was naturally dominated by the need to solve existing problems. The difficulty with the disappearing modifier was overcome by adding the modifier to the polymerization cycle gradually and replacing OEI with another group of sulphur compounds called tertiary mercaptans. A puzzling and unpredictable pause at the beginning of polymerization was traced to polyunsaturated acids in the Ivory soap used as the emulsifier. It was important to keep the butadiene–styrene ratio of GR-S constant, and William O. Baker of BTL developed a new method of measuring the styrene content of GR-S.

Once the teething problems were overcome, the researchers were able to study the chemistry of the polymerization and the structure of GR-S. A central role was played by chemical analysis, which was essential to quality control and kinetic studies. Through his analytical research, Piet Kolthoff at the University of Minnesota was drawn into the study of the various factors which affected the rate of polymerization. Frank Mayo's basic research group at U.S. Rubber converted an old silk mill in Passaic, New Jersey into a major centre for the study of copolymerization. W. D. Harkins, a retired professor at the University of Chicago, developed a detailed model for emulsion polymerization which dominated the field for many years. At BTL, Baker revealed that harmful gel particles were formed during the polymerization. The Dutch chemical physicist Peter Debye, who fled Germany in 1940 and joined Cornell University, demonstrated how the visible light scattered by polymers in solution could be used to measure their molecular weight. The novel techniques of infra-red and ultra-violet spectrophotometry were used to study the structure of GR-S.

The American research programme did not make any outstanding technological breakthroughs before the war's end but, combined with stringent quality control, it created a GR-S that was superior to IG's vaunted Buna S. The strength of American chemical research was soon confirmed by the rapid American exploitation of IG's breakthrough in redox polymerization, based on information brought back by American technical intelligence units after the German defeat in 1945.[60]

COMPARISON OF GERMAN AND AMERICAN DEVELOPMENT OF BUNA S

IG Farben's development of Buna S illustrates the difficulties faced by a successful company in one technological tradition (dyes) diversifying into new areas (synthetic rubber) with different consumers and requiring new skills. The initial success of the German dye industry, united as IG Farben after 1925, sowed the seeds of failure in synthetic rubber. Success had bred arrogance and this arrogance prevented IG from forming a close relationship with the German rubber industry, leading to a disastrous neglect of consumer satisfaction and quality control.[61] This arrogance also thwarted the attempts of other companies to form technological alliances with IG, which could have been of considerable value to the German firm. IG's unwillingness to license the Buna technology within Germany or even to allow other companies to become partners in the Buna subsidiaries prevented alternative approaches to the problems of scaling up and improving Buna S, and concentrated its production in a few factories. The strength of IG Farben's research organization also diminished the need for collaboration with academic scientists and, while IG sponsored several polymer chemists, their contributions on technical matters were usually minor.

Hitler's impatience over the erection of the first synthetic rubber factory in 1935 and 1936 forced the company to take several technical short-cuts, which reduced the quality of Buna S, and had the effect of partly 'freezing' IG's technology at an immature stage. This urgency also compelled the firm to mass-produce Buna S, which lacked the oil resistance (and hence the price premium) of neoprene and Buna N.

In the middle of the Second World War, in response to a query from the Japanese firm Mitsui, IG Farben insisted that it was impossible to build a synthetic rubber plant successfully on the basis of written instructions alone, without transferring experts and equipment.[62] The method of technology transfer from Germany to the USA varied: papers in the scientific literature, patents filed by IG Farben (Buna S, modifiers), infrequent meetings of corporate executives, informal advice from a German chemist who worked for Jasco and the intelligence-gathering operations after the Second World War. At no time did it extend to the physical transfer of technical specialists and plant, or even extensive know-how. By contrast, the transfer of cold rubber technology to West Germany in the 1950s involved the close collaboration of Firestone and Chemische Werke Hüls, and the extensive transfer of know–how.[63]

The creation of an entire industry in the USA, using little more than bare patents, also suggests that the mechanics of the actual transfer – and the volume and quality of the know-how transferred – may be less important than the environment to which the technology is transferred. An analogy with natural rubber may be appropriate. The transfer of Wickham's celebrated rubber seeds to Malaya, via Kew Gardens and Ceylon, was less than ideal, but the Malayan climate was so hospitable to *Hevea brasiliensis,* that these few trees soon became a great plantation industry.

Since the early nineteenth century, America has been fertile soil for many new industries: railways, steel, electricity, ammonia soda, petroleum refining, passenger aircraft and electronic computers.[64] The USA has had the advantages of vast natural resources and an internal market that was large in numbers and total spending power. American net imports of natural rubber was over six times greater than German net imports in 1934–8.[65] It also benefited from inflows of capital, and motivated and often gifted immigrants. Furthermore there are obvious advantages for the development of a high-technology industry in a country with large technologically advanced companies and numerous highly trained scientists (in academia and industry).

The success of the USA in creating a synthetic rubber industry stemmed not from its chemical industry, but indirectly from its large motor-car industry, which promoted the growth of the technologically sophisticated rubber and petroleum industries that developed synthetic rubber. The scale of the American rubber, petroleum and chemical industries, combined with anti-trust laws, meant that more companies were involved. This diversity aided the development of synthetic rubber in the USA by spreading the technological and economic burden over several companies, and creating a greater variety of ideas and innovations. Competition between the different firms promoted innovation at important stages in the development of synthetic rubber, including the introduction of Ameripol copolymer by Goodrich, followed by the introduction of 'cold' rubber by Phillips Petroleum, and oil-extended rubber by General Tire in the late 1940s. At the same time, however, these advances were assisted by the transfer of information. This suggests that successful innovations are often a judicious combination of competition and cooperation.[66]

The greater importance of the rubber industry relative to the chemical industry in the USA led to a higher level of involvement by the major consumers and thus a greater attention paid to quality control and compatibility with existing equipment. The high scientific standing of Bell Telephone Laboratories and the National Bureau of Standards ensured their association with the wartime rubber programme. This, in turn, heightened the programme's concern with quality control, testing and the improvement of the rubber's physical properties. The American companies often paid more attention to the marketing of synthetic rubbers than IG Farben, most notably the launching of neoprene by Du Pont.

The USA also benefited from its distance from the enemy, which prevented aerial bombing of its plants, and its enormous supplies of petroleum, coal (for styrene) and grain (for alcohol-based butadiene). The semi-tropical climate of southern California and the states around the Gulf of Mexico permitted the rapid construction of chemical plants with a minimum of brick walls and other protective structures.[67]

Most of the American companies had less experience with synthetic rubber and polymerization than IG Farben, but the rubber firms were willing to learn from IG and to seek assistance from the chemical industry. The USA also had the undoubted advantage of being second, and hence able to learn from IG's mistakes. Furthermore the USA was not forced to scale up its technology until 1942, which gave the American industry more time to study the production of butadiene and the manufacture of Buna S, without fearing the wrath of a dictator who feared that the 'hour of peril' would arrive while private industry continued to argue that the 'processes [were] not ... fully determined'.[68] This breathing-space was put to good use, particularly in the area of processibility and modifiers. The absence of mature research and development systems in many American companies, especially in the rubber industry, promoted strong links with major research universities and several academic chemists made fundamental contributions to the development of synthetic rubber.

FACING THE CHALLENGE

The successful development of Buna S (GR-S) in America during the Second World War shed light on the strategies companies can adopt towards radical innovations in their field.[69] IG Farben, with its origins in a different sector, took a gamble with the development of synthetic rubber. As we have seen, it only partly paid off before 1945, largely because of the intervention of the German government. Instead of producing a highly profitable speciality rubber (Buna N) on a modest scale, IG found itself in a race to mass-produce Buna S, virtually at cost.

To the large American rubber corporations, synthetic rubber was both a threat and an opportunity. As the world's largest consumers of natural rubber and relatively conservative organizations, they could not have relished the challenge Buna S posed to the industry's status quo. It is not surprising that Du Pont (with its links to General Motors) deliberately avoided competing with the rubber industry, to the extent of suppressing any attempt to develop neoprene as a tyre rubber. At the same time, however, the American industry had been shaken by the British rubber restriction scheme and it was becoming clear by the mid-1930s that plantations in countries such as Liberia and Brazil could offer only a partial solution, at best. They were also aware of the technical drawbacks of natural rubber, notably its modest wear-resistance.

In general, when confronted with a radical innovation in its particular field, a company can adopt a number of responses, which may overlap. It can ignore the new technology in the hope that it will fail, and aim to hinder its progress by cutting prices. This simple but high-risk approach was adopted by the British Leblanc soda industry when it was challenged by the Solvay process.[70] While this would have been an attractive strategy to the rubber industry, at a time when natural rubber prices were plummeting anyway, it did not free them from the grip of the rubber planters.

Alternatively a company with adequate research and development facilities can endeavour to outflank the other firm by introducing a competing innovation. Between 1938 and 1942, a consortium of major oil companies (and briefly IG) headed by Jersey Standard developed the Fluid Catalytic Cracking Process for gasoline to avoid taking out licences for the catalytic cracking process introduced in 1938 by the French engineer Eugène Houdry and the Sun Oil Co.[71]

However since this strategy is both high-risk and high-cost, most companies will apply for a licence to use the threatening innovation. If the firm is denied a licence and/or it considers the other company's patent position to be weak, it may seek to copy the innovation, but altering it slightly to circumvent the original patent. This was the route taken by Goodrich, which replaced the styrene (or acrylonitrile) used as the minor monomer by IG Farben with methyl methacrylate (the monomer of Perspex), thereby allowing it to launch Ameripol in 1940.

The key features of a radical innovation in chemical technology can often be no more than an alteration of a recipe or the introduction of a new catalyst, for instance the polymerizing butadiene with styrene to produce Buna S, or the addition of accelerators (iron salts and a reducing agent) to the original mutual recipe to create 'cold' rubber. Once this breakthrough is transmitted, often by way of patent applications or word of mouth, most progressive chemical (or rubber) companies with a decent research department could fill in the gaps and scale up their own version of the process. This is essentially how Goodrich and Goodyear developed their copolymer rubbers in the late 1930s and Phillips produced its 'cold' rubber a decade later. The major bar to this flanking research and development is a strong patent position, which defeated IG Farben's attempts to develop neoprene. However Du Pont also thought its patent position in the nylon field was even stronger, but by 1939 IG Farben was able to trump Du Pont's nylon 66 by developing nylon 6.[72]

For firms with significant research and development capabilities there is always a tension between technology transfer and in-house development. Goodrich and Goodyear decided to develop their own synthetic rubbers, rather than collaborate with Jersey Standard, but Firestone and U.S. Rubber opted for cooperation. In the 1950s, Chemische Werke Hüls decided to license American cold rubber technology, rather than continue to develop the German processes. The decision is often a close one, and can be influenced by numerous factors, often far removed from the technical and economic aspects of the technology, as IG's development of Buna S illustrates.

Nonetheless the central feature of this case-study is the power wielded by large innovative corporations with a strong patent position. The development of Buna copolymers in the USA was delayed for about five to six years because IG Farben refused to give Jersey Standard and the large rubber companies the necessary licences and know-how. Despite IG's enthusiasm for neoprene, it never became a tyre rubber in Germany, although it could have been, because Du Pont distrusted the German combine. IG Farben blocked the entry of any rivals into the German synthetic rubber industry, and even today Buna S production in Germany is controlled by IG's successors (Bunawerke Hüls, Buna AG and Bayer). Similarly entry into the American industry was regulated by the federal government through its supervision of IG's patents, which were handed over by Jersey Standard. Patents can encourage technology transfer by publicizing innovations and formalizing their use by others through licences. The patent specifications for Buna S and Buna N were the starting-point for the imitative research by Goodyear and Goodrich. Patents can also firmly block transfers, if the holder refuses to license foreign companies and is not compelled to do so by the issuing government. This is largely how the German dye industry crippled its British rivals in the late nineteenth century, by taking out dye patents in Britain, but neither working the patents in Britain themselves nor licensing others to use them. Their heir, IG Farben, had not forgotten this key tactic.

CONCLUSION

When Nathan Rosenberg wrote his classic paper on the history of technology transfer 20 years ago,[73] American superiority in technology was axiomatic and the pressing issue was the transfer of this technology to poorer countries. While many poorer countries are still seeking the answer to that question, the situation has changed and Japan has overtaken the USA in several high-technology industries, notably semi-conductors and, increasingly, super computers.[74] At first sight, the history of synthetic rubber supports the Japanese model. The Americans took a foreign technology and built it up using government money for research and development, and price fixing to protect the fledgling industry from natural rubber. Furthermore the basic product was improved by another transfer of technology from Germany and further government support. Within a few years the USA had replaced Germany as the industry's leader, a lead that it has retained, at least for SBR.

Nonetheless I concluded in *The American Synthetic Rubber Research Program* that the American government's involvement in synthetic rubber research slowed, rather than accelerated, innovation in peacetime. The German development of Buna S also demonstrates the negative aspects of state intervention in high technology. The USA should study the history of its own successful technology transfers, rather than attempt to imitate countries with entirely different historical and geographical backgrounds and economic structures. Goodrich and Goodyear in the pre-war years (and Phillips Petroleum and General Tire in the post-war period) displayed the characteristic American traits of independence and doggedness. Goodyear and Goodrich refused to be overawed by the threat posed by two of the world's largest corporations, or to be daunted by IG Farben's strong patent position. They pressed ahead with their own research in a field that was almost entirely new to them, and had matched the Germans (at least in the laboratory) by 1940. The virtues required to succeed with the development of a new technology, including technology transfer, are the same now as they have always been: courage, initiative, independence, determination and patience. There is no short-cut to technological and commercial success.

NOTES

1. This chapter is based on Peter J. T. Morris, 'The Development of Acetylene Chemistry and Synthetic Rubber by I.G. Farbenindustrie A.G., 1926–1945', Oxford University D. Phil. thesis, 1982, hereafter cited as Morris, 'Synthetic Rubber'; and Morris, *The American Synthetic Rubber Research Program* (Philadelphia, 1989), hereafter cited as Morris, *American Synthetic Rubber*. A preliminary version of this chapter was presented under the title 'Buna S versus GR-S: A Comparative Study of Industrial Research in Germany and the United States', at the Anglo-American (BSHS–HSS) meeting in Manchester, UK, July 1988. I would like to thank David Jeremy and Kenneth Warren for their help with this chapter, which is dedicated to the memory of the five workers killed in an explosion at Chemische Werke Buna, Schkopau, (East) Germany, on 9 February 1990.
2. Production figures for synthetic rubber are taken from the *United Nations Statistical Yearbooks* (New York, annually); R. F. Dunbrook, 'Historical Review', in G. S. Whitby, C. C. Davis and R. F. Dunbrook (eds), *Synthetic Rubber* (New York and London, 1954), pp. 51–3; and information supplied by the International Rubber Study Group, London. Synthetic rubber production in 1988 was 10 130 000 tonnes, whereas natural rubber output was 4 995 000 tonnes.

3. Peter H. Spitz, *Petrochemicals: The Rise of an Industry* (New York, 1988), pp. 141–54.
4. L. F. Haber, *The Chemical Industry during the Nineteenth Century: A Study of the Economic Aspect of Applied Chemistry in Europe and North America*, second edition (Oxford, 1969); Haber, *The Chemical Industry, 1900–1930: International Cartels and Technological Change* (Oxford, 1971); J. J. Beer, *The Emergence of the German Dye Industry* (Urbana, Illinois, 1959); A. S. Travis, *The Rainbow Makers* (Bethlehem, Pennsylvania, 1991).
5. The transfer of American technology to Hüls will be covered in a later publication. Also see Spitz, *Petrochemicals*, pp. 58–60; Raymond G. Stokes, *Divide and Prosper: The Heirs of I.G. Farben under Allied Authority, 1945–1951* (Berkeley, 1988); Stokes's forthcoming study, provisionally entitled *The Founding of the West German Petrochemical Industry*, is certain to increase our understanding of the development of the post-war West German petrochemical industry.
6. The important question of the raw materials selected for butadiene manufacture will be the subject of a future paper.
7. Austin Coates, 'World swing from wild to cultivated, 1904–1913', *The Commerce in Rubber: The First 250 Years* (Singapore, 1987), pp. 135–67.
8. Rubber prices are taken from Colin Barlow, *The Natural Rubber Industry: Its Development, Technology, and Economy in Malaysia* (Kuala Lumpur, 1978), appendix, table 2.1, and Sir Andrew McFadyean, *The History of Rubber Regulation, 1934–1943* (London, 1944), table 11.
9. Russia and Britain were also major centres of rubber research in this period. The pre-1930 origins of synthetic rubber will be covered in more detail in another paper. The best, but unpublished, account is Bettina Löser, 'Der Einfluss der Arbeiten zur Strukturaufklärung und Synthese der Kautschuks auf die Herausbildung der makromolekularen Chemie', Karl-Marx-Universität, Leipzig, PhD thesis, 1983.
10. H. Rogers, 'Development of Manufacturing Activities', in P. Schidrowitz and T. R. Dawson (eds), *History of the Rubber Industry* (Cambridge, 1952), p. 45.
11. For the development of polymer science in Germany, see Yasu Furukawa, 'Staudinger, Carothers and the Emergence of Macromolecular Chemistry', University of Oklahoma PhD thesis, 1983, chapter II, 'Hermann Staudinger and the Emergence of the Macromolecular Theory'; Yasu Furukawa's forthcoming biography of Hermann Staudinger is eagerly awaited. Also see Claus Priesner, *H. Staudinger, H. Mark und K. H. Meyer: Thesen zur Grösse und Struktur der Makromoleküle* (Weinheim, 1980); and Herbert Morawetz, *Polymers: The Origins and Growth of a Science* (New York, 1985), especially pp. 70–98. Peter Morris, *Polymer Pioneers*, Center for the History of Chemistry Publication No. 5 (Philadelphia, 1986) provides a concise overview. For the importance of colloid chemistry in Germany, see Eric Elliott, 'Colloid Chemistry in Germany; 1900–1933', University of Pennsylvania PhD thesis, 1991.
12. Wyndham Dunstan, 'Some Imperial Aspects of Applied Chemistry', *Nature*, **74**, (1906), pp. 361–6; quote on 365.
13. *Chemiker-Zeitung*, **11**, (1906), p. 313.
14. In addition to the sources listed in Morris, 'Synthetic Rubber', see Erik Verg (with Gottfried Plumpe and Heinz Schultheis), *Milestones: The Bayer Story, 1863–1988* (Leverkusen, 1988), pp. 190–3.
15. Coates, 'Political Rubber', *Commerce in Rubber*, pp. 205–63; Wilhelm Treue, *Gummi in Deutschland* (Munich, 1955), pp. 187–91.
16. Peter Hayes, *Industry and Ideology: IG Farben in the Nazi Era* (Cambridge, 1987) has already become the standard work on IG Farben during the Third Reich. Helmuth Tammen, *Die I.G Farbenindustrie AG (1925–1933): Ein Chemiekonzern in der Weimarer Republik* (Berlin, 1978) is a less effective but adequate treatment of the company during the Weimar period. Also see Fritz ter Meer, *Die I.G. Farbenindustrie AG: Ihre Entstehung, Entwicklung und Bedeutung* (Düsseldorf, 1953) for an insider's view. The firm's research and development is discussed in Morris, 'Synthetic Rubber', pp. 38–55.
17. For the synthetic rubber research in IG between 1926 and 1945, see Morris, 'Synthetic Rubber'; Claus Heuck, 'Ein Beitrag zur Geschichte der Kautschuk-Synthese: Buna-

Kautschuk I.G. (1926–1945)', *Chemiker-Zeitung*, **94**, (1970), pp. 147–57; Heino Logemann and Gottfried Pampus, 'Buna S – Seine grosstechnische Herstellung und seine Weiterentwicklung – ein geschichtlicher Uberblick', *Kautschuk und Gummi, Kunststoffe*, **23**, (1970), pp. 479–86. Gottfried Plumpe, 'Industrie, technischer Fortschritt und Staat: Die Kautschuksynthese in Deutschland, 1906–1944/5', *Geschichte und Gesellschaft*, **9**, (1983), pp. 564–97, places this research in its political and economic context.

18.   David A. Hounshell and John K. Smith, *Science and Corporate Strategy: Du Pont R&D, 1902–1980* (Cambridge, 1988), pp. 233–6, 251–7, which is based on John K. Smith, 'The Ten-Year Invention: Neoprene and Du Pont Research, 1930–1939', *Technology and Culture*, **26**, (1985), pp. 34-55.

19.   Smith, 'The Ten-Year Invention', p. 51.

20.   The classic accounts of Hitler's autarkic designs are generally misleading on the topic of synthetic rubber. Nonetheless see Berenice A. Carroll, *Design for Total War: Arms and Economics in the Third Reich* (The Hague, 1968), especially p. 128; D. Petzina, *Autarkiepolitik im Dritten Reich: Der Nationalsozialistische Vierjahresplan* (Stuttgart, 1968); Burton H. Klein, *Germany's Economic Preparations for War* (Cambridge, Mass., 1959). Also see A. Hitler, *Hitler's Table Talk, 1941–1944: His Private Conversations* (London, 1973), p. 73 (18 October 1941) for his views on synthetic rubber.

21.   E. Konrad to F. ter Meer, 6 June 1933, ZA 2362, Firmenarchiv Hoechst, Frankfurt, Germany (FH).

22.   Frank A. Howard, *Buna Rubber: The Birth of an Industry* (New York, 1947), p. 39; O. Loehr to ter Meer, 1 May 1934, ZA 2362, FH.

23.   As reported by Erich Hammesfahr, Reich Commissioner for Rubber, at a meeting in the Überwachungstelle für Kautschuk und Asbest, 30 October 1943, ZA 1446, FH.

24.   Report in *The Times* (London), 12 September 1935, 12, col.5.

25.   Adolf Hitler, memorandum on the Four Year Plan, August 1936; translation in Jeremy Noakes and Geoffrey Pridham (eds), *Documents on Nazism, 1919–1945* (London, 1974), p. 406.

26.   I intend to publish a paper on the Du Pont–IG neoprene negotiations. In the meantime, see George W. Stocking and Myron W. Watkins, *Cartels in Action* (New York, 1947), pp. 107–13; Hounshell and Smith, *Science and Corporate Strategy*, pp. 206–7; O. Loehr, 'Materialien zum Komplex Buna/U.S.A.', 29 August 1947, ter Meer defence exhibit no. 176, in *U.S. v. I.G. Farben*, reel 74 of US National Archives microfilm M-892.

27.   Morris, 'The Planning of a Synthetic Rubber Industry, 1934–1939' and 'The Buna Planning in Wartime, 1939–1945' in 'Synthetic Rubber'. For an independent but similar account, see Hayes, *Industry and Ideology*, pp. 148–51,188–93, 339–40, 347–58; also see Plumpe, 'Industrie, Technischer Fortschritt und Staat', *passim*. For the history of Hüls, see Franz I. Wünsch, 'Das Werk Hüls: Geschichte der Chemische Werke Hüls AG in Marl, 1939–1949', *Tradition*, **9**, (1964), pp. 70–9; Paul Kränzlein, *Chemie Im Revier: Hüls* (Düsseldorf and Vienna, 1980), pp. 29–41. For Auschwitz, also see the commendable thesis by Joseph Robert White, 'The Politics of Labor Utilization: I.G. Farben, the SS and Auschwitz', Georgia State University M.A. thesis, 1989, and Robert Simon Yavner, 'IG Farben's Petro-Chemical Plant and Concentration Camp at Auschwitz', Old Dominion University M.A. thesis, 1984).

28.   R. L. Bebb and L. B. Wakefield, 'German Synthetic Rubber Developments', in Whitby, Davis and Dunbrook (eds), *Synthetic Rubber*, p. 939.

29.   Claus Heuck, 'Buna-Kautschuk IG', p. 151 and Table 8.

30.   'Summary Report on the Production and Performance of German Synthetic Tires and Other Transportation Items', Rubber Bureau, War Production Board, and Office of Rubber Reserve, Reconstruction Finance Corporation, August 1945, CC–31, pp. 2, 9; there is a copy of this report in Record Group 243, United States Strategic Bombing Survey, European War, Oil Division, section 110b63, Modern Military Branch, National Archives, Washington. Later reports were generally more positive about the quality of Buna S3. For an excellent review, see Bebb and Wakefield, 'German Synthetic Rubber Developments', pp. 950–4.

31. Morris, 'Synthetic Rubber', pp. 304–13.
32. 'Summary Report', p. 9.
33. W. J. S. Naunton and R. Hill, 'Synthetic Rubber: Interrogation of Dr. W. Becker ... 20th and 29th August 1946', Part II, BIOS 1119, p. 10.
34. Herbert Morawetz, *Polymers*, p. 173.
35. Bebb and Wakefield, 'German Synthetic Rubber Developments', p. 982.
36. *Trials of War Criminals before the Nuremberg Military Tribunals under Control Council Law No. 10*, Case VI, 'The IG Farben Case' (Washington, DC, 1953), vol. VII, 860, English transcript page 6792, reel no. 7, M-892, direct examination of ter Meer by the defence.
37. Morris, 'Synthetic Rubber', pp. 111–16, 123–33 and Peter J.T. Morris, 'The Technology–Science Interaction: Walter Reppe and Cyclooctatetraeme Chemistry', *British Journal for the History of Science*, forthcoming.
38. Morris, 'Synthetic Rubber', pp. 252–3, 256, 296–7.
39. An annotated bibliography of the history of the American oil and chemical industries, including company histories (by Eric Elliott), can be found in Jeffrey L. Sturchio (ed.), *Corporate History and the Chemical Industries. A Resource Guide*, Center for the History of Chemistry Publication No. 4 (Philadelphia, 1985), pp. 11–33.
40. Alfred Lief, *The Firestone Story* (New York, 1951); Goodyear: Hugh Allen, *The House of Goodyear: Fifty Years of Men and Industry* (Cleveland, Ohio, 1949); Maurice O'Reilly, *The Goodyear Story* (Elmsford, New York, 1983); M. J. French, 'The Emergence of a U.S. Multinational Enterprise: The Goodyear Tire and Rubber Company, 1910–1939', *Economic History Review*, second ser., **40**, (1987), pp. 64–79. United States Rubber: Glenn D. Babcock, *History of United States Rubber Company: A Case Study in Corporation Management* (Bloomington, Indiana, 1966).
41. Wilhelm Treue, *Gummi in Deutschland*, p. 219; H. Rogers, 'Development of Manufacturing Activities', in Schidrowitz and Dawson (eds), *History of the Rubber Industry*, p. 47.
42. The standard (but dated) work is Williams Haynes, *American Chemical Industry: A History*, six volumes, (New York, 1945–54); volume six contains over 200 company histories collected by Haynes. Also see Hounshell and Smith, *Science and Corporate Strategy*; and Peter H. Spitz, *Petrochemicals*.
43. *United Nations Statistical Yearbook* for 1948; *Statistical Abstract of the United States, 1938* (Washington, DC, 1939); Treue, *Gummi in Deutschland*, p. 262.
44. The complex and highly controversial relationship between IG Farben and Standard Oil of New Jersey, surprisingly, still awaits a complete, balanced and accurate treatment by historians. The standard (and reasonably accurate) apologia is Frank A. Howard, *Buna Rubber*. A rather muted account is provided by Charles Popple, *Standard Oil Company (New Jersey) in World War II* (Standard Oil, 1952), pp. 49–76; Henrietta Larson, Evelyn Knowlton and Charles Popple, *New Horizons, 1927–1950* (New York, 1971), pp. 153–9, 170–4, 412–18. A clutch of books deliver the classic anti-cartel homily, namely, Stocking and Watkins, *Cartels in Action*, pp. 91–117, 491–505; Ervin Hexner, *International Cartels* (London, 1946), pp. 313–21, 344–5; Guenter Reimann, *Patents for Hitler* (New York, 1942), pp. 158–201; and Richard Sasuly, *I.G. Farben* (New York, 1947), pp. 141–60. Joseph Borkin delivered a blistering attack on IG and Jersey Standard during the Second World War, with Charles A. Welsh, in *Germany's Master Plan: The Story of Industrial Offensive* (New York, 1943) and returned to the fray with *The Crime and Punishment of I.G. Farben* (London, 1979), pp. 46–52, 76–94. Much of the source material for this literature came from the published hearings of two US Senate committees, the Bone Committee on patents (1942), and the Truman Committee on the National Defense Program (also 1942). The prosecution exhibits (No. 942–998) in *U.S. v. I.G. Farben* also touch upon this relationship, and can be found on reel 25 of M-892.
45. John L. Enos, *Petroleum, Progress and Profits: A History of Process Innovation* (Cambridge, Mass., 1962) is a superb analytical history of gasoline manufacture.
46. Wolfgang Birkenfeld has provided excellent accounts of the hydrogenation research in 'Leuna, 1933', *Tradition*, **8**, (1963), pp. 97–111, and *Der Synthetische Treibstoff, 1933–1945* (Göttingen, 1964). Also see Raymond G. Stokes, 'The Oil Industry in Nazi

Germany, 1936–1945', *Business History Review*, **59**, (1985), pp. 254–77; A. N. Stranges, 'Friedrich Bergius and the Rise of the German Synthetic Fuel Industry', *Isis*, **75**, (1984), pp. 643–67; Thomas Parke Hughes, 'Technological Momentum in History: Hydrogenation in Germany, 1898–1933', *Past and Present*, **44**, (1969), pp. 106–32; Tammen, *I.G. Farben*, pp. 46-56, 94–112; Arnold Krammer, 'Fuelling the Third Reich', *Technology and Culture*, **19**, (1978), pp. 394–422; A. von Nagel, *Methanol, Treibstoff* (Ludwigshafen, 1970), pp. 37–71.

47. Hexner, *International Cartels*, p. 300; Stocking and Watkins, *Cartels in Action*, pp. 478–80.

48. Howard, *Buna Rubber*, pp. 47–58; Robert M. Thomas, 'Early History of Butyl Rubber', *Rubber Chemistry and Technology*, **42**, (1969), G90-G96.

49. Reimann, *Patents for Hitler*, pp. 178–89.

50. The most complete history of the American synthetic rubber programme was compiled by the Reconstruction Finance Corporation in 1948. The first volume covered the natural rubber projects and the second recorded the history of the synthetic rubber programme (and the scrap rubber programme). The original typescript is stored at the National Archives, Washington, Record Group 234, Office of the Secretary, Entry 26, PI-173. Howard, *Buna Rubber*, presents an insider's account. Vernon Herbert and Attilio Bisio, *Synthetic Rubber: A Project That Had to Succeed* (Westport, Conn., 1985) provide a clearly written and compact history. Robert Solo, *Synthetic Rubber: A Case Study in Technological Development under Government Direction*, Study No. 18 for the Sub-Committee on Patents, Trademarks and Copyright, Committee on the Judiciary, U.S. Senate, 85th Cong., 2d sess., 1959, Committee Print, 93, reprinted as *Across the High Technology Threshold: The Case of Synthetic Rubber* (Norwood, Penn., 1980) contains a well-written and informative account of the pre-war and wartime synthetic rubber programme; it is much weaker on the post-war period and the technological aspects generally. This monograph was based on Solo's 'The Development and Economics of the American Synthetic Rubber Industry', Cornell University PhD thesis, 1952, which contains a wealth of information about the political aspects. Also see Davis R. B. Ross, 'Patents and Bureaucrats: U.S. Synthetic Rubber Developments before Pearl Harbor', in Joseph R. Frese, SJ, and Jacob Judd (eds), *Business and Government* (Tarrytown, New York, 1985), pp. 119–55; William M. Tuttle, Jr., 'The Birth of an Industry: The Synthetic Rubber "Mess" in World War II', *Technology and Culture*, **22**, (1981), pp. 35–67.

51. Two former Jersey Standard chemists, Willard Asbury and A. Donald Green, stated in a 1985 interview with Peter Morris (for the Beckman Center) that no Buna know-how had been transferred, but Hans Beller, an IG chemist working at Jasco, had explained the patents (especially those relating to modifiers) to the Jersey Standard chemists; Howard, *Buna Rubber*, pp. 105,108; Ross, 'Patents and Bureaucrats', p. 143.

52. In addition to the hostile commentators in note 58, also see Charles F. Phillips, Jr., *Competition in the Synthetic Rubber Industry* (Chapel Hill, NC, 1963), pp. 32, 37–8. For a thoughtful presentation, see Solo, 'The Development of the American Synthetic Rubber Industry', pp. 24–9.

53. For the Reich Ministry of Economics' view in 1938, see the minutes of a meeting at the Reich Ministry of Economics about 'Buna in U.S.A.', 18 March 1938, *U.S. v. I.G. Farben*, prosecution exhibit 960, NI-10455, and Löb to IG, 8 October 1938, prosecution exhibit 967, NI-10459, both on reel 25 of M-892; a good summary is provided by Loehr, 'Komplex Buna/U.S.A.', p. 6.

54. For an overview of IG's relationship with potential synthetic rubber producers in other European countries during the Second World War, and the government's mercurial attitude to such projects, see Morris, 'Synthetic Rubber', pp. 345–56.

55. Howard, *Buna Rubber*, pp. 79–91; Joseph Borkin, *Crime and Punishment*, pp. 84–8; Larson, *et al.*, *New Horizons*, pp. 405–7. At Nuremberg, ter Meer said he decided to block the transfer of know-how on his own initiative, because there was no prospect of the German government agreeing to it; *Trials of War Criminals*, vol. VII, p. 1328: cross-examination of ter Meer by the defence; this is supported by Howard, *Buna Rubber*, p. 108. Borkin's statement that the government blocked the transfer, accepted by Hayes

(*Industry and Ideology*, p. 336), is based on *J. Robert Bonnar et al.* v. *the United States*, No. 293–63 (Ct. Cl. 1971), defendant's exhibit 399, 'Report on Transfer of I.G. Patents to Third Parties'.

56. Exports to all countries from Germany did not amount to much until the third quarter of 1937, 'Perbunan-Umsatz in Ausland, 1937' 11 November 1937, folder 151/3, Bayer Werksarchiv, Leverkusen, Germany, which also contains the trademark registration for Perbunan, 30 December 1937. A total of 50.8 tonnes of Perbunan were exported to the USA in 1938.

57. Mullaly to Koch, 27 June 1938, folder 5, ZA 377, FH. Howard, *Buna Rubber*, p. 45 claimed that Du Pont asked IG to supply its customers with Buna N, but this is refuted by the Mullaly letter. He also places the Deepwater explosion in early 1937, but it clearly occurred in January 1938; see Smith, 'The Ten-Year Invention', p. 47, and a telegram from Kühne to Konrad, 25 January 1938, *U.S.* v. *I.G. Farben*, ter Meer defence exhibit 204, reel 75 of M-892; Mullaly states that Du Pont was shut down from February to May (1938).

58. Herbert and Bisio, *Synthetic Rubber*, pp. 128 and 168, state that the capacity was 60 000t, a figure found in other sources, but Smith, 'The Ten-Year Invention', p. 54, gives a figure of 40 000t.

59. Morris, *American Synthetic Rubber*, provides a complete history of the research programme and gives detailed references to the technical literature.

60. 'Redox polymerization' was a more rapid polymerization system which permitted the manufacture of Buna S/GR-S at much lower temperatures, thereby producing the superior 'cold' rubber. It was initially developed by Heino Logemann at Leverkusen during the war, but first brought to the industrial scale in the USA in the late 1940s. I intend to publish a paper on the transfer of redox polymerization know-how to the USA, one of the major successes of the post-war technical intelligence-gathering programme, and its return to West Germany in the 1950s.

61. IG Farben's arrogance was described by Jasper E. Crane, Du Pont's expert on international matters, in a talk to Du Pont's chemical directors, 26 May 1930, Hagley Museum and Library, Acc. 1416, Box 7. I am indebted to David Hounshell for this reference.

62. Minutes of a meeting with Ayai of Mitsui, 17 December 1942, ZA 1503, FH.

63. I am grateful for the assistance of Dr Frederico Engel, formerly of Hüls AG, with the history of this transfer.

64. Nathan Rosenberg, *Technology and American Economic Growth* (New York, 1972); Rosenberg and Luther E. Birdzell, Jr., *How the West Grew Rich: The Economic Transformation of the Industrial World* (New York, 1986). For the chemical industry, also see Ralph Landau and Nathan Rosenberg, 'America's High-Tech Triumph', *Invention and Technology*, (Fall 1990), pp. 58–63.

65. Net imports taken from McFadyean, *The History of Rubber Regulation*, pp. 234–5, Table 6. The consumption figures for 1937–39 in Treue, *Gummi in Deutschland*, p. 262 (1937), p. 300 (1938 and 1939), and the figures for American consumption in McFadyean, *The History of Rubber Regulation*, p. 238, Table 7 also give a six-fold ratio.

66. Morris, *American Synthetic Rubber*, pp. 50–9. See R. R. Nelson and S. G. Winter, *An Evolutionary Theory of Economic Change* (Cambridge, Mass., 1982), pp. 275–307, for a critical discussion of dynamic competition and innovation.

67. Spitz, *Petrochemicals*, pp. 95–6.

68. Hitler's remarks in Noakes and Pridham (eds), *Documents on Nazism*, p. 406.

69. This section has been influenced by Richard N. Foster, *Innovation: The Attacker's Advantage* (London, 1986).

70. Kenneth Warren, *Chemical Foundations: The Alkali Industry in Britain to 1926* (Oxford, 1980); W. J. Reader, 'Solvay Triumphant', in *Imperial Chemical Industries: A History*, vol. 1, *The Forerunners, 1870–1926*.

71. Enos, *Petroleum, Progress and Profits*, pp. 187–224.

72. Basil Achilladelis, 'A Study in Technological History. Part I: The Manufacture of "Perlon" (Nylon 6) and Caprolactam by I.G. Farbenindustrie', *Chemistry and Industry*, (5 December 1970), pp. 1549–54.

73. Nathan Rosenberg, 'Economic Development and the Transfer of Technology: Some Historical Perspectives', *Technology and Culture*, 11, (1970), pp. 550–75.

74. For evidence of American worries about Japan, see almost any recent issue of *Harvard Business Review* and *Fortune*, (26 February 1990), a special issue on American perceptions of Japan.

APPENDIX: HOW TO MAKE SYNTHETIC RUBBER

To make a synthetic rubber you need a *monomer*, a chemical compound with a special feature called a double bond. For the manufacture of most synthetic rubbers, the monomer has two double bonds and these compounds are called *dienes*. Natural rubber is constructed of building-blocks of a diene with five carbon atoms, called isoprene. Unfortunately isoprene is expensive to synthesize, and chemists soon turned to other dienes, such as methylisoprene. Methylisoprene contains six carbon atoms and can be prepared by combining two molecules of acetone, a comparatively cheap compound with three carbon atoms. Isoprene and methylisoprene are derivatives of the simplest diene, butadiene, which has four carbon atoms. Isoprene has one methyl group – a single carbon atom surrounded by three hydrogen atoms – attached to the second carbon atom of butadiene, and methylisoprene has a second methyl group joined to the third carbon atom. By the mid-1920s, butadiene became the preferred monomer for synthetic rubber, but Du Pont's neoprene used chlorobutadiene. This monomer is similar to isoprene, with the methyl group replaced by a chlorine atom.

However Buna S (GR-S) – the major subject of this chapter – is made from a 7:3 mixture of butadiene and another monomer, styrene. Polystyrene is a well-known plastic, which is quite different from rubber. Styrene contains only one double bond but, combined with butadiene, it can produce a synthetic rubber which marries the elasticity of polybutadiene with the hard-wearing characteristics of polystyrene. Polymers produced from two monomers are called copolymers. Buna N is a copolymer of butadiene and acrylonitrile (the basis of acrylic sweaters).

The process of converting the monomer(s) into a synthetic rubber is called *polymerization*. The monomer molecules react with each other, in turn, to produce a long flexible chain of monomer units, rather like the beads in a necklace. This process can happen spontaneously, as in Bayer's process for methyl rubber or Du Pont's original process for neoprene. More often, however, an *initiator* is used to start the polymerization reaction. The first initiator used on a large scale was the reactive metal, sodium. Firestone returned to *metallic polymerization*, using sodium's close relative, lithium, to make synthetic 'natural rubber' in the 1950s. The initiator for Buna S (and GR-S) was potassium persulphate, a compound similar to hydrogen peroxide (which is used to bleach hair). To prevent the chains becoming too long, a *modifier* was added. IG Farben's original modifier for Buna S was linoleic acid (the unsaturated acid of linseed oil) but this was replaced in GR-S and Buna S3 by sulphur compounds. The modifier halts a growing polymer chain by donating a hydrogen atom, but it is thereby converted into a reactive fragment, which starts a new chain. In *redox polymerization*, a single

Figure 4.3   Manufacture of American GR-S (Buna S-similar)

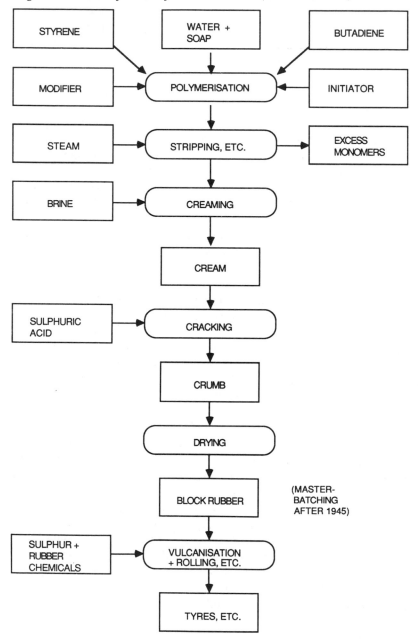

initiator compound was replaced by a more powerful mixture of two compounds, an oxidizing agent (usually a peroxide) and a reducing agent (compounds which donate hydrogen, for example glucose) catalyzed by ferrous sulphate (also found in the iron tablets given to blood donors).

It is possible to polymerize the monomer(s) on its (their) own (*bulk polymerization*) but this often creates technical problems, especially with build-up of heat during the reaction and the extraction of the polymer from the reactor. An alternative is solution polymerization, dissolving the monomer in an organic solvent, but the inevitable escape of solvent usually makes this option too expensive and environmentally hazardous. The best solution in the case of Buna S (GR-S) is *emulsion polymerization,* using soap or detergent to suspend the virtually insoluble monomers in water. The initiator can be either water-soluble (potassium persulphate) or monomer-soluble (organic peroxides). Emulsion polymerization permits greater control over the operating temperature, eliminating local hot-spots, and produces an easily handled emulsion of small polymer particles (latex). Unfortunately it could not be combined with metallic polymerization, because sodium reacts violently with water. Once the polymerization has reached the desired stage, when about two-thirds of the monomers have reacted, it is halted by use of special compounds called *short-stops*. The excess monomers are removed, and the latex is then converted into rubber crumbs and dried. The Germans converted the crumb into long bands which were then baled, but the Americans compressed the crumb into blocks.

5. Aspects of the Anglo-American Transfer of Computer Technology: The Formative Years, 1930s–1960s

Geoffrey Tweedale

INTRODUCTION

Modern computer history begins after the Second World War with the development of the electronic stored-program digital computer. In another sense, though, the history of computers commences with the invention of the first calculating machines.[1] The humble abacus, which probably originated in Babylonia (now Iraq) five thousand years ago, was perhaps the first device to embody a momentous idea – the notion of using a machine to perform intellectual work. Through the ages numerous philosophers, mathematicians and inventors, amongst them the English mathematician Charles Babbage (1791–1871), who embarked upon the construction of his ill-fated Difference Engine in the 1820s, devised increasingly sophisticated machines. In the late nineteenth century, as calculating problems grew, an American, Herman Hollerith (1860–1929), built punched-card machinery to mechanize the tabulation of the 1890 US Census, so establishing the data-processing industry.

By the early twentieth century, mechanical calculation, either in the office or the mathematical laboratory, was well established. Punched-card machinery, analogue devices for solving complicated equations and manual desk calculators were commercially available for 'computing', though it should be noted that prior to 1940 this term meant only one thing – a clerk equipped with a hand-calculating machine, who could 'compute' the standard calculations required for wages, actuary tables and ballistics. During the period 1935–45 the application of better engineering techniques, especially in electronics, began to speed up calculations for specific problems. In the 1930s, firstly in America and then in England, the first differential analysers were built for the solution of differential equations. During the Second World War new challenges spurred two major developments: the COLOS-

SUS, a code-breaking machine constructed for the British Government at Bletchley Park; and the ENIAC (Electronic Numerical Integrator and Computer), which was commissioned late in 1945 for the US Army Ordnance Department for ballistics calculations.

Though these machines were an important step along the way, none were computers in the modern sense of the word. Some, such as the differential analyser, were analogue machines: these expressed numerical quantities by analogue instead of digital representation and were usually built for specific problems, such as simulating aircraft behaviour. None were *universal*: that is, machines capable of solving any problem that could be solved by mathematical means, once an appropriate program had been inserted. Above all, they lacked a key feature of modern computers – an internal store (or memory), which could hold both instructions (the program) and data, and whose contents could be selectively altered automatically during computation. Soon after the end of the Second World War both the conceptual and engineering problems involved in constructing and utilizing such a memory were solved, so ushering in the era of the stored-program digital computer. By the end of the 1960s, the computer revolution was well under way: digital computers were commercially available in increasing numbers, the market for punched-card machinery was rapidly declining, analogue machines were being phased out, and the silicon integrated circuit (or 'chip') had arrived.

During these formative years, leaving aside the importance of the military in virtually all aspects of computer development, a notable feature was the remarkably close relationship between Britain and the USA. It is a commonplace that during the heyday of the 'Atlantic Economy' in the nineteenth century, America drew heavily on British technologies in founding its own industries. Some aspects of this transfer have been well studied by historians: textile technologies, mechanical engineering, the pottery industry, silk manufacture and special steels have all been the subject of detailed case-studies.[2] Generally these accounts have emphasized how successfully and swiftly America absorbed foreign technologies (though some have highlighted US backwardness in certain areas). By concentrating on the nineteenth century they have also implied that technological transfer – at least from Britain to America – was largely over by the early twentieth century. More studies will be needed, however, before any final conclusions can be reached. What can be stated with certainty is that in computing technology the Anglo-American connection was far from moribund, even after 1945, and was of great importance for the emerging computer industry. The nature of this linkage has never been systematically explored: indeed in many recent accounts, which have tended to focus on American advances, it has been underplayed. This account aims to rectify this deficiency.

DEVELOPMENTS BEFORE THE SECOND WORLD WAR

Charles Babbage is usually regarded as a decisive figure in the early history of computing, yet there is little evidence that his ideas were very widely disseminated. Many of the twentieth-century pioneers were admirers of Babbage, but this was often a retrospective interest and there is little evidence that Babbage influenced the design of the modern computer. One American who it is usually said was inspired by Babbage's ideas was Howard Aiken (1900–73), who began building the Harvard Mark I in 1937, and who often linked himself with Babbage and liked to present himself as his heir. According to one account, Aiken 'felt Babbage was addressing him personally from the past'. But Aiken's machines show no similarity to Babbage's designs, which were in any case unavailable to Aiken.[3] Inventors usually discovered Babbage's ideas afresh. Babbage may have influenced the American inventor and businessman, Herman Hollerith, but it seems more likely that his punched cards owed more to the Jacquard loom than to the Englishman.[4] It was with Hollerith, however, that transatlantic transfers of computer technology began.

By the 1900s, Hollerith's punched-card machines were being produced commercially by his Tabulating Machine Co. in New York. In 1904, Hollerith began exploiting his inventions in Britain, where he established a subsidiary which had the right to market and manufacture the American machines. The transfer of technology to the British company – which became the British Tabulating Machine Co. Ltd (BTM) in 1907 – was effected by C.A. Everard Greene, the first general manager of the British company, who visited the USA during 1902–4. He later recalled: 'My training consisted of getting an insight into the manufacture of parts, the assembly and wiring of machines, the making, planning and drawing up of cards for jobs, the investigation and organising necessary for installing and operating machines on the job.'[5] BTM purchased exclusive rights to manufacture and sell the machines, but the company was not without competition. In the early 1900s, rivalry over the US Census punched-card machine business developed between Hollerith and another inventor, James Powers, with the latter winning an important share of government business. This rivalry was transferred to Britain when, in 1915, an American-owned subsidiary of the Powers company was formed, the Accounting & Tabulating Corporation of Great Britain Ltd – often known as the 'Acc & Tab'.

In the heyday of the punched-card business in the inter-war period both BTM and the Acc & Tab prospered. Before the 1920s these two companies had essentially marketed and maintained machines which were largely American made. But gradually British manufacture and design prevailed: by 1920 Acc & Tab had opened a factory at Croydon and two years later BTM had begun manufacturing operations at Letchworth. R & D activity in these companies began shortly afterwards, though there was some patent activity before this time. Probably the most significant invention in the development of punched-card machinery, and unquestionably the most important British contribution, was the alphabetical printing unit, the work of Acc & Tab engineer, Charles C. Foster. This invention transformed punched-card accounting, since prior to alphabetical machines only figures could be printed, whereas henceforth names, addresses and descriptive material could be produced. Foster's unit was patented in 1916, but the First World War hindered its development, so that the prototype was not demonstrated until 1921. This led to a swift (and rare) reverse transfer of technology to the USA, since the American Powers company was eager to exploit it.

Documentation on other technical developments is scanty or non-existent at this time. But the broad picture is clear: British firms built upon the base of American technology, for which they sometimes paid dearly (BTM had to pay the patent holders – by that time IBM – 25 per cent after tax of its net revenues). American developments usually soon found their way to Britain. A good example was the introduction in the USA in 1928 of IBM's 80-column punched card with slotted holes in place of the standard 45-column card with round holes. The greater capacity of the new card was further extended by Remington-Rand, which offered a 90-column card soon after. These new-sized cards were adopted by BTM and Acc & Tab within a year or two of their appearance on the American market. However, on their own terms the British firms were able to make important contributions to punched-card design. One of the notable British achievements during the inter-war period was a smaller punched card, which after its introduction in 1932 by the British Powers Co. (by then known as Powers–Samas) enabled a range of low-cost machines to be marketed for small and medium-sized businesses. Another important development was the 'rolling total' mechanism developed at BTM by H.H. ('Doc') Keen. This device enabled values to be 'rolled' from one counter to another, so boosting the calculating possibilities of the machine. The BTM rolling total tabulator launched in 1936 was functionally superior to its IBM counterpart.

These machines were used for commercial applications. The first use of Hollerith tabulating equipment for large-scale scientific computations was pioneered in England by L.J. Comrie (1893–1950), who headed HM Nautical Almanac Office in London. In 1923–5, he had taught at two American universities, where he pioneered the introduction of computation as part of the curriculum. Comrie devised a method for calculating Fourier series on standard punched-card machines, and used this to calculate the motions of the moon for the years 1935 to 2000. These calculations were based on Brown's *Tables of the Moon* and, when E.W. Brown visited England in 1928, he was shown the computations in progress. Brown returned to the USA with the technique and discussed it with his friend Wallace J. Eckert, a mathematician and astronomer. Eckert was later able, in 1930, to persuade the president of IBM, Thomas J. Watson, to fund an Astronomical Computing Bureau at Columbia University, so that work could be done along similar lines to that of Comrie in London. It was not long before standard punched-card accounting equipment was modified to further facilitate large-scale calculation. In 1932, Comrie managed to persuade the Hollerith firm to modify their equipment so that the contents of one register, which previously had been limited to taking part in addition operations, could now be transferred to other mechanical registers in the machine. IBM equipment was modified in the same way about ten years later.[6]

The appearance of punched-card machinery in Britain in the early twentieth century was a visible symbol of the Anglo-American transfer of technology. Less apparent, but perhaps of greater importance for the subsequent history of computing, were linkages concerning analogue machines for mathematical calculations. Among the most important analytical tools in science and engineering are differential equations: a branch of calculus, these equations enable the prediction of the behaviour of moving objects by relating them to certain variables. They are very difficult to solve, but Lord Kelvin (1824–1907) argued in a remarkable paper published in 1876 that a mechanical 'differential analyser' capable of solving complicated differential equations was theoretically possible. His brother, Professor James Thomson, had first thought of the idea. Basically the machine used an 'integrator' – a wheel and disc arrangement with attached drive shafts – to effect the mathematical process of integration. But the technology of the day was incapable of realizing Kelvin's ideas and so his machine was never built.

In about 1930, however, Vannevar Bush (1890–1974), a professor of engineering at the Massachusetts Institute of Technology, returned to the problem and constructed a working differential analyser. Bush overcame the technical problems that had defeated Kelvin. In particular he was able to incorporate into his machine a 'torque amplifier', an indispensable device which 'stepped up' the smallest forces of the numerous shafts and gears. How much this design was based on Kelvin's previous published work is difficult to establish. According to Bush's memoirs, his project was original and he did not read Kelvin's paper until after he had built his machine.[7] Be that as it may, Bush's device was soon imitated.

In the summer of 1933, Bush received a visit from Professor Douglas R. Hartree (1897–1958), who at that time held the Chair of Applied Mathematics at Manchester University, and whose career highlighted not only the transition from analogue to digital techniques but also the importance of the Anglo-American connection. Hartree had realized that Bush's machine would much lighten the enormous calculations involved in his own work on quantum theory regarding self-consistent fields and he therefore decided to build such a machine for himself. The plans were generously given to him by Bush, who hoped that Manchester would produce an even better machine. With the help of a Manchester undergraduate, Arthur Porter, Hartree had constructed his first machine from *Meccano* (a child's construction set) by January 1934. Hartree and Porter then began building a full-scale machine, which was completed in 1935, having been engineered by Metropolitan Vickers. For a time it was the largest, most sophisticated and widely used differential analyser outside America.[8]

In 1937, Arthur Porter was awarded a Commonwealth Fund Fellowship, which enabled him to study at MIT under the supervision of Vannevar Bush. By now Bush had a new machine under way, the Rockefeller Differential Analyser, which made increasing use of electronics and high-precision engineering. Porter was to examine the problem of loading information into the machine using punched tape.[9] The first demonstration of the incomplete analyser was made in December 1941 and in the following year it was used for important war work on the calculation of firing tables and the profiles of radar antennas. By then, however, computing was swiftly developing in other directions.

THE SECOND WORLD WAR AND THE ADVENT OF THE STORED-PROGRAM DIGITAL COMPUTER

After 1940, military needs were the overriding influence on the development of computers, as the war threw up a host of computational problems. Computing devices were needed for gunnery control, bomb aiming, flight simulation, radar signal processing, atomic weapon calculations and code-breaking. In Britain a number of centres, such as the Telecommunications Research Establishment (TRE) and the Post Office Research Station, provided new ideas and, above all, the personnel, who were to direct post-war British efforts in this area.

Of particular interest is the special-purpose 'computer' named COLOSSUS, produced in great secrecy by the Post Office Research Station for the Government Code and Cipher School, Bletchley Park, Buckinghamshire. This machine, which was operational by the end of 1943, was built to crack German coded messages, which it did with great success. Absurdly, these operations are still classified, though the secrecy surrounding the project has relaxed sufficiently for the broad details to be known. Apart from its impact on the allied war effort, two aspects are particularly important. Firstly, although it is clear that the COLOSSUS was in no sense a modern computer, the final version of the machine contained all the necessary elements except an internal program store. Since it used almost 1 500 thermionic valves, it was also a remarkable demonstration that large numbers of electronic circuits could be made to do reliable calculations at speed. Secondly, the project brought together mathematicians and engineers in a fruitful collaboration, which alerted them to the possibilities inherent in computing. As one of them later commented: 'The value of the work ... was that we acquired a new understanding of and familiarity with logical switching and processing because of the enhanced possibilities brought about by electronic technologies which we ourselves developed. Thus when stored program computers became known to us we were able to go right ahead with their development.'[10] Amongst those involved with the building of the COLOSSUS were the mathematicians M.H.A. (Max) Newman (1897–1984) and Dr Alan M. Turing (1912–54), both of whom were to play an important role in subsequent British computing developments.

COLOSSUS was independent of American efforts. However the US armed forces had established contacts with the British cryptanalysts well before the USA came into the war, and there were regular missions for the exchange of information. Certain members of the COLOSSUS team, such as Alan Turing, were already familiar with the American scene. A Cambridge-trained mathematician, Turing had first visited the USA during 1936–8, when he held a visiting fellowship at the Institute of Advanced Study at Princeton University (IAS). This brought him into contact with that other major figure in twentieth-century computing, John von Neumann (1903–57). The visit coincided with the publication of a famous mathematical paper by Turing, 'On Computable Numbers', in which he outlined his idea for a theoretical universal automaton. The impact of this abstract and, to some, incomprehensible paper, is difficult to assess, though it now takes its place as a significant milestone in computer history. Personal contact between Turing and von Neumann appears to have been slight, though apparently by 1939 von Neumann knew and admired Turing's ideas and, certainly, Turing's paper was known at Bletchley Park.[11] At the end of 1942, Turing was in America again, charged with liaising with the Americans in connection with his work on COLOSSUS. This trip included a visit to Washington, followed by a tour of the Bell Laboratories, where he immersed himself in the electronic technology of speech encipherment and discussed matters relating to his work with prominent engineers, such as Claude Shannon. This was probably the only journey Turing made to America during the war, though the legend grew up that he and von Neumann met during the conflict, and that this was somehow an important event in the evolution of the modern computer.[12] There is no evidence for this, however: the modern computer evolved from the mainstream of developments in twentieth-century mathematics and engineering and did not need a meeting between Turing and von Neumann to bring it about.

Nevertheless, John von Neumann's involvement with the development of the computer was crucial. It stemmed from his introduction to the work on the ENIAC at the Moore School of Electrical Engineering at the University of Pennsylvania, which was a major source of technical and computational support for the US Army's Ballistics Research Laboratory. The ENIAC contained 18 000 valves and 1 500 relays, weighed over 30 tons and was built by a team of 200 people between 1943 and 1945. Significant less for its achievements – it did not become operational until some months after the war – than for what it promised, ENIAC gave scientists and the public their first dramatic glimpse of the computer age. It was a development in which British scientists played a part. Douglas Hartree had visited the USA again in 1945, as soon as the European war was over, and had seen the ENIAC, which was still incomplete. In the following year he was invited for a second visit so that he could advise on its use. According to Herman Goldstine, the representative of the Ballistics Laboratory, Hartree 'was of great help to the ENIAC group coming when he did, because he helped keep up the morale and intellectual tone of the ENIAC operating staff'.[13] Hartree was able himself to use the ENIAC for a problem in laminar boundary flow, though a program error was later found to have vitiated the results. Nevertheless he had shown that ENIAC had a broad range of applicability. On his return to England, where he took up a chair in mathematical physics at Cambridge University, Hartree was able to publicize American activities in *Nature* and in his inaugural lecture. His support for US computing continued in 1948, when he spent three months as acting director of the Institute for Numerical Analysis, newly established by the Bureau of Standards on the UCLA campus. A series of lectures he gave at the University of Illinois on this trip was repeated in Cambridge on his return and also published.[14] Hartree continued this championing both of American advances and computers throughout his life.

The development of the ENIAC and the personalities involved – notably, the driving force behind the project, J. Presper Eckert and John Mauchly – have been well described elsewhere.[15] Here attention will be confined to its impact on Anglo-American technology, which was profound. The ENIAC team were to be responsible for the sudden flowering of the stored-program concept, when they began work on their next machine at the Moore School, the EDVAC (Electronic Discrete Variable Automatic Calculator). Before then it had always seemed logical to store data outside the machine, but this became increasingly difficult once machines such as the ENIAC could process thousands of instructions per second. The ENIAC engineers took the crucial step of considering storing data *within* the machine. Building on Eckert's and Mauchly's work (though unfortunately not acknowledging them), von Neumann elucidated the concept of the stored-program digital computer –

one in which both data and instructions would be held in a memory – in his document, 'First Draft of a Report on the EDVAC' (1945).[16] Available in a limited number of copies, this report began percolating into the scientific community at about the same time as a special summer course was run at the Moore School in 1946. The course was entitled, 'Theory and Techniques for the Design of Electronic Digital Computers', which attracted 28 people from both sides of the Atlantic.[17] Together with von Neumann's report, these seminars helped trigger the post-war development of the stored-program computer both in Britain and the USA. By the late 1940s, the race was on to overcome the engineering problems involved in building such a computer. England, with its wartime experience with electronics and code-breaking machinery, was well placed to take up the challenge with a number of major initiatives. These projects and especially their relationship to American developments will now be considered.

MANCHESTER UNIVERSITY MARK I

After the war the key problem facing engineers was the construction of a satisfactory computer memory. Clearly whoever solved this problem stood a good chance of being the one to build the world's first operational stored-program computer. In the event, the prize was to be claimed by a team at Manchester University, led by Professor (Sir) F.C. Williams (1911–77) and (Professor) Tom Kilburn. Both men had acquired a wartime grounding in radar electronics at the Telecommunications Research Establishment at Malvern. In 1946, Williams accepted a chair at Manchester University and with the help of Kilburn (who was seconded from the TRE) began work on a novel form of computer storage using the cathode ray tube (crt). This was at a time when a number of mathematicians and engineers with expertise in the fields of electronics and mathematics had contrived to secure jobs at Manchester University. These eventually included Max Newman (who had secured a Royal Society grant to set up a 'Computer Laboratory'), Alan Turing and I.J. Good, all former COLOSSUS men. The development of the Manchester University project, and its relationship to American activities, is known in some detail because of later patent litigation.[18]

During the war Williams had visited the USA in connection with his radar work. He was one of the editors of a Radiation Laboratories multi-volume reference work (known as the 'five-foot shelf' because of its bulk) and to discharge his responsibilities in this direction he visited the Laboratories in Boston in November 1945, where he observed that there was much discussion of crt storage. In June 1946, Hartree had secured an invitation for him to view the ENIAC, which in Williams's words was the first time he 'personally came across computation in terms of numbers'. Methods of storage using crt's were being explored at this time in the USA, particularly at the Moore School, but without any success. On his return to England in July 1946, however, Williams, whose own background and inventive genius had given him a unique insight into the technical difficulties involved, began work on crt storage at the TRE. The result of his efforts, which by 1947 had been transferred to Manchester University, was the Williams tube – the first electrostatic random-access memory for a computer – in which Williams discovered a relatively simple method to regenerate, and thus store, electronic pulses. The device became the basis for a prototype machine (the forerunner of the Manchester Mark I) which was built at Manchester University and on 21 June 1948 became the world's first stored-program computer to operate.

As for the logical design – the stored-program concept – that had been explained to Williams by Newman in 'all of half an hour'. It is not known if this reflected American influence, though Newman was certainly aware of US progress after the war. The Royal Society grant enabled him to send a member of the Manchester group, David Rees, to the famous Moore School lectures and, in 1946, Newman himself visited the Moore School and saw ENIAC, later spending a term at Princeton where he discussed computers with von Neumann. On the other hand, Newman professed ignorance of American ideas before that date: after all, he was able to draw on the theories of his student and fellow COLOSSUS worker, Alan Turing. Williams and other members of his team always emphasized that their work was an independent growth and owed nothing to US precedents: as Williams was wont to say, 'it was all in Babbage'.

A provisional patent on the Williams tube was filed on 11 December 1946 and by the end of the following year Kilburn had produced an unpublished report, 'A Storage System for Use with Binary Digital Computing Machines', which summarized their findings. This was duplicated in considerable numbers and taken by Hartree to the USA, where Williams refused permission for it to be copied too widely because it would pre-empt publication in the *Journal of the Institution of Electrical Engineers*. 'Nonetheless,' as Williams stated, 'there is no doubt that the information spread through the United States.' This had two results. Firstly, in 1950, Williams found himself defending his crt patent against American inventors led by Eckert, who refused to acknowledge Williams's work and implied that previous US efforts along those lines were responsible for the regenerative technique. With the help of the National Research Development Corporation (NRDC), which had taken the Manchester work under its wing on behalf of national interests, Williams successfully refuted this claim.[19] Secondly, since for a brief period the Williams tube represented the best available storage device, it was used under licence in some of the first US computers.

In 1949, recalled Williams, he was invited to IBM with his wife and son 'and given the VIP treatment. They went in for c.r.t. storage in a big way and, of course, offered me a lucrative job, which I refused, much to Mr. Watson's surprise.' Here Williams scandalized IBM workers with a jibe at their president's THINK motto, when at a lecture someone asked him:

> Can you explain to me how it comes about that you with one scientific colleague and two technical assistants have managed to build a computing machine, and we with all our resources have not succeeded? I said yes, it's very simple: we pressed on regardless, without stopping to THINK too much.

In July 1949, negotiations took place between Lord Halsbury of the NRDC and IBM, which licensed the use of the Williams tube in early IBM computers. In 1952, IBM introduced the 701 design, the first large scientific calculator made in any quantity, which incorporated 144 Williams tubes. By 1955, IBM had taken over six of Manchester's US patents and this was eventually to earn the NRDC £125 712 in royalties. IBM became involved in research to improve the technical capabilities of the crt store, but magnetic core storage soon made the Manchester invention redundant.[20]

The Williams tube was also used in the machine built at the IAS in Princeton, which was the result of an initiative by John von Neumann in 1946. Finding an adequate storage device had proved a headache, since American ideas had run into technical problems. At this point the Princeton team heard about the work at Manchester University and Julian Bigelow, the project leader, travelled to Manchester in 1948. Here he met Williams – according to Bigelow 'a true example of the British "string and sealing wax" inventive genius'[21] – and became acquainted with the Williams tube. Eventually the IAS machine incorporated a 40-tube Williams memory, arranged in something like a 'V-40' engine configuration. Thus it appears in a famous photograph, with von Neumann standing in front of the computer. The Manchester store was also used in the American ILLIAC, SWAC and SEAC and was initially the preferred memory in the Whirlwind.[22]

Meanwhile at Manchester University, Williams and Kilburn developed their own machine – the Manchester Mark I – which became the basis, at the government's prompting, for a series of collaborative commercial ventures with the local electronics firm of Ferranti Ltd. This company's interest in computers had begun in earnest in the summer of 1948, when it dispatched one of its technical experts, Dr D.G. Prinz, to America to report on computer activities. Prinz toured all the major US computer centres, discussed technical matters with scientists and engineers, collected printed material and assessed the possibility of an alliance with a US firm. Reported Prinz:

A few words may be said about the reaction of the various people to the F.C. Williams tube of which I had taken a description along with me. Patterson and Snyder (EDVAC, Moore School) were greatly impressed; they pointed out that they had worked on similar lines some years ago, but gave it up in favour of the mercury delay line, and they appreciated that Williams had discovered some trick that they themselves had not found. Similarly, Eckert and Mauchly were very much interested. Rajchman thought the Williams tube 'the second-best'. Klemperer (formerly Raytheon, now MIT) was impressed because he knows the difficulties inherent in secondary-emission storage tubes such as those developed by Haeff and himself (the charge tends to spread out on the screen). Only Aiken dismissed the idea.[23]

An oft-repeated story, that on his visit Prinz was told to his surprise that the world's most advanced computer project was on his doorstep, was perhaps apocryphal: probably Prinz learned about Williams's work at an IEE (Institution of Electrical Engineers) lecture. Nevertheless the burden of his report was that Ferranti should utilize the work of Manchester University in building its own computers. The first result of this collaboration was the Ferranti Mark I, a commercial version of the University machine, and this was followed by a number of influential computers.

The Williams–Kilburn partnership (which continued until about 1952, when Kilburn assumed direction of computer projects, as Williams turned to other research) was responsible for a number of pioneering innovations in computer design – to say nothing of the work of those such as Gordon Black, who pioneered the *use* of computers for such tasks as optical ray tracing. Of particular importance was the Manchester invention of index registers (or B-lines, as they were known by the designers), a feature now seen on every modern computer, and the early combination of a small, but fast, random-access store backed by a slower (but larger-capacity) sequential store, which was to produce significant Manchester innovations in the ATLAS computer (considered below). These ideas had their impact on American design, though documenting individual transfers of technology is not always possible. The Anglo-American connection remained close in the 1950s. Kilburn visited America in 1952 and admitted to being 'fairly familiar' with US projects, though his designs followed a very independent line. The US influence on Manchester was perhaps strongest in terms of hardware: by the early 1950s, Williams was requesting samples of the first American transistors to arrive in the UK and, by the end of 1953, Kilburn had built the world's first transistorized computer (an experimental model).[24] American interest in Manchester University and Ferranti computers remained strong and Kilburn remembers regular visits by IBM staff. In the mid-1950s, when he was engaged in work on the Ferranti Mercury computer, 'the fact that we were well on the way with this floating-point [arithmetic] startled IBM at one time when they visited us'.

Manchester innovations also reached the USA via Ferranti's activities in Canada. In September 1952, Ferranti sold a copy of the Mark I (named FERUT) to the University of Toronto, where it helped with design calculations for the St Lawrence Seaway. Lord Bowden (1910–89), Ferranti's first computer salesman, attested to the impact the success of this venture had on IBM. At Ferranti Electric Ltd (later Ferranti–Packard) in Toronto, engineers under Arthur Porter (Hartree's co-worker) were responsible for important pioneering designs in the mid-1950s. They built a naval data acquisition and target tracking system that included the first computer network in which three physically separate processing systems were interconnected through radio channels and operated as a single system. This was copied by the Americans. Ferranti–Packard also built the FP6000, the world's first time-sharing, multi-tasking machine, which in the UK in the mid-1960s was used as the basis for International Computers Ltd's 1900 series.[25]

THE CAMBRIDGE UNIVERSITY EDSAC (ELECTRONIC DELAY STORAGE AUTOMATIC CALCULATOR)

The EDSAC was perhaps the most influential of the post-war British computer projects. Although Manchester University had run the first stored program, it was the Mathematical Laboratory at Cambridge University that was the first centre in the world to provide a useful and reliable computing service. The EDSAC is particularly interesting, since it was inspired directly by American example.

The EDSAC team was headed by Professor Maurice V. Wilkes, whose experience in mechanical calculating had been provided by the Cambridge differential analyser and the friendship of Douglas Hartree. In May 1946, L.J. Comrie gave him a copy of von Neumann's report on the EDVAC and Wilkes 'recognised this at once as the real thing, and from that time on never had any doubt as to the way computer development would go'.[26] Armed with introductions from Hartree, Wilkes next attended the Moore School meetings and even whilst in Philadelphia began formulating ideas for the EDSAC. The keynote was pragmatism: on his return Wilkes intended to build a usable machine, rather than one which attempted to experiment with the most advanced techniques. For the memory he followed the EDVAC idea for a store using mercury delay lines, even though a working version had not yet been built even in the USA. EDSAC ran its first calculation at the Mathematical Laboratory, Cambridge, in May 1949, almost a year behind the Manchester team, but still well ahead of the Americans. However, the Cambridge machine was more than simply a testbed: by the end of the year it was able to offer a useful computer service.

A significant feature of the Cambridge approach was the attention paid to user convenience and programming. No sooner had EDSAC been completed than work began at once on the development of a programming system and a library of subroutines. Here the expertise of the Cambridge team's programmers, such as (Professor) Stanley Gill and particularly (Professor) David J. Wheeler, became evident. Besides providing a well-stocked library of subroutines, a report on the preparations of programmes and subroutines was also prepared and sent by Wilkes to interested users throughout the world. This was especially useful because, until then, only theoretical studies on programming had been available and these had not been based on practical experience. This report aroused a good deal of interest, particularly in the USA. At about this time, Wilkes received a visit from Zdenek Kopal, then at MIT and later a professor of astronomy at Manchester University, who took the report away with him and brought it to the attention of Addison-Wesley, then a small-scale publishing operation in Cambridge, Massachusetts. In 1951, Addison-Wesley published the report under the authorship of Wilkes, Wheeler and Gill as *The Preparation of Programs for an Electronic Digital Computer: With Special Reference to the EDSAC and the Use of the Library of Subroutines*. The economy and elegance of the EDSAC programming, largely the work of Wheeler, was much in advance of any US or British group and the book (usually referred to as Wilkes, Wheeler and Gill, or simply as WWG) was very influential.

Wheeler's work, which included the use of a symbolic notation for programming, the so-called 'initial orders', subroutines, the subroutine library, and debugging techniques, was recognized in America as the 'leading example of programming virtuosity'.[27] In the USA the programming system developed for the MIT Whirlwind by Charles W. Adams was strongly influenced by the Cambridge group. In 1951–3, Wheeler joined the University of Illinois at Urbana as an assistant professor, at a time when the University was constructing the ILLIAC computer (and its 'twin' the ORDVAC, which was later transferred to Maryland) for the Ballistics Research Laboratories. Wheeler, as the only member of the team with any practical experience of stored-program computers, influenced the programming system of the machine, which was based on the EDSAC. He also influenced aspects of the design, such as extending the address space, though the conservatism of the chief engineer of the project, Ralph Meagher, meant that Wheeler's suggestion that they double the power of the machine by installing index registers was not utilized.[28] Nevertheless the ILLIAC influenced several other computers in the USA, besides those in other countries, such as Israel (the WEIZAC) and Australia (the SILLIAC). After Wheeler's return, the Cambridge connection at the University of Illinois was maintained by Stanley Gill and (Professor) A.S. Douglas. The latter was closely involved in studying the library routines in order to advise on the design of ILLIAC II. Douglas and a US programmer, David Muller, produced a report outlining their conclusions regarding word-length and the number of registers in the mill, as well as their cross-connections. Of particular importance was the idea that all registers on the mill should be interconnected in such a way that numbers could be moved from one to the other directly, via shift paths or through adders under micro-program control – a scheme that was later implemented on the MANIAC III, constructed at the University of Chicago in the late 1950s. Douglas concludes, however, that British influence was strongest on the programming side:

> David, Stan and I taught successive classes of 50 using the techniques we had developed (cf. Wilkes, Wheeler & Gill). My instructors (i.e. assistants) were Gene Golub (now a senior professor at Stanford), Werner Frank (sometime vice-president of a major software house, Informatics Inc.), and my students went all over the US – one turned up in an LP team at IBM some ten years later – whilst we certainly influenced many whom we talked to on our travels.[29]

Wheeler also highlights the importance of this 'grapevine' aspect in the spread of computer technology. It was fostered by the integration of the ILLIAC and the EDSAC into teaching courses and the operation of these computers in an 'open shop' manner. Users were expected to programme their own calculations, assisted where necessary by staff, and this facilitated the flow of information. While users waited their turn at the machine, problems and new procedures could be discussed. Lectures were given to newcomers and the first summer school for training outsiders was held in Cambridge in 1950. Notes Wheeler: 'The use of the computer spread rapidly as successful users infected their friends.'[30]

Naturally these men, and also Wilkes, who remained a regular visitor to the USA at this time and was present when the electrostatic core memory was run on the Whirlwind in August 1953,[31] returned from the USA with fresh ideas, which proved useful in the design of EDSAC II. The ILLIAC II ideas were also directly reflected in the English Electric machine, the KDF9.

Cambridge University, too, developed links with industry. This was in the unlikely form of a close relationship with the catering firm of J. Lyons & Co., whose forward-looking management had become interested in the latest developments in computing as a way to free the firm from the cost and tedium of its enormous accounting operations. The link was spurred by American developments. In May 1947, representatives of Lyons visited Princeton, where they met Herman Goldstine who, besides explaining projects such as the EDVAC and the new IAS machine, told them of Wilkes's computer at Cambridge. Following a communication from Goldstine to Hartree, the latter then wrote to Lyons inviting their representatives to Cambridge. After their visit in the summer of 1947, Lyons agreed to support the Cambridge project and began building the LEO (Lyons Electronic Office). It was the beginning of an involvement in computing which was eventually to see the catering firm, somewhat incongruously, enter the field as computer manufacturers themselves.[32]

THE NPL PILOT ACE (AUTOMATIC COMPUTING ENGINE)

The projects at Manchester and Cambridge were by far the most successful in the early history of British computing; as such, their relationship with America is relatively easy to assess. This is less true of another post-war effort centred at the National Physical Laboratory at Teddington.

In 1944, a Mathematics Division was established in the NPL, in order to coordinate facilities and techniques related to machine-aided computation. Douglas Hartree and L.J. Comrie were father figures in the foundation of the Division, but, as regards the building of a stored-program computer, the NPL received most of its impetus from the disbanded COLOSSUS team from Bletchley Park, particularly Alan Turing.

The NPL project is of particular interest, since at the end of the war it became the centre of what it was hoped would be a national attempt to build a computer. The superintendent of the Mathematics Division, J.R. Womersley, began canvassing support and recruiting staff in 1945 and was responsible for Turing's appointment. Events in the USA had undoubtedly inspired Womersley's actions. Early in 1945, he had visited America and had been one of the first foreigners to see the ENIAC and be given a copy of the EDVAC report. The threat of America moving ahead in the computer race provided the impetus for his plans, though it should be noted that a strong, independent line was already evident. Womersley had read Turing's paper 'On Computable Numbers' before the war and was well acquainted with the idea of 'Turing machines'. Hence his desire to have Turing join the NPL.

The fragmentation of British technical personnel and resources after the war, however, meant that Womersley's plans for a national machine were never realized, but an NPL computer did emerge, based on a draft report submitted by Turing to the executive committee of the NPL in 1946. Turing's report detailed the design and operation of an electronic universal machine, christened the ACE (Automatic Computing Engine). From this blueprint emerged the Pilot ACE, so named because the prototype became the completed version of the machine. In recent years this draft report has become the subject of renewed interest, mainly because of Turing's far-sighted recognition of the possibilities of the stored-program computer. Among the topics discussed in Turing's report, but not found in that of von Neumann, are address mapping, instruction address register and instruction register, microcode, hierarchical architecture, floating point arithmetic, hardware bootstrap loader, subroutine stack, modular programming, subroutine library, link editor, symbolic addresses and the ability to treat programs as data. Turing's vision was also apparent at a London Mathematical Society lecture he gave in February 1947. Before the first stored-program computer had even been demonstrated, he predicted the end of the human computer, the use of terminals connected over telephone lines, analysts, programmers, operators, on-line curve followers and – perceptively – the protective mystique and gibberish affected by systems programmers.[33]

The relationship of Turing's ideas to US developments is obscure. On the one hand, Turing made no great claims to the originality of his ideas, recommending that his proposal should be read 'in conjunction' with von Neumann's EDVAC report. The hardware for the memory of the ACE, the mercury delay line, was also an American idea. Indeed, at Hartree's suggestion, a member of the ENIAC team, Harry D. Huskey, had joined the ACE project to introduce expertise on the hardware side. On the other hand, a biography of Alan Turing has argued persuasively that his ideas were original and owed most to his idea of a universal machine outlined in his paper 'On Computable Numbers'.[34] Significantly Turing resisted Womersley's suggestion that he cooperate with Wilkes on an EDVAC-style machine, scathingly arguing that Wilkes's plans were 'in the American tradition of solving one's difficulties by means of much equipment rather than by thought'. When Turing himself visited the USA at the end of 1946 to attend a Symposium on Large Scale Digital Calculating Machinery held at Harvard and also met the ENIAC and von Neumann groups, he later commented that he had not 'brought any very new technical information to light'. He thought the numerous American projects were dissipating their energies over too wide an area and concluded: 'We ought to be able to do much better if we concentrate all our effort on the one machine, thereby providing a greater drive than they can afford on any single one.' Jim Wilkinson (1919–86) and Donald Davies, members of the ACE team who brought the project to a successful conclusion after Turing prematurely left the NPL (he appears to have become disillusioned with bureaucratic indecision there), also emphasized the independence of the NPL work.[35] Wilkinson highlighted the fact that, although they had the EDVAC report to hand, they made little use of it in the design for the ACE, which had an idiosyncratic design with user convenience, never one of Turing's priorities, sacrificed for speed. Moreover he believed that Huskey, with whom Turing violently disagreed, had brought little to the project, apart from basic circuitry.

Whatever the assessment of American influence on the ACE may be, there is little doubt that Turing's work represented a considerable achievement: when completed the 800-tube Pilot ACE had a computational speed several times better than the 3000-tube EDSAC. Hartree took a copy of the ACE report to the ENIAC group in 1946 and Turing's work was also known at Princeton, which he himself visited in January 1947. But the ACE design, as was often the case in England, was too far outside the mainstream of computer development to have any widespread impact, whatever admiration Turing's ideas may arouse today. Nevertheless it is worth recording that, when Huskey returned to the USA to work on the SWAC (taking with him, as it happened, the technology of the Williams tube, which he recommended for use in that machine), he utilized the ideas of the ACE. During a sabbatical year at Wayne State University in 1953, he designed a computer for the Bendix Corporation that was strongly influenced by Turing's ideas. This computer, the Bendix G-15, was produced successfully – over 400 were eventually sold – and its speed made it a favourite for certain classes of engineering design.[36]

A.D. BOOTH AND THE ARC (AUTOMATIC RELAY COMPUTER)

In the early days of stored-program computing there was still room for the old-style 'tinkerer', working with very limited resources. Such an individual was Dr Andrew D. Booth, who had first become involved in automatic calculators during the Second World War, while working on the determination of crystal structures using X-ray diffraction data. The computations involved were extremely tedious and there was ample incentive for automating the process. Booth was employed as a mathematical physicist in the X-ray team at the British Rubber Producers' Association (BRPRA), Welwyn Garden City, Hertfordshire, from August 1943 to September 1945. Subsequently he moved to Birkbeck College, London University, though he was still retained as a consultant by BRPRA. This consultancy later proved fortuitous in respect of workshop facilities for his Automatic Relay Computer (ARC), which he designed during 1947–9.

Booth's interest in universal automatic digital computers was fostered by contact with the indefatigable Douglas Hartree, who looked him up after reading some of Booth's mathematical papers. Booth was already working on a digital calculator, but Hartree gave him his first knowledge about what was going on in the wider world of computing, especially in the USA. Booth was to be heavily influenced by the logical design of American machines. In the summer of 1945, he crossed the Atlantic, funded by the Rockefeller Foundation, London University and the proceeds of a lecture tour on which Booth was after-dinner speaker to 'earnest old ladies'. He visited a number of groups, including that of von Neumann and Goldstine at Princeton, J.W. Forrester at MIT, Howard Aiken at Harvard, Eckert and Mauchly in Philadelphia and Morris Rubinoff at the Moore School. After this visit, which had enabled Booth to evaluate the respective merits of the various projects, the Rockefeller Foundation offered him a fellowship to work at an American institution of his own choice. Booth had by now read the EDVAC report, courtesy of Hartree, and he had no hesitation in choosing the IAS at Princeton, 'not because I had seen anything of the hardware of their project, which I had not, but because the rigorous knowledge and precise thought of von Neumann attracted me: it had none of the airy imprecision of other workers'.[37] This visit to the IAS, during March to September 1947, firmly launched Booth on the design of a stored-program computer.

At Princeton, besides exploring the joys of von Neumann's approach, Booth was also able to refine some of his own earlier ideas on electronic storage, which he regarded as 'the whole key' to computing technology. He believed that magnetic processes were the only ones that had any potential for large-scale, long-term storage and while in America sketched out, but took no steps to construct, various magnetic storage devices.

On his return to the UK, Booth and his assistant, Miss Kathleen Britten (later Mrs K.V.H. Booth), began to build a machine. The project was tiny: apart from his future wife, Booth never had more than one engineer and he was dependent for facilities on the BRPRA, since no laboratories were available at Birkbeck College. Booth's first experiments concerned a 'floppy-disc'-type memory, using oxide-coated paper discs from the US firm which manufactured 'Mail-a-Voice' recording machines. Though the principle was very similar to that used for modern disc drives, Booth's device proved unstable and he had no resources to overcome the technical problems. So, with the help of his father, who was a fine mechanical engineer, he returned to his original idea, the magnetic drum. This was more successful and by 1948 he had installed a working magnetic drum in the experimental ARC. Booth and his father continued to experiment and by 1952 they were producing large drum memories for others. Some of these drums were exported to the USA, where they performed reliably for as long as ten years. Closer to home, Booth's attempt to design low-cost computers that would be useful to smaller scientific organizations attracted the interest of BTM. Eventually, the firm used Booth's designs to build the HEC (Hollerith Electronic Computer), which was later marketed as the BTM 1200 series.

By 1962, Booth's work in England was complete: in that year he took his expertise to Canada, where he continued his computing career.

THE ANGLO-AMERICAN COMPUTER RACE

Within a decade of the pioneering projects outlined so far, the frame of reference had changed drastically. By the end of the 1950s, the race for computing supremacy was no longer being run in technical terms in university laboratories, but in the market-place where British and American electronics firms competed for the rapidly growing world business in computers.

In the late 1940s and early 1950s, Britain rivalled American firms in innovation. The first operational stored-program computer, the first computer service, the first transistorized computer and the first commercially available computer – these were a string of remarkable technical achievements, especially considering the acute shortages of manpower and resources in post-war Britain. The way in which several companies – Ferranti, Elliott Bros, Lyons, English Electric, GEC and Marconi – soon became involved in production shows also that the commercial potential of the computer was not overlooked. However, the vulnerability of these firms to the large US corporations was soon apparent. By 1964, it was estimated that there were almost 22 000 computers installed in the USA, including approximately 1 767 in civil government, 2 000 in the Department of Defense, and another 2 000 or so used by government contractors at the state's expense. In contrast, less than 1 000 computers had been installed in the UK by the same date, of which only 56 were in civil government departments.[38] Thus the American companies set the agenda for the commercial development of the computer in the 1960s. Yet British scientists and firms continued to make important contributions to computer design in this period and Anglo-American transfer of computing technology therefore continued unabated.

American competition operated across the board, but the threat was perceived initially in terms of large computers for scientific use. By the mid-1950s, it had become clear that Britain was rapidly falling behind in this field and that a concerted effort would be needed if the country was to stay in the computer race. This fear was inspired by an awareness of several major computer projects to build high-speed computers, such as the IBM STRETCH. In the summer of 1956 a team of British experts – A.S. Douglas from Cambridge, D.W. Davies and J.H. Wilkinson from the NPL and Jack Howlett from Harwell – had visited the USA and had confirmed America's rapid progress for themselves. It was felt that Britain needed its own fast computer project, responsibility for which was assumed by the NRDC, which had become closely identified with the progress of the British computer industry. But NRDC attempts to nurture such a project amongst computer firms and government establishments had only limited success and resulted in costly delays and only a half-hearted commitment to a cooperative project. Eventually a close approximation to a national computer emerged in the form of the

Ferranti–Manchester University ATLAS, under the direction of Tom Kilburn. This machine was to be a commercial failure and only three ATLAS computers were ever installed after deliveries began in 1963. Whether this was because of the greater resources of the Americans or of bureaucratic indecisiveness remains debatable.[39] What is certain is that ATLAS was a technical achievement of great importance. A number of innovations in its architecture were to be very influential in later computer developments around the world. Amongst these were: multiprogramming, job scheduling, spooling, extracodes, interrupts, pipelining, interleaved storage, autonomous transfer units, virtual storage and paging. Virtual memory and the ATLAS operating system – by which blocks of information could be swapped between different stores to increase the speed and capacity of the machine – were especially influential. ATLAS proved that it was possible to build a multiprogramming machine with a paged memory and sophisticated operating system (there was even a pioneering provision for time-sharing, which had to be discarded owing to budget limitations). These ideas eventually featured in US machines.

Meanwhile the early 1960s also saw a 'technology gap' and a rapid escalation of US competition in the commercial sector. In the 1950s, American competition in the European market was almost non-existent, but by 1967 the leading US computer manufacturers such as IBM, NCR, UNIVAC, Burroughs and Honeywell had nearly a 70 per cent share of the British market. The dominant company was IBM, which had 40 per cent of the market in that year. In the electronic data-processing market British firms had fallen well behind. By 1960, virtually all US computers had second-generation transistorized processors; their software and programming languages (such as FORTRAN and COBOL) were in advance of Europe; and their magnetic tape and disc storage technology were vastly superior. Not surprisingly, British firms, such as ICT (formed in 1959 as a result of a merger of BTM and Powers–Samas), had to go to America for their technology. In 1961, ICT signed an agreement with RCA, which gave the British firm a licence to use RCA computer technology. Another arrangement allowed ICT to import the RCA model 301 computers, to be resold as the ICT 1500. (English Electric was another firm which had a long-standing technology-sharing agreement with RCA: in 1961, it introduced a version of the RCA 501 which was known as the KDP10 and also adopted the RCA Spectra 70 architecture for its System 4 in the late 1960s.) In the following year, ICT made a similar deal with UNIVAC to import and resell their model 1004 calculating tabulator.

American dominance was underlined in 1964, when IBM launched its highly successful System/360 range of computers. This event, which is regarded as a watershed in the history of commercial computing, saw the introduction of the first compatible family of third-generation computers. The range encompassed six distinct processors and 40 peripherals, which were intended to replace all of IBM's current mid-range computers. The concept of compatibility and the several-fold increase in price/performance offered by the System/360 range sent shock waves through the industry. In IBM the brilliance and success of the range took on a symbolic significance. Yet, even here, transatlantic influences were at work. An important feature of System/360 computers was the use of control stores. This was a key hardware feature that allowed computers with very different hardware implementations to appear identical to the user, except for different costs and speeds. Such stores were based on the idea of 'microprogramming', first presented in 1951 by Maurice Wilkes at Cambridge. An important part of the development work for the control store was directed by John W. Fairclough, a graduate of Manchester University who had worked on STRETCH at IBM's Hursley Laboratory in the UK. This was the first time an important aspect of machine development had been undertaken by one of IBM's overseas subsidiaries. Thus 'the existence of control-store technology and system design experience in the Hursley Laboratory facilitated an important achievement in IBM System/360: first use of read-only control stores in a series of commercial computers'.[40] Several serious shortcomings in the System/360, particularly a weakness in virtual memory address translation, later resulted in the model 67. Although this model was not entirely compatible with the /360 line, it did introduce an ATLAS-like paging system with the hardware address translation and other facilities that were necessary for efficient operation of a machine via time-shared terminals.

Almost immediately after the IBM announcement of the System/360, the other large computer companies followed with their own 'families' of compatible machines. The two larger British firms responded with the ICT 1900 series and the English Electric–Leo–Marconi System 4. The story of these computers, and that of the eventual merger of the British industry into ICL in 1968, has been recently documented.[41]

CONCLUSION

Herman Goldstine remarked that, in 1945, 'a number of British visitors came to the Moore School, and from these visits stemmed the computerization of Great Britain'.[42] Although this statement contains an element of the truth, the discussion above has shown that it is also a gross simplification. In fact it might be more accurate to argue that the development of the computer in the UK (and in the USA) would have proceeded independently, whatever was occurring across the Atlantic. As it happened, US events did exert a powerful influence on British computerization; but then so, too, did UK technology on its US counterpart. A more complete picture would aim to show that the development of the computer in these two countries was a product of a complex interaction. This has been attempted here, though it should be emphasized that it is an impressionistic picture. The international diffusion of computer technology is a huge field and more research needs to be done to delineate fully the web of Anglo-American links.[43] Nevertheless, a number of significant trends and conclusions have emerged.

Perhaps the overriding impression is of the speed of the Atlantic transfer of computing technology. This was due to a number of factors. Firstly, a common military cause focused both British and American minds on crucial areas of electronics technology, providing the seedbed for the development of the stored-program computer. This in itself spurred transatlantic exchanges of technology. British and American electronics engineers not only spoke a common everyday language they also spoke a common scientific language – one that shared an involvement with radar work, valve and crt storage technology, and weapons development. The military, both during and after the Second World War, also underwrote all the major projects. To this extent, the transfer of computer technology was not, as it was for nineteenth-century technologies, a product of 'free enterprise'.

Secondly, information could be passed relatively swiftly and freely between interested parties, especially university and research institutions. Although many computer projects were funded by the military, once the war was over there were surprisingly few restrictions on the dissemination of technical information. It is interesting to note, for example, the ease with which Dr D.G. Prinz on his post-war tour of American computer establishments was granted unrestricted access virtually everywhere, despite his German nationality. The latest ideas and news of projects could be transferred by articles in technical journals, newsletters (notably those of the Office of Naval Research and the National Bureau of Standards), patents, lecture courses (especially at the Moore School), the activities of overseas subsidiaries and, above all, by personal contacts. Often the lag between British and American developments was no more than the time it took for a technical paper to be posted across the Atlantic or for a scientist to arrive by sea (or, towards the end of this period, by air). Gradually, as computer science developed, the opportunity for contacts increased (in fact, an interesting feature of the growth of information technologies is that their very success facilitates the further spread of the technology). Soon major international scientific meetings on computing technology were a regular event. One of many such meetings was the Joint AIEE–IRE Computer Conference at Philadelphia in December 1951, where Maurice Wilkes and Fred Williams reviewed progress in their respective projects.

Thirdly, as in the nineteenth century, it was the individual technologist who was paramount in the spread of transatlantic information in the early stages. The computing fraternity was a very small one in the late 1940s: in England at that time the leading scientists could all meet comfortably in one room, such as at the Cambridge Mathematical Laboratory's regular colloquia. Maintaining contacts was relatively easy, especially before the mid-1950s, so that in reviewing this period one is impressed by the closeness of the transatlantic scientific community. As Sandy Douglas has remarked:

> It would be wrong to underestimate the importance of personal contacts at that time, since we were not a large group world-wide and many ideas 'floated' from place to place with whoever moved around. Ideas from EDSAC I, Manchester Mark I and ACE were a 'common heritage' in the UK. Whilst I was in the US, I visited the Whirlwind at MIT, SEAC at the National Bureau of Standards, SWAC in UCLA, ORACLE at Oak Ridge, JOHNNIAC in Princeton, the MANIAC II in Los Alamos and so on, where we exchanged ideas freely – and I know David Wheeler and Stan Gill did the same. Monty Phister, who was at Hughes and later became chief engineer of Max Palevski's group at Xerox, was an old Cambridge alumnus and had several ex-Ferranti people working for him, like Ted Braunholtz. Another alumnus was Tony Oettinger from Harvard and ideas even went via Australia, where John Bennett, also ex-Cambridge and Manchester, built SILLIAC (a copy of ILLIAC I), so that his engineer, Barry Swire, was at Illinois when I was, picking up technology. Whilst no one intentionally plagiarised, we tended to treat knowledge as internationally available and not necessarily attributable – sometimes one didn't know who had a particular idea first anyway. Also, of course, we were far from being the only transatlantic travellers. Douglas Hartree, Maurice Wilkes and, after 1954, Jim Wilkinson visited frequently, as did Freddie Williams. Only Tom Kilburn seemed to expect everyone to come to him![44]

A truly comprehensive study would examine more fully the transfer of personnel, which has continued to the present day. It was particularly intense during the 'brain-drain' era of the 1960s, when the dominance of American firms in both semi-conductor and computer technology had reached new heights, and when many British graduates and computer engineers were attracted to the USA by better pay and job prospects. There they seem to have revelled in the more open managerial and scientific ambience of American firms, occasionally returning to the UK with fresh ideas.[45]

The speed with which knowledge on computing is disseminated, the openness of the Western research community, the fact that individual engineers hold much of the most important technological information, and that patents have little protection for a firm's innovations (often patent cases are economically moot by the time they are settled) – all these ensure both the necessity of continuous heavy investment in new technology and the inevitability of the internationalization of the industry.[46] This study has highlighted aspects of the international nature of computing technology – in particular, the continuing importance of the Anglo-American connection in the twentieth century. It shows that the development of a technology can rarely be considered in isolation, by viewing that technology solely within a national boundary. If this is true of the development of the computer, which in the popular mind is strongly associated with a single country (that is, the USA), then how many other industries might repay closer attention from an Anglo-American perspective?

NOTES

This chapter draws on a wide range of secondary literature. In addition, I have been able to use the documentary material I have been collecting and cataloguing on behalf of the National Archive for the History of Computing, Manchester University. During the course of this work I have also benefited from discussions with many key individuals, whose comments have informed this study. I am particularly grateful to: Professor Gordon Black, the late Lord Bowden, Professor Tony Brooker, Professor Sandy Douglas, Professor Dai Edwards, Professor W.S. Elliott, Professor Tom Kilburn, Dr D.G. Prinz, Professor Bernard Richards, Professor David Wheeler and Professor Maurice Wilkes. Dr Martin Campbell-Kelly kindly read my initial draft and made several useful suggestions.

1. For general background, see Stan Augarten, *Bit by Bit: An Illustrated History of Computers* (New York, 1984); Michael R. Williams, *A History of Computing Technology* (Englewood Cliffs, NJ, 1985). *Annals of the History of Computing* (Arlington, Va., 1979) also contains much that is relevant to Anglo-American technology transfer. Simon H. Lavington, *Early British Computers* (Manchester, 1980), provides the essential story of UK developments, with an expert appreciation of the technology. G. Tweedale, *Calculating Machines and Computers* (Aylesbury, 1990) is a brief, illustrated account.
2. For details of these case-studies, see my annotations in Lewis Hanke (ed.), *Guide to the Study of United States History outside the US, 1945–80*, 5 vols. (New York, 1985); and my *Sheffield Steel and America: A Century of Commercial and Technological Interdependence, 1830–1930* (Cambridge, 1987).
3. I. Bernard Cohen, 'Babbage and Aiken', *Annals of the History of Computing,* **10,** (1988), pp. 171–93. The American philosopher Charles Sanders Peirce was also aware of Babbage's work and saw that his concept could be realized electromechanically, with relays. But Peirce's ideas had no impact on computing technology. See Alice and Arthur Burks, *The First Electronic Computer: The Atanasoff Story* (Ann Arbor, Mich., 1988), p. 260 and *passim*.
4. Geoffrey D. Austrian, *Herman Hollerith: Forgotten Giant of Information Processing* (New York, 1982), pp. 16–17; Anthony Hyman, *Charles Babbage: Pioneer of the Computer* (Oxford, 1984), pp. 254–5.
5. C.A. Everard Greene, *The Beginnings – Reminiscences* (1958), p. 3. For the subsequent account, I have relied on Martin Campbell-Kelly, *ICL: A Business and Technical History* (Oxford, 1990).
6. Williams, *Computing Technology*, p. 254. See also Mary Croarken, *Early Scientific Computing in Britain* (Oxford, 1990).
7. V. Bush, *Pieces of the Action* (New York, 1970). However Kelvin's work was common currency amongst engineers at this time. See Larry Owens, 'Vannevar Bush and the Differential Analyzer: The Text and Context of an Early Computer', *Technology and Culture,* **27,** (1986), pp. 63–95; and 'Straight Thinking: Vannevar Bush and the Culture of American Engineering', Princeton University PhD thesis, 1987. For useful surveys

on the pre-digital era, see Paul Ceruzzi, *The Prehistory of the Digital Computer, from Relays to the Stored-Program Concept, 1935– 45* (Westport, Conn., 1983); and James Small, 'Analogue Computers: Technical Change and Designer History', Manchester University MSc, 1988. Small is presently working on the definitive study of analogue computers, a neglected area in the literature.

8. Douglas R. Hartree and Arthur Porter, 'The Construction and Operation of a Model Differential Analyser', *Memoirs of the Manchester Literary and Philosophical Society,* **79**, (1934–5), pp. 51–73.

9. Arthur Porter, recorded by Dr Christopher Evans for the 'Pioneers of Computing' (Science Museum, London, 1976), tape no. 20.

10. T.H. Flowers quoted in Brian Randell, 'The COLOSSUS', in Nick Metropolis, Jack Howlett and Gian-Carlo Rota (eds), *A History of Computing in the Twentieth Century* (New York, 1980), p. 87. Another member of the team, W. Gordon Welchman, later went to work in the USA, joining the Whirlwind project at MIT and then various US and British companies.

11. According to S. Frankel, who worked on the atomic bomb at Los Alamos and was one of the first to use the ENIAC, von Neumann 'firmly emphasised to me, and to others I am sure, that the fundamental conception [of the computer] is owing to Turing – insofar as not anticipated by Babbage, Lovelace and others'. See Randell, 'COLOSSUS', p. 79.

12. See Lord Halsbury, 'Ten Years of Computer Development', *Computer Journal*, **1**, (1959), p. 154, who refers to the cross-fertilization of Turing's and von Neumann's ideas when they met during the war.

13. H.H. Goldstine, *The Computer from Pascal to von Neumann* (Princeton, NJ, 1972), p. 246. Sir Charles G. Darwin wrote in Hartree's obituary in *Biographical Memoirs of Fellows of the Royal Society*, **4**, (1958), p. 109, 'I do not think it would be an exaggeration to say that it was he who taught [the Americans] the way in which advantage could be taken of [the ENIAC's] extreme rapidity of action.'

14. D.R. Hartree, 'The ENIAC, an Electronic Computing Machine', *Nature*, **158**, (1946), pp. 500–6; also *Calculating Machines: Recent and Prospective Developments and Their Impact on Mathematical Physics* (Cambridge, 1947); *Calculating Instruments and Machines* (Urbana, Ill., 1949, and Cambridge, 1950): these two books have been reprinted, with an introduction by M.V. Wilkes (Cambridge, Mass., 1984).

15. Nancy Stern, *From ENIAC to UNIVAC: An Appraisal of the Eckert-Mauchly Computers* (Bedford, Mass., 1981).

16. The Report is partly reprinted in Brian Randell (ed.), *The Origins of Digital Computers* (Berlin and New York, 1975), pp. 355–64. See also W. Aspray, *John von Neumann and the Origins of Modern Computing* (Cambridge, Mass., 1990).

17. Martin Campbell-Kelly and Michael R. Williams (eds), *The Moore School Lectures* (Cambridge, Mass., 1985).

18. For this account I have relied upon Simon H. Lavington, *A History of Manchester Computers* (Manchester, 1975); the Williams and Kilburn 'Pioneers of Computing' tapes (n. 9), nos 5 and 7; and the papers of Manchester University Department of Computer Science, deposited in the National Archive for the History of Computing (NAHC/MUC/ Series 1–3). Particularly useful are documents relating to the Williams tube interference suit, 1946–52 (NAHC/MUC/Series 1. C. 1a).

19. Eckert, however, continued to imply that his crt store (which he called the 'iconoscope') was responsible for the electrostatic storage tube. In 1976 he wrote: 'I worked on a storage-tube device at the University of Pennsylvania modeled on the ideas of the iconoscope. I showed this work to F.C. Williams, who came over from England when the Moore School Lectures on Computer Design were given in 1946. Williams went back to Manchester and applied for patents on iconoscope ideas, first in England and then in the US.' See *Metropolitan History of Computing*, p. 534.

20. Charles J. Bashe *et al.*, *IBM's Early Computers* (Cambridge, Mass., 1986); Bryon E. Phelps, 'Early Electronic Computer Developments at IBM', *Annals of the History of Computing*, **2**, (1980), pp. 253–67; Emerson W. Pugh, *Memories that Shaped an Industry: Decisions Leading to IBM System/360* (Cambridge, Mass., 1984).

21. Julian Bigelow, 'Computer Development at the Institute for Advanced Study', in *Metropolitan History of Computing*, p. 304.

22. The Whirlwind was operational by 1953 at MIT and pioneered the magnetic core store of Jay W. Forrester, which was the next major advance in computer memories. Though the machine was planned with crt storage, Forrester later wrote that it 'inherently lacked the high signal levels, the high signal-to-noise ratio, the ability to give good signals from the noise, that we would require for our high-reliability application ... [so] ... we did not stay with the Williams tube idea for very long'. See Kent C. Redmond and Thomas M. Smith, *Project Whirlwind: The History of a Pioneer Computer* (Bedford, Mass., 1980), p. 181.

23. Papers of Dr D.G. Prinz. NAHC/PRI/C.1a. Report of a visit made by Prinz to US, September 1948, p. 3.

24. On 24 January 1952, F.C. Williams wrote to E. Cooke-Yarborough at the Atomic Energy Research Establishment, Harwell: 'I saw Sir John Cockcroft the other day in London and he said that you were the proud possessor of about a dozen American-made transistors, and that you had high hopes of more to come. I probed him on the possibility of your sparing us a representative sample from relatively speaking your abundant wealth.' NAHC/MUC/Series 1. B.1d.

25. Author's interview with Lord Bowden, 1 November 1988. See also Beverley J. Bleakley and Jean LaPrairie, *Entering the Computer Age: The Computer Industry in Canada: The First Thirty Years* (Agincourt, 1982), pp. 10–12, 51–2; NAHC/FER/C.32. Records of Ferranti–Packard Electric Ltd, c. 1962–8.

26. M.V. Wilkes, *Memoirs of a Computer Pioneer* (Cambridge, Mass., 1985), p. 109.

27. Charles W. Adams, quoted in Wilkes, Wheeler and Gill, *The Preparation of Programs etc.* (Cambridge, Mass., 1982; reprint of 1951 edition). Introduction by Martin Campbell-Kelly, p. xviii.

28. Author's interview with David Wheeler, 28 February 1989. See also James E. Robertson, 'The ORDVAC and the ILLIAC', in *Metropolitan History of Computing*, pp. 347-64.

29. Letter to author, 12 October 1988.

30. D.J. Wheeler, 'Programmed Computing at the Universities of Cambridge and Illinois in the Early Fifties', in Stephen G. Nash (ed.), *A History of Scientific Computing* (Reading, Mass., 1990), pp. 269–79.

31. Wilkes, *Memoirs*, admits to having had a 'love-affair' with the USA ever since he met Americans in Germany during the Second World War. In 1980, he became senior consulting engineer at Digital Equipment Corporation in Massachusetts and an Adjunct Professor at MIT.

32. John Hendry, 'The Teashop Computer Manufacturer: J. Lyons, LEO and the Potential and Limits of High-Tech Diversification', *Business History*, **29**, (1987), pp. 73–101. John Pinkerton, who helped develop the LEO, remembers a visit by an IBM vice-president: 'The gossip that got around was that they thought, well, if a tea company in Britain can do it, well surely we ought to be able to do it. The impression was that it was rather disgraceful for a company which was already the dominant company in office machinery at that time, not to be able to supply what people were going to ask for.' Quoted in Peter Pagnamenta and Richard Overy, *All Our Working Lives* (London, 1984), pp. 254–5.

33. B.E. Carpenter and R.W. Doran (eds), *A.M. Turing's ACE Report of 1946* (Cambridge, Mass., 1985).

34. Andrew Hodges, *Alan Turing: The Enigma of Intelligence* (London, 1983). Uncited quotations in this paragraph are from this source. See also the comments by Mike Woodger, 'The Foundations of Computer Engineering', *Radio and Electronic Engineer*, **45**, (1975), pp. 598–602.

35. Davies and Wilkinson, 'Pioneers of Computing', nos 1 and 10. See also 'The Birth of a Computer: An Interview with James H. Wilkinson on the Building of a Computer Designed by Alan Turing', *Byte,* (February 1985), pp. 177–94.

36. Martin Campbell-Kelly, 'Programming the Pilot ACE: Early Programming Activity at the National Physical Laboratory', *Annals of the History of Computing*, **3**, (1981), pp.

133–62; Huskey, 'Pioneers of Computing', no. 13; 'The SWAC: The National Bureau of Standards Western Automatic Computer', in Metropolis *et al.*, *A History of Computing*, pp. 419–31.

37.   Metropolis *et al.*, *A History of Computing*, p. 553. Other material on Booth is derived from 'Pioneers of Computing', no. 9, and reports and working drafts in the Papers of Andrew D. Booth, NAHC/BOO.

38.   Barry White, 'State Intervention in Technology in the Post-War Years: Case Studies in Technology Policy', Aston PhD thesis, 1985, p. 124.

39.   John Hendry, 'Prolonged Negotiations: The British Fast Computer Project and the Early History of the British Computer Industry', *Business History*, **26**, (1984), pp. 280–306; *Innovating for Failure: Government Policy and the Early British Computer Industry* (Cambridge, Mass., 1989). See also Paul Drath, 'The Relationship between Science and Technology and the Computer Industry, 1945–1962', Manchester PhD thesis, 1973. An unpublished history of Ferranti computers provides an interesting comment on the relative size of UK and US computer projects: 'One of the remarkable features of the ATLAS project was the small number of staff employed compared with the large numbers used by IBM on STRETCH and by the Bull Company on the Gamma 60. We have seen that, probably, the former had some 300 graduates and the latter about 200 programmers. ATLAS never had more than ten programmers on the supervisor and about 15 working on compilers. The total number of engineers on one computer must have been of the same order.' See Bernard Swann, 'The Ferranti Computer Department' (1975). Copy in NAHC/FER/C.30.

40.   Pugh, *IBM System/360*, p. 202. See also Emerson W. Pugh *et al.*, *IBM's 360 and Early 370 Systems* (Cambridge, Mass., 1991). IBM (UK) Ltd was founded in 1951 and has since become the largest British computer manufacturer.

41.   Campbell-Kelly, *A Business and Technical History*.

42.   Goldstine, *From Pascal to von Neumann*, p. 217.

43.   William Aspray, 'International Diffusion of Computer Technology, 1945-1955', *Annals of the History of Computing*, **8**, (1986), pp. 351–60.

44.   Douglas (n. 29).

45.   Pagnamenta and Overy, *Working Lives*, pp. 256–7. See generally P. Stoneman, *Technological Diffusion and the Computer Revolution: The UK Experience* (Cambridge, 1976).

46.   Kenneth Flamm, *Creating the Computer: Government, Industry and High Technology* (Washington, DC, 1988), pp. 203–34, has a particularly useful chapter on technology transfer and international competition. Rapidity of technological transfer also typified the semi-conductor industry. See John E. Tilson, *International Diffusion of Technology: The Case of Semiconductors* (Washington, DC, 1971).

6. Oil Production Technology, West to East

John Hassan

INTRODUCTION

The offshore oil industry covers a wide range of complex activities. In order to restrict a discussion of the transfer of offshore oil technologies into and out of the North Sea to a reasonable length, it is necessary to adopt a ruthlessly selective approach. While important developments in other European countries are acknowledged, this chapter will therefore concentrate upon transfers of production technologies affecting the British sector of the North Sea.

The vast nature even of North Sea production technology as a subject area, let alone offshore technology in general, is reflected in the fact that bibliographical studies list literally thousands of items in the field. One guide to such *sources* of information extends to 70 pages.[1] The theme of technology transfer is rarely the focus of offshore publications. A North Sea historiography does not really exist, hardly surprising as North Sea oil only began to flow into Britain as recently as 1975. There are, however, a number of surveys, published in the 1970s, which provide invaluable introductory material on the North Sea oil and gas industries, notably those by Callow, Cooper and Gaskell, and Chapman.[2] Highly useful guides to the industry have also been written by M. Lovegrove, while M. Jenkin has provided an authoritative study of the role of state intervention in the 1970s.[3] Trade journals may be consulted for information on current or future developments.

In the following sections the broad context within which the North Sea oil industry expanded is outlined; there is a description of the way in which British offshore activities in the 1960s involved the application of technologies which had been developed in the western hemisphere; and an explanation is given for the need to discover new techniques if activities were to continue into deeper water. In the closing sections of the chapter the actors responsible for technology transfer and innovation in the North Sea are identified; examples of a world-wide diffusion of deepwater technologies pioneered in the North Sea are cited; and an attempt is made to explain these patterns of technological development.

THE CONTEXT OF NORTH SEA TECHNOLOGY TRANSFER

Systematic exploration of the British sector of the North Sea was delayed until the UK ratified the 1958 Geneva Convention on sea-bed rights in 1964. A series of discoveries of large natural gas accumulations was made between 1965 and 1967, with BP's rig 'Sea Gem' making the first successful strike in the West Sole field. Uninspired by the price offered by British Gas and believing that the large natural gas discoveries had already been made, in the late 1960s the oil companies' attention moved to northern waters. In April 1970, Phillips announced its discovery of the major Ekofisk oilfield in the Norwegian sector. Close to the median line, this stimulated heightened interest in the adjacent British zone, with BP's rig 'Sea Quest' making the first offshore commercial discovery of British Oil, that of the Forties field. The discovery of the Brent, Piper and Claymore fields rapidly followed.

The drilling rigs shifted northward along the structural features of what is known as the Viking Graben. A cluster of important new finds was made between 1971 and 1974, including Brent, Argyll and Montrose. By the end of the decade 17 oilfields were producing or under development, and Britain was on the brink of achieving net self-sufficiency in oil. The scale of the investment had been enormous. Brent had been the biggest single private engineering project carried out in the UK. In the 1970s and into the early 1980s offshore spending accounted for between 20 and 28 per cent of total UK industrial investment.

This development may be set in a global and historical context. The first attempts to recover oil from underwater reservoirs were prompted by a desire to increase output from established oilfields which appeared to extend under the sea. The first well drilled offshore was at Santa Barbara, California, from a short pier constructed from the beach in 1897. Lankford describes the subsequent expansion of offshore activity – to Lake Maracaibo, Venezuela, and later to the shorelines of Texas and Louisiana – and associated technical advances.[4] The extent of progress in the first half-century of the offshore oil industry's existence should not be exaggerated. The first offshore platform placed in the Gulf of Mexico was erected in 1945 in 18 feet of water. It was made of timber and supported a converted land rig which drilled a dry hole. Soon, however, the use of steel in the Gulf of Mexico became practically universal. The basic design of the fixed steel production platform, although

Plate: Concrete production platform in Chevron's Ninian Field

operating in fairly shallow waters, proved itself in a variety of locations before the North Sea.

A brief reference to developments in exploration drilling should be made. By the early 1960s, a number of different types of vessel had achieved considerable mobility and flexibility, craft selection being determined by the design features and offshore conditions. Drill ships could operate in very deep water, but had poor motion characteristics in rough weather. Semi-submersible rigs (which had evolved from submersible barges operating in the Gulf of Mexico) are floating units which can be partly submerged by flooding underwater pontoons. They were working successfully by 1962.[5] Capable of working in very deep water, the design is utilized not only for drilling rigs, but also for production purposes (see Figure 6.1) and multi-purpose vessels. The invention of the self-elevating, jack-up rig was significant. While storm conditions stop work on most rigs, the retractable legs not only allow it to be moved from site to site, but also make it possible for the (floating) platform to be raised above the waves and for drilling to proceed. The jack-up rig became the preferred exploratory tool in the 1950s in many locations.

Various surveys have traced the enormous advances achieved in offshore technologies between 1945 and 1970, not only for production work but also for areas such as diving and underwater techniques for welding, metal-cutting and painting.[6] The spatial diffusion of the new technologies made possible an important growth in the offshore oil industry, accounting for a negligible proportion of world oil output in 1950, but rising to 19 per cent by 1971, and the number of countries significantly involved growing from two to 21. The advent of activity in the North Sea was part of a world-wide trend. Geological and geophysical knowledge establishes that partially enclosed marine, sedimentary basins (such as the North Sea, the Gulf of Mexico and the Mediterranean) are favourable regions for finding oil. The North Sea, however, is particularly important. By 1974, it was second only to the Gulf of Mexico in terms of exploration activity. 'The North Sea,' it was stated in 1980, 'is now established as the most important offshore area in the world in terms of hydrocarbon potential and deep water production technology.'[7] Globally, by 1982, about 25 per cent of oil production came from offshore fields, rising to 39 per cent in 1985, of which about one-quarter was produced in the North Sea.

Much has been written about the role of the state in the North Sea oil and gas industries. Potentially the state did have powerful instruments at its disposal to influence developments. An appropriate legal framework was created with the passing of the Continental Shelf Act in 1964, and government controlled the process of licensing grounds, imposed taxes upon operators, and participated directly in the production and disposal of hydrocar-

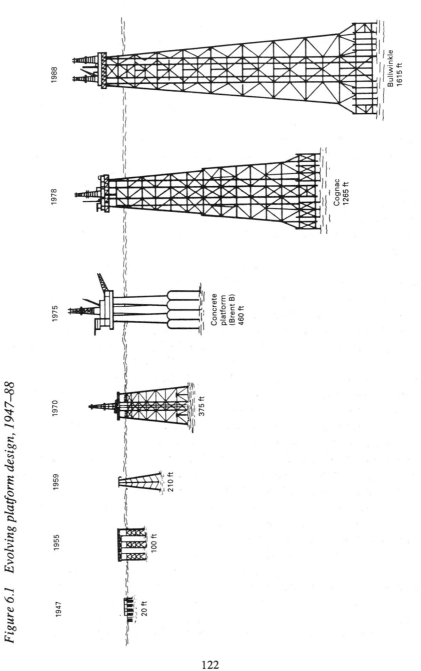

Figure 6.1 Evolving platform design, 1947–88

1947

1955

1959

1970

1975

1978

1988

20 ft

100 ft

210 ft

375 ft

Concrete platform (Brent B) 460 ft

Cognac 1265 ft

Bullwinkle 1615 ft

bons, especially through the BNOC (British National Oil Corporation), set up in 1976. The period of large-scale, direct involvement, however, was restricted to 1977–83. The total public-sector share of licensed territory in 1983 had fallen back to 7 per cent. An evaluation of the evidence leads one to conclude that the government's fiscal, depletion or participation policies made little impact upon technological innovation. Until the mid-1970s the state effectively left private-enterprise operators in the North Sea to achieve their own solutions to the technological problems confronting them, and technological innovation has been achieved largely thanks to their efforts.

Some qualifications are necessary. Depletion and fiscal policies may have unintended consequences. Until the early 1970s they were constructed so as to accelerate the coming on stream of oil and natural gas fields. This encouraged the over-hasty design and implementation of untried technologies, with costly consequences for, for example, reservoir recoverability.[8] On a more positive note, the 1983 budget did introduce fiscal changes which encouraged the development of new, marginal fields, and therefore indirectly stimulated research into ways of overcoming the problems of producing oil from such fields. This achieved fruition in the application of innovational methods by Texaco and Shell/Esso in the development of their marginal Highlander, and Tern and Eider fields respectively. The one area where the state played a more discernibly active role relates to its policies towards the offshore supply industries. These will be considered later.

Climatic and physical conditions presented unprecedented challenges to the oil industry in the North Sea. There was limited experience of operating in up to 150 feet of water in southern waters, still less at the much greater depths – up to 800 feet – to be encountered further north, a problem compounded by the adverse weather conditions of the region. Materials and structures had to be designed to withstand the effects of low temperatures, rain, wind and the properties and movement of sea-water. In the southern North Sea waves might exceed eight feet (the limit at which supply boats could safely discharge cargo offshore) for only 6 per cent of the time, but this occurred 35 per cent of the time in northern waters. More fearful conditions than this had to be anticipated, even the 'once-in-a-century' 100-foot waves and 150 mph winds which occurred in 1953. 'Down-time', when work had to be suspended because of bad weather, affected development costs substantially, the summer 'window' for platform installation in the early days being as little as three months. This had design implications, leading to the search for a platform type with a rapid installation time.

THE APPLICATION OF OFFSHORE TECHNOLOGY TO THE NORTH SEA

The initial development of the North Sea, that is of the natural gas fields located in the southern regions, was able to proceed rapidly by drawing upon technologies which had evolved in other offshore areas. For example, Shell and BP carried out the task of physically surveying the region, applying experience gained in the Middle East, and in Venezuela and Nigeria.[9] This expertise may explain their apparent good fortune in applying for good licence blocks and rapidly discovering the super-giant oilfields, Brent and Forties.

As previously indicated, considerable progress had been achieved across the whole spectrum of offshore technologies since 1945, especially as applied in the Gulf of Mexico. Nevertheless some of the earliest structures erected in the North Sea were rather primitive and contrived in conception. BP's 'Sea Gem' was basically a pontoon, originally constructed in the USA in 1952. It had been employed in various parts of the world for several purposes, until significant modifications were carried out in 1964 and 1965. The risks of the North Sea were emphasized when 'Sea Gem' toppled into the waves during a manoeuvre, with the loss of 13 lives, in December 1965.[10] The first platform built in the North Sea in the West Sole field was 'not dissimilar in basic principles to piers at the sea-side'.[11] Nevertheless a suitably advanced offshore technology had come into existence, making the exploitation of oil and gas in the North Sea commercially feasible.

Exploration drilling, for example, proceeded rapidly. The mobility of jack-up rigs, their re-use facility and operability in rough weather conditions, and adaptability for production purposes led them to be used extensively in the southern North Sea. When first employed, jack-up rigs operated as temporary installations in water depths up to 150 feet. In certain circumstances jack-up rigs can be employed for production purposes, as at Ekofisk in the early 1970s.[12]

The most favoured type of production unit in the offshore industries is the fixed, piled steel platform. Originally these were uncomplicated structures, pinned to the seafloor by steel piles. As long as structures remain simple and cheap and water depths shallow it has been usual to install multi-platform systems, with separate units for drilling, production and living quarters, usually connected by bridges. This solution facilitates fabrication and installation; it also simplifies safety precautions and enables production and drilling to be carried on simultaneously from separate platforms. Multi-platform complexes were typical of the Gulf of Mexico in the 1950s and 1960s. They were extensively used also in the natural gas fields of the southern North Sea.

The techniques of directional drilling proved particularly relevant in the North Sea. By drilling as many wells as possible at an angle more of a reservoir can be tapped from a single production platform, hence maximizing its use. In fact sea extensions of oilfields in southern California were exploited by directional wells from the beach as early as the 1920s. Until recently a 'whipstock', a tapered steel wedge, was used to kick off the well in a diagonal direction. The introduction of powered devices and more accurate instrumentation permitted more accurate results.[13] The pre-existing technology of directional drilling was very significant for the North Sea, as platform costs rise with increasing water depths. It enabled appreciable scale economies to be achieved, especially in large, deep fields with several wells being drilled from one platform. Only four platforms were required to drain Brent, Britain's biggest oilfield. This was because they were equipped to drill a total of up to 154 wells, the paths of some being two miles away from the platform.[14]

Just as techniques for offshore production had been developed in the Gulf, so had techniques for underwater pipelaying been sufficiently developed to permit experienced American contractors like Brown & Root to overcome at least the initial North Sea hazards they would face. Cooper and Gaskell concluded:

> When BP made the first gas discovery in the North Sea in September 1965, the oil industry had already been producing oil and gas from underwater fields for many years. A wealth of experience had been gained ... and both equipment and expertise existed to drill and produce oil and gas for use offshore.[15]

Consequently initial operations in the North Sea were conducted within the existing technological frontier and no technological bottleneck threatened the rapid early development of the region's hydrocarbons in the shallower, southern waters.

Any explanation for the successful transfer of offshore technology into the North Sea must (a) consider the role of multinational enterprise as a vehicle of technology transmission, and (b) emphasize that the offshore oil industry has evolved structures favourable to the dissemination of engineering knowledge.

The particular difficulties in operating offshore have led the great international oil companies to dominate offshore oilfield development. Relative to their onshore activities the offshore role of the smaller, independent companies is much less. In the Gulf of Mexico the 20 largest American oil producers were responsible for 97.7 per cent of output in 1971.[16] In the UK continental shelf, while large players have not displayed such dominance, they do exhibit a large profile. BP, Shell and Exxon have been the main companies throughout (See Table 6.1), with a group of about seven more American companies and Britoil also playing an active role. UK interests accounted for 43.63 per cent of licence ownership in the British sector of the North Sea in 1985, American enterprise for 41.61 per cent.[17]

Table 6.1   A summary of UK continental shelf interests of the 'main players', 1985

	Licence Interests	Field Rem	Recov Res	Annual Production			
	Gross (sq km)	Oil (mn barrels)	Gas (bn cu ft)	Oil ('00b/d) 1983	1985	Gas (mmcfd) 1983	1985
British							
Gas	13 372	176	6 364	34	52	293	483
BP	12 774	1 750	1 967	482	454	173	205
Britoil	36 722	793	2 441	148	148	197	208
Exxon	14 404	1 556	3 291	326	393	620	683
Shell	14 999	1 556	3 291	326	393	620	683

Source: M. Lovegrove, *Lovegrove's Guide to Britain's North Sea Oil and Gas* (Cambridge, 1985), p. 16, citing James Capel & Co., UK Petroleum Database.

An explanation of the pre-eminence of large international companies in the North Sea can be drawn to a certain extent from earlier studies of multinational enterprises, such as those of Wilkins. It is apparent that multinational, frequently US, enterprise enjoyed advantages in the 1950s and 1960s in technology and product design in the offshore sector. This helps to account for its important role in early exploration and production activities in the North Sea. Wilkins noted that an important method of technology transfer is where a multinational enterprise transfers its technology abroad with its investment. This method involves an export, or rather an extension, of the firm itself abroad. There are certainly cases in the North Sea which conform to this pattern. Wilkins also believed that the absence of infrastructural or cultural obstacles to American businesses operating in Britain facilitated the receipt of American investment and technology in Britain in the 1950s and 1960s.[18] To be truthful, though, the oil industry has long been used to working internationally, the language factor rarely, if ever, constituting an important problem. Furthermore in the oil industry, multinational enterprise includes two (partly) British-based companies, BP and

Royal Dutch/Shell, easing the transfer of offshore technology into the North Sea. Significantly among the constituent companies of the latter group was Shell Oil, in the 1980s 'the leading offshore oil producer in the US with major production activity in the Gulf of Mexico and offshore California'.[19]

The financial commitment required to develop offshore fields was awesome. This has led companies to spread risks in consortia. This solution, very characteristic of the Gulf of Mexico, was also relevant in the North Sea, given the novel scale of operations, the physical distribution of fields, the division of the North Sea into blocks, and finite human resources. Companies with 100 per cent participations in projects were the exception rather than the rule. The outstanding example of resource-pooling is the 50/50 partnership set up in July 1964 by Shell and Esso (who had previously worked together in Holland) – Shell UK Exploration and Production (Shell Expro) – to exploit oil and gas in the North Sea. The magnitude of undertakings in the North Sea was unprecedented. Shell Expro's Brent development claimed £1.6 billion each from the two partners by 1978. By 1984, the partnership had contributed over a quarter (£12 billion) of the UK oil industry's offshore capital and expenditure.

The early successes in finding major fields such as Brent led to a surge of investment in the mid-1970s which 'stretched the resources of the oil and supplying industries to the full'.[20] In principle any operator can hire subcontractors, drawing from the international pool of expertise, and participate in North Sea ventures. Indeed smaller companies are present. However in practice, the advantage tends to lie with bigger players, for example in buying concession acreage, simply because of the sheer size of projects. As Jenkin says, 'virtually all of the ten companies', which were responsible for *all* of the discoveries actively under development in 1975, 'possess financial resources which place them amongst the largest corporate entities in the world'.[21] This was highly significant, given the resources required to develop North Sea fields commercially. Unlike the smaller, independent companies, with this financial strength they were able to finance North Sea projects largely from their own world-wide resources – from cash flow (retained profits plus depreciation). Smaller participating firms in consortia relied more on loans from UK-based banks. By 1980, three-quarters of North Sea financing came from the oil companies' own resources.[22]

The offshore oil industry has therefore created structures for sharing risks and expertise, for example through consortia. Further subcontracting has an important role. There is a general pattern of engaging subcontractors to undertake tasks specified by the client. Kash noted of the oil firms:

From initial seismic surveys, through drilling and field development to transporting and feeding offshore production crews, they rely on low bidders or negotiated contracts with old corporate friends. The result has been a proliferation of speciality firms, many with headquarters in the Gulf Coast area, which are prepared to undertake a wide variety of assignments up to and including complete field development.[23]

North Sea operators draw from a pool of technological knowledge, which has accumulated through the growing experience of the offshore oil industry and its R & D programmes. Collaborative R & D and the use of subcontractors is part of an industry-wide pattern of technical cooperation. The oil companies also share their knowledge as members of bidding consortia. There are, as well, numerous forums for the exchange and dissemination of scientific and engineering information. The annual Offshore Technology Conference at Houston, first held in 1969, is simply the foremost among many such conferences. Kash concludes that engineers and scientists have a tradition of patent sales and cross-licensing which makes available a common pool of knowledge and facilitates the transmission of new technologies throughout the offshore industry.[24]

THE DEVELOPMENT OF NEW TECHNOLOGY IN THE NORTH SEA

Offshore technology transferred from the western hemisphere was generally sufficient for the first operations in the southern North Sea. As activity shifted into the deeper, remoter, rougher waters of the northern oilfields the situation altered. In fact the North Sea taxed the oil industry's existing technology to the limits, and became the proving ground for the development of not simply a modified, but of an entirely *new* offshore technology.

In early operations equipment was tested to the limits of tolerance. Divers placed sandbags around the legs of jack-up rigs as a defence against strong currents. In the development of the Argyll field 'design and fabrication often went hand-in hand – at times a frustrating, but always a highly educative process'.[25] Learning by doing, however, involved risks. Several accidents underlined the strains imposed on rigs brought in from less inhospitable environments, and the southern fields claimed three rigs in the first three years of work in the mid-1960s. The combined forces of wind and wave imposed unaccustomedly severe shocks and fatigue loading on production platforms. In 1973, the British government helped set up the UK Offshore Steels Research Project to ascertain the design requirements of North Sea structures, particularly relating to the issue of steel fatigue. Its range of findings from the 43 studies comprising the project indicates that the scientific and technological knowledge necessary for the fabrication of steel structures for the North Sea simply did not exist when operators first moved into deeper waters. It had to be acquired and developed, even at the level of basic physical research.[26] The North Sea, therefore, forced the pace of technological change – in drilling, pipelaying, in the perfection of dynamic positioning (computer-based systems for maintaining floating vessels in a desired position) and seismic surveying.[27]

Production rather than exploration technology, however, was potentially the most serious bottleneck. Supply constraints had been perceived as increasing with distance from mainland bases, but the principal constraint was water depth. In 1950, the effective limit on offshore operations was 20 feet. By 1973, up to 350 feet was not considered abnormal, but it was apparent that even greater depths would have to be tackled if the oilfields of the north were to be developed. The decision to employ conventional, fixed platforms in the fairly shallow waters of the southern North Sea was based on rational criteria. When operations moved further north, fixed piled steel platforms continued to be used. They were, however, much bigger, specially strengthened and much more costly relative to previous experience in the Gulf of Mexico. Space limitations prohibit any exhaustive description here of the challenges involved in the construction of unprecedentedly heavy steel-jacket structures and their installation in unusually deep water in the early 1970s, as in the Forties field (see Figure 6.1). 'First-generation' northern North Sea production structures, such as the Thistle steel platform, standing in 530 feet of water 'did not use any obviously new technology', but 'did involve untried extensions of technology in many areas'. Costly design errors were made at Thistle, including an underestimation of the implications of a 25-year production life, and insufficient operating capacity.[28] High installation costs and a view that steel-jacket platforms were beginning to approach their operational limits in terms of water depths led to radical new departures being developed in production platform technology. While steel structures are typically pinned to the sea-bed by piling, gravity-based concrete structures sit directly on the sea-floor under their own weight. The gravity structure incorporates a hollow base, which can be used as a buoyancy chamber on transit to site, and offers an oil-storage facility afterwards. The use of concrete in platform construction in the North Sea in the 1970s was a major innovation. The structures which resulted from this approach were so striking in design and scale that for a while it appeared that the future of production platform technology would lie in this direction. They appeared to offer a number of advantages over steel platforms, especially in fabrication onshore and installation. They promised to reduce costs, as capital costs increase with the greater quantities of steel (particularly the highly specialized steel used for jackets) required for bigger structures.

After Phillips Petroleum had demonstrated the potentiality of concrete as an offshore constructional material with their gigantic sea-bed storage tank at

Ekofisk in 1974, a considerable impetus was given to the promotion of concrete platforms. The spectacular designs employed, particularly in the Brent development (production commencing 1976), inspired many euphoric assessments. 'The frontiers of technology have been pushed back to such an extent that the development of the Brent field,' it was said, 'can only be compared to the US space shuttle programme both in terms of technological progress and cost.'[29] The Brent B platform, for a while the largest, heaviest and most expensive offshore production unit ever built, weighed 348 000 tons, and measured 815 feet from top to bottom. It was followed by the colossus constructed for Chevron at Loch Kishorn for their Ninian field: arriving on site in 1978, with a total tow-out weight of 620 000 tons and total height of 776 feet, the entire structure represented the world's heaviest platform and largest movable object.

Subsequent experience suggests that the specifications of the concrete platforms erred on the side of caution, and that they were built on an overmassive scale. They had their limitations, being simply enormous structures, suitable only for large-field developments and particular sea-bed conditions. Project delays proved very expensive. The storage facility was not a particular advantage in most circumstances. Furthermore Timor's forecast that continuous design improvements would lead steel platforms to continue to represent a viable solution to oil-production problems in even deeper, more hostile waters has proved correct,[30] particularly following the design of more slender structures and the development of powerful, floating cranes which has facilitated installation. By 1980, new slim-line steel structures were being built again in preference to concrete platforms, in comparison with which they were very light-weight indeed. By the end of this decade Shell's 590-foot Eider steel jacket had a launch weight of only 19 000 tons.

The high cost and difficulty of installing fixed structures nevertheless led oil companies to search for alternative – or supplementary – methods of producing oil offshore. The economic and physical conditions which had rendered the exploitation of the early giant oilfields financially rewarding by conventional methods did not apply for smaller accumulations located beneath deeper waters. The latter were likely to become increasingly important in subsequent offshore developments. Abandoning the attempts to imitate onshore techniques, engineers, 'adapting to rather than resisting the sea', took the decisive step of going underwater at the well-head, and began to develop a whole range of underwater production systems.[31]

Rather than try to do justice to the different systems which have evolved over the last dozen years or so, a brief résumé of the main approaches will be supplied, and one innovation (the tension leg platform – TLP) will be singled out for slightly fuller comment.

Subsea production systems eliminate the need for a fixed platform, with well-heads being placed on the sea-bed rather than the platform, and the oil may be transferred to an adjacent platform or loaded onto a tanker by a mooring system. A variety of approaches is illustrated in Figure 6.2. Early subsea completions were Hamilton's Argyll field and Mobil's Beryl field, from 1975. A later breakthrough was the underwater manifold concept (UMC) developed by Shell Expro, and installed in the Central Cormorant field in 1982. The UMC is a complex, multifunctional, sea-bed unit, linked to and controlling a cluster of satellite wells (connected to the UMC by marine flowlines) and other subsea units, including a remote-controlled maintenance vehicle.

Subsea solutions were combined with mobile surface supports connected to floating production units. The Argyll development, incorporating a converted semi-submersible rig as a production unit, exemplified this approach. BP developed the Buchan field in a similar way in 1982. The salient feature of a variety of floating production concepts which have evolved is the delivery of oil to shuttle tankers by 'catenary anchored floating' systems. Mobil's Beryl and Shell Expro's Fulmar developments represent variants of this method.

The proliferation of subsea well-head systems relatively remote from larger structures and the concomitant laying of vast networks of marine flowlines has been associated with significant advances across a range of subsea techniques. Innovative developments have been achieved in subsea welding and inspection, flexible flowlines and risers (the pipes connecting sea-bed installations to a production unit), the use of computers to control and monitor facilities and the employment of unmanned, remote-controlled equipment. Expro's Eider development is a prototype of an unmanned production platform.

Compliant platforms represent a hybrid solution between fixed and floating structures (avoiding the undue stiffness of one and flexibility of the other). Figure 6.3 illustrates different types. Compliant platforms float on the surface and are linked to sea-bed installations by a moving articulated column, guyed tower, or steel mooring lines. The latter is the TLP concept, and the first project in the world using it was Conoco's Hutton oilfield, 90 miles north-east of Shetland, which started production in 1984. The Hutton development was relatively small, the water depth of 485 feet being unexceptional. It was, however, a most significant technological development, as it offered a relatively inexpensive, easily installed method of exploiting numerous less accessible or smaller offshore fields in very deep waters throughout the world.[32]

Many of the radical innovations in offshore technology noted above were pioneered in the North Sea. The challenge of overcoming its problems led to the acquisition of 'frontier knowledge' and the emergence of a 'state of the art technique' in the region.

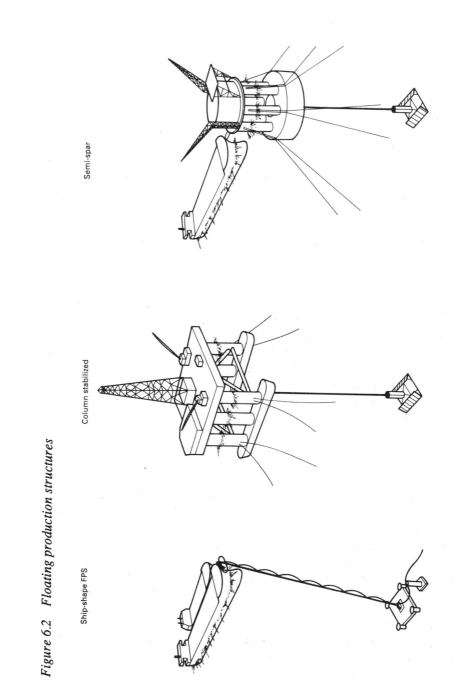

Figure 6.2   Floating production structures

Ship-shape FPS

Column stabilized

Semi-spar

132

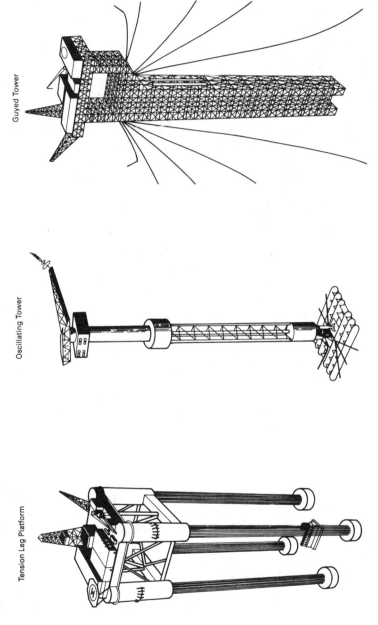

Figure 6.3 Compliant production structures

Guyed Tower

Oscillating Tower

Tension Leg Platform

133

THE AGENTS OF TECHNOLOGICAL INNOVATION

The technology developed in the North Sea oilfields was to a considerable extent contrived specifically to overcome the North Sea's unusually difficult conditions. Multinational enterprise and various consortia in which British capital was strongly represented were the customers of the new technology. Yet, particularly at first, much of the actual hardware was designed and built elsewhere, especially in the USA and to a lesser extent in Europe, or installed by American companies. In the early 1970s British industry supplied only 25–30 per cent of the goods and services used in the UK offshore sector. From the mid-1970s, factors inhibiting a stronger indigenous participation in the offshore supply industry were overcome, and British industry assumed an increasingly important role in this market.

The initial British underperformance is well documented. During the first ten years of North Sea activity the number of drilling rigs increased from about 150 to 500, the vast majority being made in the USA, some in Norway. British Steel was apparently unwilling or unable to produce specialized steel required for pipelines, leaving the market to Japan (supplying 83 per cent of North Sea needs in 1972), Germany (9.5 per cent) and France (7.5 per cent). Of the pipelines, 95.5 per cent were laid by American contractors. Of 26 production platforms placed in the North Sea by 1970, 95 per cent were made in the Netherlands and 4 per cent in Germany.[33]

Even when subsequently more of North Sea construction and installation work was carried out by British (and European) firms, much of the design and development activity continued to be done by American companies, or was carried out in the Gulf of Mexico. For example, the earliest proving of subsea technology was carried out in this region. A number of consortia bringing together American and European partners (such as BP, Shell Oil also being involved) were actively pursuing tests or production simulations of subsea production systems in the early 1970s. Later Exxon's R & D work for the UMC was based in the Gulf.

The involvement of British firms in the North Sea offshore market improved quite substantially in the mid-1970s, the British contribution to the supply of goods and services increasing from no more than about 30 per cent in 1972 to over 60 per cent by 1977. This was evident in the establishment of consortia to build steel platforms, whose members included British firms such as Laing Offshore, Wimpey and British Steel. The trend can also be illustrated with reference to the even more radical departures in concrete platforms.[34] Among the designs with significant British interests were

McAlpine Sea Tank (a group consisting of Newarthill, through its wholly owned subsidiary Sir Robert McAlpine, and the French company, Sea Tank) and ANDOC (in which Tarmac and British Insulated Callender Cables had stakes). Some of their work is listed in Table 6.2.

Table 6.2   Fixed oil production platforms installed in UKCS by 1978

Field	Operator	Platform contractor	Site	Steel/ concrete	Installation
Auk	Shell	Redpath Dorman Lang	Methil	S	July 1974
Beryll	Mobil	Norwegian Contractors	Stavanger, Norway	C	July 1975
Brent A	Shell	Redpath Dorman Lang	Methil	S	July 1976
B	Shell	Norwegian Contractors	Stavanger	C	Aug. 1975
C	Shell	McAlpine/Sea Tank	Ardyne Point	C	June 1978
D	Shell	Norwegian Contractors	Stavanger	C	July 1976
Claymore	Occidental	Union Industrielle et d'Entreprise	Cherbourg, France	S	July 1976
Cormorant	Shell	McAlpine/Sea Tank	Ardyne Point	C	May 1978
Dunlin	Shell	Andoc	Rotterdam	C	July 1977
Forties FA	BP	Laing Offshore	Teeside	S	June 1974
FB	BP	Laing Offshore	Teeside	S	June 1975
FC	BP	Highland Fabricators	Nigg Bay	S	Aug. 1974
FD	BP	Highland Fabricators	Nigg Bay	S	June 1975
Heather	Uncoal	McDermott Scotland	Ardersier	S	May 1977
Montrose	Amoco	Union Industrielle et d'Entreprise	Le Havre, France	S	Aug. 1975
Ninian 1	Chevron	Howard Davis	Loch Kishorn	C	May 1978
2	Chevron	Highland Fabricators	Nigg Bay	S	July 1978
Piper	Occidental	McDermott Scotland/ UIE	Ardersier/ Le Havre	S	June 1975
Thistle	Britoil	Laing Offshore	Teeside	S	Aug. 1976

Source: Department of Energy, *Development of the Oil and Gas Resources of the United Kingdom, 1987* (London, 1988), pp. 107–8.

Thus during the mid-1970s the indigenous response in supplying the offshore sector improved, particularly in capital goods, the UK content of offshore orders placed increasing from 37 to 50 per cent for concrete platforms between 1974 and 1975, and from 64 to 95 per cent for steel platforms. The supply of services was less good, with only an 11 per cent UK content for pipelaying orders in 1975 and 18 per cent for installation operations.[35]

Though some weaknesses persisted, an analysis of orders placed in 1978 and 1987 (Table 6.3) reveals that British industry was improving its performance over a broad front. Previous shortcomings, as in deepwater pipelaying, were being rectified. A considerable investment programme equipped the British Steel Corporation with modern plant capable of producing high-quality steel required for offshore needs, as in steel jackets.[36] Perhaps more significantly, UK enterprise was building up a reputation for world technical leadership in a number of offshore production areas. Brown Brothers of Edinburgh, a Vickers subsidiary, for example, won the contract for supplying design proposals for Conoco's Hutton field TLP. Subsequently

Table 6.3   Orders placed for goods and services for the development of the UKCS

	Total value of orders placed (£ million)		Of which UK content (%)	
	1978	*1987*	*1978*	*1987*
Exploration				
Surveying	11	50	73	82
Exploration and appraisal drilling	72	102	19	91
Development				
Production platform	401	373	74	94
Installation operation	147	88	41	85
Plant and equipment	132	267	74	88
Submarine pipeline	42	104	38	71
Development drilling	30	46	70	91
Terminals	232	30	85	90
Production				
Maintenance and production	73	159	73	94
General Services				
Transport	206	188	84	88
Diving and underwater equipment	30	57	77	89
Drilling tools and equipment	71	297	52	76
Support of personnel onshore	67	72	30	92
Miscellaneous	60	36	33	94
Total	1 574	1 869	63	87

Source: Department of Energy, *Development of the Oil and Gas Resources of the United Kingdom, 1979* and *1988.*

Vickers Design and Projects Division supplied anchoring equipment for this, the first commercial TLP in the world.[37] In the 1980s, British firms have been active in providing the design engineering services and constructing the equipment for a number of innovational projects, especially in subsea technology, such as the UMC (for Shell Expro) and diverless deepwater production systems (BP).

TECHNOLOGY TRANSFERS: FROM EUROPE WORLD-WIDE

By the 1980s, the potential had emerged for the wider diffusion of offshore technologies, proven in the North Sea, to other offshore provinces. By 1977, it was already claimed that technological leadership was passing from the Gulf of Mexico to the North Sea region: 'London and Aberdeen are fast becoming oil centres offering experience and expertise back to centres such as Houston.'[38] By the late 1980s, indeed, the USA had become a net importer of subsea technology from the North Sea.[39]

The first large-scale production platforms of the early 1970s were designed for North Sea use. But the capacity to operate in depths up to 550 feet clearly had potential applications outside the North Sea. It is striking that it is the two companies with extensive experience in the North Sea, Exxon and Shell, which have become leaders in extending the depth of what was considered practical for fixed platforms. A variety of design improvements (such as the use of lighter materials and the automation of equipment) has made such progress possible. Building on their North Sea expertise, Exxon in the 1980s installed a steel production platform in over 730 feet of water in the Honda field off California, and Shell achieved successive world records with their Cognac platform in the Gulf of Mexico standing in over 900 feet and the Bullwinkle platform operating in 1 250 feet in the same region. (See also Figure 6.1, which gives platform heights).

The growing European expertise in developing cost-saving methods of exploiting marginal fields and supplying services capable of surviving transportation costs also illustrates the theme of technology transfer from the North Sea. By 1988 it was claimed that British companies were world leaders in areas such as computer-aided seismic survey work and computer-aided design and management techniques for application in small-field developments, and were attracting the interests of 'international clients in their overseas operations'.[40]

The innovatory production technologies pioneered in the North Sea during the 1980s were also on the point of wider application. Shell, for example, had acquired operational experience of floating, tanker-loading systems in the North Sea, which was subsequently employed in their operations off Spain in 380 feet of water and the Tazerka field off Tunis in 460 feet.[41]

The technological diffusion of the TLP production concept, first used in Conoco's Hutton field, is on the point of taking off. A TLP is under development for use in 2 700 feet in the Adriatic Sea, and Conoco anticipate that production based on the system will commence from the Heidrun field in 1 150 feet in Norwegian waters, just 70 miles from the Arctic circle, in 1992.[42] Conoco is developing the Jolliet field in the Gulf of Mexico employing the same principles, working in 1 760 feet of water. Amoco, Exxon and Shell are also studying the practicality of exploiting the Green Canyon find, in the Gulf of Mexico, in about 3 500 feet of water. It has been stated that TLPs could be used in up to 10 000 feet of water. 'Applications of these may be in the Gulf of Mexico, the North Sea, Brazil, the west coast of Africa, and the west coast of the US.'[43]

EXPLANATION

Historians such as Jeremy and Wilkins who have studied international technology diffusion have developed concepts and frameworks for modelling the mechanisms of diffusion, particularly in the context of processes operating in the originating and receptor economies. The concepts developed in such studies have proved useful in this investigation of the offshore oil industry, especially in the identification of potential barriers to, and channels of, technology transmission. The explanation for technology diffusion offered here, however, places as much emphasis upon the fully international character of the oil industry, the role of consortia and the dynamic relationships between enterprises (especially subcontractors and their clients) as on the specific characteristics of the originating and receptor economies.

The findings of a number of officially sponsored investigations provide the basis for an exhaustive analysis of the relative underperformance of British industry in the offshore sector up to the early 1970s.[44] Among the causal factors were the following: the poor financial position of potential builders of offshore equipment; losses incurred by constructors of drilling rigs; lack of suitable plant and facilities; ignorance of the offshore operators' requirements; inadequate educational and training facilities; possible resistance by management and labour to new technologies; and, crucially, the entrenched position of American offshore contractors. At the outset there were no firms in Britain remotely capable of matching American firms' expertise and established position in domestic and international markets.

Although this analysis will concentrate upon explaining how British industry subsequently improved its position in the offshore market, the early

American pre-eminence deserves further comment. The American impact, from the British point of view, was not wholly negative: American strength did not necessarily equate with British weakness outside the short term.

American enterprise played an important role, not only in the initial transmission of offshore technology to the North Sea, but also in the development and application of new techniques. The facility with which American (or European) multinational enterprise in the offshore sector might be able to transcend possible cultural or institutional impediments to technology transfer in the receptor economy, and the initial American advantage in product design and productive capacity in the offshore field, have already been noted. In 1972, for example, the USA (plus US-owned yards in Singapore) accounted for nearly 70 per cent of world orders for drilling rigs. Writers therefore considered it natural that British industry should hesitate and American firms dominate in the early North Sea offshore business, an area of uncertainty for one, but of commercial strength and technical familiarity for the other.[45]

An important dimension to the advantageous position of established American enterprise was the characteristically close relationship which existed between operators and contractors. The two sides developed a close understanding of each other's requirements and worked together in design and development. In 1972 it was said:

> The sources of supply of equipment and materials of all kinds ... rests essentially on who specifies and who buys. At present these functions are mainly in the hands of US and US-experienced engineers who tend naturally to favour proven equipment from known and trusted suppliers.[46]

It is understandable that the oil companies when first embarking on North Sea operations should like to do business with established American contractors like Brown & Root, with its 53 years' experience of marine engineering and technological leadership in many areas of offshore work. It was the first firm to lay an offshore pipeline in the 1930s, to construct an offshore platform in open water in the Gulf of Mexico in the 1940s, to develop floating drilling methods in the 1950s, to install offshore pipelines and fixed platforms in the North Sea in the 1960s, and to install structures in the first commercially productive oilfield in the North Sea in the 1970s.[47]

From the mid-1970s there was a pronounced improvement in British industry's contribution to offshore supplies, reflected in Table 6.4, and technological innovation. The 1987 share of 87 per cent of the market was an all-time high. A number of arguments can be advanced to explain the transformation.

Although American firms enjoyed a number of important advantages with respect to their strength in offshore technology, equally British–Euro-

Table 6.4   British contractors' share of UKCS orders

	1974	1975–9	1980–6	1987
Value of orders placed annually (£ billion)	1.28	1.56	2.66	1.87
British share (%)	40	66	75	87

Source: Department of Energy, *Development of the Oil and Gas Resources of the United Kingdom*, various.

pean enterprise, including significantly the two European-based majors, did have the capacity to respond to the challenge, not only by importing the technology, but by advancing it a stage forward. A vital means whereby technology and skill were absorbed and diffused in the host region was through the mechanism of British-American partnerships. There are numerous instances of such collaboration, and one example must suffice. BP worked in close liaison with Brown & Root in the development of steel platforms for the Forties field, the contract for the basic design being given to Brown & Root, with developmental appraisal being carried out at Rice University, Texas, prior to construction on Teeside.[48] 'Although some of these firms may have foreign ownership or shareholding,' it was said of the first offshore suppliers established in Britain, 'which was essential to effect the initial transfer of technology, they generally now have very few expatriate staff and are providing long-term employment opportunities for British citizens.'[49]

Conditions in the North Sea were radically different from those in the region in which American suppliers had been accustomed to operate, and there was a limit to the extent to which the transatlantic flow of expertise could be counted upon to provide solutions to the technological problems awaiting companies in northern waters. A number of reasons account for the local, European strength in concrete platform technology. They include the existence of capable European firms experienced in heavy reinforced concrete construction, which could draw upon local technological traditions and expertise, and the availability of suitable deepwater sites for platform fabrication.

More generally some consideration must be given to the British government's policy of promoting the interests of the UK offshore supply industry. The government's adoption of an active policy dates back to 1975, with the establishment within the Department of Energy of the Offshore Supplies Office and Offshore Energy Technology Board. The essence of governmental objectives has been to help the British offshore supply industry improve its ability to compete in domestic, and eventually export, markets through (a) ensuring that British contractors obtain 'full and fair opportunity' to tender for orders pursued through various policy instruments, particularly a contract auditing procedure, and (b) supporting research. In 1976/77 government funds available to offshore R & D were £9.6 million, rising to £18 million by 1980/81. The Department of Energy funds projects up to 50 per cent; it does not undertake research itself.

Jenkin, in his authoritative study, is circumspect in his evaluation of the technological impact of government intervention in the 1970s (at a time when its power to influence purchasing, for example through the British National Oil Corporation, is greater than today). The application of available policy instruments did not necessarily promote technological innovation. 'Many offshore suppliers,' Jenkin explains, 'are engaged in activities which do not depend upon access to advanced technology. Even those firms which make use of advanced technology can often obtain it fairly easily on licence.' [50] Jenkin believes that the increase in British industry's share of the offshore market was mainly due to the internal improvement in the competitive capacity of British industry. He acknowledges, however, that the government did have a role in broadening the receptivity to British goods and services of the oil companies, who became aware of the importance attached by government to offshore supplies.[51] The limited research spending supported by the government appears to have been shrewdly deployed to target areas with strategic growth potential. Nevertheless compared to the massive national programmes pursued under the aegis of public authorities in Norway and France, the state's role in Britain is small and informational. Final authority on purchasing decisions lies with the oil companies themselves. One concludes that the improvement in British industry's share of the offshore market had less to do with government interference and more to do with a dynamic process of response by private enterprise to opportunities which emerged.

There was the sheer incentive to capture part of a very large market on its doorstep. By the mid-1980s, the total capital investment in the UK oil exploration and production industry was exceeding £3 billion annually. Esso alone was spending close to £1 billion per annum for capital and replacement items and services, their purchasing power being important to 'hundreds of companies'.[52] Of £1.3 billion invested in BP's Magnus project, over 80 per cent was spent in the UK. Two main contractors, six major fabricators and over 1 400 subcontractors and suppliers were involved in the project.[53] Thus many British firms gained experience in offshore technology.

British offshore specialist firms, because of the relationships built up in North Sea operations, especially with big enterprises like Shell, BP and Exxon, are potentially in a not dissimilar position to that enjoyed by American contractors first entering the North Sea market 25 years ago. Exxon Corporation, for example, operates in more than 80 countries. Because the international oil companies like doing business with known contractors who have performed satisfactorily in the recent past, British offshore suppliers of, for example Exxon, have 'a real advantage in bidding elsewhere in the world'. A reasonable number of British firms who have won important contracts from Exxon in its world-wide activities illustrate this opportunity. When Exxon Company USA, for example, installed the world's first commercial guyed tower to produce oil and gas from the Lena field in 1 000 feet in the Gulf of Mexico, British firms were able to win contracts for the supply of equipment.[54]

CONCLUSION

As previously indicated, concepts drawn from historical studies of technology transfer have proved useful in elucidating the role of multinational enterprise, contractors, consortia and other systems as vehicles of technology transmission. The offshore technology transferred to the North Sea, however, soon had to be transformed out of all recognition, if the region's challenges were to be overcome. And it is doubtful whether the concept of 'reverse flows' accurately describes the subsequent diffusion of new technologies which had been developed in the North Sea. In this fully international industry it does not seem altogether appropriate to associate the mastery of offshore technology with a particular region. Technological leadership is possessed by enterprises who operate globally and who, through collaborative ventures (often involving local interests), can apply that expertise almost anywhere. While the first TLP was sited in the North Sea, Marathon Oil's contract for design and appraisal work for application in the Gulf of Mexico went to a San Francisco firm.[55] Much stimulus to offshore technological development is currently coming from Brazil. Brasnor, a Norwegian/Brazilian subsea specialist firm, is threatening the highly regarded French firm, Coflexip's, dominance of flexible risers and pipelines. Brasnor had previously acquired a majority stake in the German company, Pag-O-Flex.[56] Shell has a massive R & D expenditure in the UK, but application of the ensuing knowledge will not be restricted to North Sea operations. It is international consortia, which can combine local know-how and resources with the financial power and technological experience of established oil companies or contractors, which are able to achieve a very swift world-wide diffusion of best-practice technique in the offshore oil industry.

NOTES

The author is grateful to Mr Francis Goodall for numerous comments and corrections of perspective. Permission to reproduce material supplied by the following is gratefully acknowledged: Shell UK Limited for Figures 6.1–6.3 and Chevron UK Limited for Plate.

1.   R. Adern, *Offshore Oil and Gas: A Guide to Sources of Information* (London and Edinburgh, 1978).
2.   C. Callow, *Power from the Sea: The Search for North Sea Oil and Gas* (London, 1973); B. Cooper and T.F. Gaskell, *The Adventure of North Sea Oil* (London, 1976); K. Chapman, *North Sea Oil and Gas: A Geographical Perspective* (London, 1976).
3.   M. Lovegrove, *Our Island's Oil: A Study* (London, 1975); M. Lovegrove, *Lovegrove's Guide to Britain's North Sea Oil and Gas* (Cambridge, 1985). M. Jenkin, *British Industry and the North Sea: State Intervention in a Developing Industrial Sector* (London, 1981).
4.   R.L. Lankford, 'Marine Drilling', in J.E. Brantly (ed.), *History of Oil Well Drilling* (Houston, Texas, 1971). This is a major historical survey which, however, could only anticipate North Sea developments.
5.   Ibid., p. 1401.
6.   P.E. White, 'Diving for Oil', *Petroleum Review*, **23**, (June 1968), pp. 61–4; P.M. Aagaard and C.P. Besse, 'A Review of the Offshore Environment – 25 Years of Progress', *Journal of Petroleum Technology*, **25**, no. 12, (December 1973), pp. 1355–60.
7.   P. Hinde, *The Exploration for Petroleum and the Prospective Areas of Britain* (Institute of Petroleum Symposium, Aberdeen University, for British Gas, 21 September 1972, revised September 1980), p. 10.
8.   *Lovegrove's Guide*, p. 38.
9.   Callow, *Power from the Sea*, p. 56.
10.   Ibid., pp. 123–4.
11.   Cooper and Gaskell, *Adventure*, p. 141.
12.   Chapman, *North Sea Oil*, pp. 112–13.
13.   J.W. Jenner, 'Drilling for Oil', in G.D. Hobson and W. Pohl (eds), *Modern Petroleum Technology*, (London, fourth edition 1975), p. 128.
14.   M.F. Shepherd, 'The Brent Oil-Field – From Discovery to Refinery', paper presented to *The Royal Institution of Naval Architects* (25 April 1979), p. 241.
15.   Cooper and Gaskell, *Adventure*, p. 137.
16.   D.E. Kash *et al.*, *Energy under the Ocean: A Technology Assessment of Outer Continental Shelf Oil and Gas Operations* (Folkestone, 1974), p. 94.
17.   *Lovegrove's Guide*, p. 64.
18.   M. Wilkins, 'The Role of Private Enterprise in the International Diffusion of Technology', *Journal of Economic History*, **34**, no. 1, (March 1974), p. 167; *The Maturing of Multinational Enterprise: American Business Abroad from 1914 to 1970* (Cambridge, Mass., 1974), pp. 341–2.
19.   The 'Shell' Transport and Trading Company plc, *Annual Report 1982*, p. 8.
20.   Shell UK, *Oil Industry Investment in the UK* (Background brief, London, 1984), p. 2.
21.   Jenkin, *British Industry*, p. 150.
22.   Department of Energy, *Development of the Oil and Gas Resources of the United Kingdom 1980* (London, 1981), p. 20.
23.   Kash *et al.*, *Energy under the Ocean*, p. 99.
24.   Ibid.
25.   W.A. Thomas, 'Floating Production and Subsea Completions', in *A Guide to North Sea Oil and Gas Technology* (Proceedings of the Institute of Petroleum 1977 Annual Conference, London, 1978), p. 80.
26.   Proceedings of *European Offshore Steel Research Seminar* (held Cambridge, November 1978; Weldings Institute for Dept. of Energy, 1980).
27.   Cooper and Gaskell, *Adventure*, p. 83.

28. C.R. Bond and P.G.H. Shaw, 'Lessons from 8 Years' Operation of a First Generation North Sea Platform', in *Proceedings of the 16th Annual Offshore Technology Conference* (Houston, Texas, 1986), pp. 73–9.
29. Shell UK Limited, *Brent and Beyond* (London, n.d.), p. 2.
30. J. Timor, 'Platforms – Steel Structures', in *A Guide to North Sea Oil Technology*, pp. 64–5.
31. F. van Daalen, 'Offshore Engineering: The Next Decade', in *Understanding North Sea Oil: Operations, Prospects and Policy* (Bank of Scotland/Institute of Petroleum, Edinburgh, 1977), pp. 23, 28.
32. J. Huxley, 'How They Could Drain the North Sea Dry', *The Sunday Times*, 18 November 1984, p. 80.
33. For some of this evidence, see Cooper and Gaskell, *Adventure*, p. 115; Callow, *Power from the Sea*, p. 87.
34. Lovegrove, *Our Island's Oil*, pp. 47–50.
35. M. Gaskin and D.I. McKay, *The Economic Impact of North Sea Oil on Scotland* (Aberdeen University for Scottish Economic Planning Dept., 1978), p. 21.
36. K. Forrest, 'Answering the Offshore Challenge', in *British Business Enterprise Offshore*, 4 September 1981, p. 13.
37. 'Establishing a Track Record', ibid., p. 7.
38. Foreword in *A Guide to North Sea Oil Technology*, p. ix.
39. J.R. Huff, cited in 'Can Europe Stay on Top?', in *Noroil*, **16**, no. 8, (August 1988), p. 82.
40. Department of Energy, *Development of the Oil and Gas Resources of the United Kingdom, 1987* (London, 1988), p. 77.
41. Shell UK, *New Ideas for North Sea Development* (London, 1987), p. 8.
42. *The Times*, 28 September 1987.
43. *Lloyds List*, 6 May 1988.
44. For example: International Management and Engineering Group of Britain Limited, *Study of Potential Benefits to British Industry from Offshore Oil and Gas Developments* (London, 1972).
45. Callow, *Power from the Sea*, p. 85; Cooper and Gaskell, *Adventure*, p. 137.
46. IMEG, *Study of Potential Benefits to British Industry*, p. 8.
47. 'Marine R & D Plays Key Role in Industry', *Brownbilt* (Winter 1982), pp. 19–21.
48. BP, *Our Industry: Petroleum*, fifth edition (London, 1977), p. 153.
49. *United Kingdom Offshore Operators' Association* (London, n.d.), p. 10.
50. Jenkin, *British Industry*, pp. 106–7.
51. Ibid., pp. 178–85.
52. K. Taylor, 'Openings for British Industry: International Opportunities', *Esso Magazine*, no. 137, (Spring 1986), p. 2.
53. R. Dafter, 'Satellite Send-off: Magnus Oil Field', *Financial Times*, Special Survey, 14 September 1983, p. 9.
54. Taylor, 'Openings', pp. 2–5.
55. *Lloyds List*, 28 September 1987.
56. 'Can Europe Stay on Top?', p. 82.

PART II

Transfers from Japan

7. The Local Competitiveness and Management of Japanese Cotton Spinning Mills in China in the Inter-war Years

Tetsuya Kuwahara

JAPANESE COTTON SPINNERS' IN CHINA: ESTABLISHMENT AND INVESTMENT

From its beginnings in the 1890s, the Japanese cotton industry depended heavily for its growth on overseas markets. By 1914, Japanese cotton spinners exported about 40 per cent of their total sales, most to the Chinese market, where they established a dominant position, especially in coarse cotton yarn and coarse cotton cloth. They exported to China 520 000 bales of cotton yarn (value 60 million yen), which was 58 per cent of the total amount of yarn imported by China in 1914. They also exported coarse cotton cloth (sheeting, drill and T cloth), total value 25 million yen, which was 56 per cent of the total amount imported by China. The Chinese cotton spinning industry, which had been slow to develop since its inception, began expansion of its production capacity during the First World War. Cotton exports from Lancashire to China fell and the price of cotton goods rose. Under these favourable market conditions many native entrepreneurs entered cotton spinning, their spindles increasing in number from 800 000 in 1913 to 1.1 million in 1918. The Chinese market became self-sufficient in coarse cotton yarns (cotton yarns of 20 count and downward) and coarse cotton cloth. Imports of cotton yarns to China decreased from 900 000 bales in 1914 to 400 000 bales in 1918. Imports of sheeting and drill decreased, sheeting from 120 million yards in 1915 to 80 million in 1918. This change in the Chinese coarse cotton goods market had a serious impact on the Japanese cotton industry, which had had a dominant position there.

Most major Japanese cotton spinners built local mills to defend their position in the Chinese market.[1] Eight Japanese cotton manufacturing firms

– Dainippon Cotton Spinning Co., Nisshin Cotton Spinning Co., Osaka Godo Cotton Spinning Co., Kanegafuchi Cotton Spinning Co., Fuji Gasu Cotton Spinning Co., Toyo Cotton Spinning Co., Nagasaki Cotton Spinning & Weaving Co. and Fukushima Cotton Spinning Co., – opened new cotton spinning mills in China. If we include Naigaiwata & Co., which had been engaged in local production in Shanghai since 1911, nine Japanese cotton spinning firms had local mills in China. Major Japanese cotton trading firms and merchants also had local cotton spinning mills in China. Mitsui & Co. began cotton spinning in Shanghai in 1902. Nihon Menka Co. and Ito Chu & Co. undertook local production around the end of the First World War. Sakichi Toyoda, inventor of an automatic weaving machine, built a cotton spinning mill in Shanghai in 1921. Having Japanese investments, the Chinese cotton industry increased its number of spindles and weaving machines, from 800 000 spindles and 4 000 looms in 1913 to 2 400 000 spindles and 13 000 looms in 1922.

The depression following the First World War caused cut-throat competition in the Chinese cotton industry. From 1923 to 1930, 15 Chinese mills ceased to exist because of bankruptcy. Of these, 13 were sold out and two were reorganized (Table 7.1). Out of the 66 Chinese firms existing in 1930, nine suspended operation, four were under the control of creditors, 12 were leased and five commissioned. Though some Chinese firms, such as Shen Xin Cotton Spinning & Weaving Co. and Yung-an Cotton Spinning & Weaving Co., grew, few could follow them.

There were six Western firms, with 246 000 spindles and 1 900 weaving looms, in China in 1915: Iwo Cotton Spinning & Weaving Co., Lao Kungmace Cotton Spinning Co., International Cotton Spinning & Weaving Co., Soychee Cotton Spinning Co., Kun-i Cotton Spinning Co. and Yang Shu-pu Cotton Spinning Co.[2] Iwo and the last two firms represented the cotton manufacturing division of Jardine Matheson & Co. Kun-i and Yang Shu-pu were merged into Iwo in 1921. These Western cotton firms were rather slack, as were most of the native firms. International was sold to Japanese cotton merchants in 1918, Lao Kungmace to the Japanese firm, Kanegafuchi Cotton Spinning Co. in 1925, and Oriental Cotton Spinning & Weaving Co. (who had bought Soychee Co. in 1916) to a Chinese firm, Shen Xin Cotton Spinning & Weaving Co., in 1929.

While many cotton spinning firms suffered dull performance in China during the 1920s, most Japanese local mills established a firm position in the Chinese cotton spinning industry and grew steadily. Their profitability was good from the beginning.[3] The number of Japanese local spindles increased from 1.3 million in 1925, equivalent to 37.5 per cent of the total spindles in China, to 1.8 million in 1930, equivalent to 40 per cent. The number of Japanese weaving machines increased from 6 000 (equivalent to 26 per cent

Table 7.1 Number of cotton spinning firms in China, 1912–30

| | Chinese firms | | | | | | | | | | Western firms | Japanese firms | Total firms |
| | Foundation | | | | | Expiration | | | | End of year | | | |
	Beginning of year	By mill construction	Purchasing existing mills	Reorganization	Total	Fire	Sold out	Reformation	Total				
1912	20	0	0	0	0	0	0	0	0	20	5	3	28
1913	20	0	0	0	0	0	0	0	0	20	5	3	28
1914	20	0	0	0	0	0	0	0	0	20	6	3	29
1915	20	1	0	0	1	0	0	0	0	21	6	3	30
1916	21	3	1	0	4	0	0	0	0	25	6	2	33
1917	25	1	0	2	3	1	1	2	4	24	6	2	32
1918	24	4	0	0	4	0	1	0	1	27	5	3	35
1919	27	4	0	0	4	0	0	0	0	31	5	3	39
1920	31	6	1	0	7	1	1	0	2	36	5	3	44
1921	36	16	0	0	16	0	0	0	0	52	5	6	63
1922	52	8	0	0	8	0	0	0	0	60	3	9	72
1923	60	2	1	0	3	0	1	0	1	62	3	11	76
1924	62	1	1	0	2	0	2	0	2	62	3	12	77
1925	62	0	0	0	0	0	1	0	1	61	2	15	78
1926	61	2	0	0	2	0	1	0	1	62	2	15	79
1927	62	0	2	1	3	0	2	1	3	62	2	15	79
1928	62	1	2	0	3	0	3	0	3	62	2	15	79
1929	62	3	1	0	4	0	1	0	1	65	1	15	81
1930	65	1	2	1	4	0	2	1	3	66	1	15	82
Total		53	11	4	68	2	16	4	22				

Note: Year of foundation represents the year of beginning of operations.

Sources: On Chinese firms, see Yen Chungping, *The History of Modern Chinese Industrial Development* (1966) pp. 443–70. On Japanese firms, see T. Kuwahara, 'Overseas Operations', *Rokkodai Ronshu*, vol. 22, no. 12, (1975).

of the total in China) to 14 000 (equivalent to 42 per cent of the total) over the same period.[4] On the other hand, the share of spindles held by native mills decreased from 62.4 per cent in 1925 to 58.5 per cent in 1930, and the Western mills from 7.2 per cent to 4.1 per cent over the same period.[5]

To compete successfully with the native firms, the Japanese local mills had to develop advantages more than to offset the costs of distant operations. These costs arose from communication and travel between head offices and local mills, allowances for employees' foreign service, delays and distortions in information and decision making, and unfamiliarity with the local Chinese situation. This chapter will explore the competitive advantages by means of which Japanese spinning firms overcame the economic and social costs of distant operations in China. The focus is on the production process inside the mills and their local purchasing and selling in China. What was the strength of Japanese mills and how did they realize it?

JAPANESE MANAGEMENT AND ORGANIZATION OF LOCAL MILLS IN CHINA

The Japanese domestic mills had widened the productivity gap with competitors in China since the 1890s.[6] They increased exports of cotton goods to China based on their untiring improvements to mill operation. It was crucial for the Japanese local mills in China to maintain a higher level of technology than their competitors, in order to survive and grow there. But Japanese local mills in China faced difficulties in satisfying these requirements because they faced an unfamiliar business environment with local production.

To cope with these problems, the Japanese cotton spinning firms dispatched many Japanese employees and let them reside in China. In 1930, Naigaiwata & Co. sent 402 personnel and managed 15 000 Chinese labourers; Kanegafuchi Co. (its local subsidiary was called Shanghai Silk Manufacturing Co.), 260 personnel, 8 500 Chinese; Dainippon Co., 160 personnel, 5 500 Chinese; Toyo Co. (Yuhon Cotton Spinning Co.), 70 personnel, 2 300 Chinese; Osaka Godo Co. (Dong Shing Cotton Spinning and Weaving Co.), 75 personnel, 2 000 Chinese (see Table 7.2). The role of the managers and technicians can be seen by looking more closely at Toyo Co.'s subsidiary, Yuhon Cotton Spinning Co., in Shanghai.[7] Yuhon Co.'s top management consisted of six directors: a president, a managing director and four directors. Five of the six directors were from Toyo Co.'s board of directors, and the other one was an employee. The managing director and one of the four directors resided in Shanghai, while the other four stayed at the parent company's office in Osaka. Toyo Co. dispatched 70 personnel (one director and 69 employees) to the local subsidiary. One director was the managing director of the subsidiary, while one employee was the director and mill manager of the subsidiary. Of the other 68 employees who were sent to subsidiary, 46 (including seven college graduates) were in charge of engineering, one of construction, one of office work, one of the warehouse, two of supplies, one of accounting, eight of labour and personnel affairs, five of medical and health affairs and three of selling and purchasing.

All of the posts in the management organization of the Yuhon Cotton Spinning Co. that required expertise and professional decision making were staffed by the personnel dispatched from Toyo Co. The organizational structure is shown in Figure 7.1. The organization was similar to that of the home mills in terms of the composition of engineers and experienced workers as a core group, and of a hierarchy based on academic training and length of service. A major difference from the home mill organization was the appointment of Chinese 'number ones' (no. 1) between the Japanese front-line manager and the Chinese labourers. The Chinese no. 1 worked as assistant and translator for the front-line manager. Particularly important was the need to achieve smooth communication with labourers. The system of direct control was more effective with the no. 1.

At the mill the front-line manager (process chief) responsible for a specific process surveyed the attendance of millhands, prepared setting for the work, assigned millhands to positions, directed them, supervised their work and controlled the humidity and temperature according to spinning conditions. The operating shift chief was in charge of scheduled operations of the whole process and coordination of the flow of semi-finished goods. The chief engineer was in charge of maintenance of machines, the safety of operation and standardized routines of workers. The mill manager was responsible for the efficiency of the mill as a whole.[8]

The Japanese local mills ran continuously, except for 12 hours from 6pm to 6am every Sunday. During these 12 hours they removed ash from the boiler, repaired electrical facilities and checked fire protection systems. The Japanese personnel were on duty for 12 hours, day or night, and took the lead in operations inside the mill. They improved the efficiency of mill operation based on statistical data.[9] The Shanghai Cotton Spinning & Weaving Co. inspected the semi-finished goods on the twenty-fifth of every month in the 1930s. They compared the amount with the result obtained by subtracting the output of product, and estimated amount of cotton waste and fly (from the input of raw cotton per month). They evaluated the mill efficiency using the difference.

The local mills gathered information on productivity and latest engineering know-how from domestic mills. They tried to catch up with the technology and productivity of the home mills. The output of 20 count cotton yarn per hour at the local mill in China was 0.039 lb in 1929, and at the home mills 0.050 lb.[10] The chief engineer in the spinning section at Tsingtao Mill

Table 7.2   Japanese personnel dispatched and Chinese workers in local mills, January 1930

Local name of firms	Location of mills	Top management of local mills[1]
Naigaiwata Cotton Spinning Co.	Shanghai	2
	Tsingtao	General manager
		n.a.
Shanghai Silk Manufacturing Co.	Shanghai	m.d.1 d.1
	Tsingtao	d.1
Dainippon Cotton Spinning Co.	Shanghai	0
	Tsingtao	0
Dong Shing Cotton Spinning and Weaving Co.	Shanghai	m.d.1
Yukon Cotton Spinning Co.	Shanghai	s.m.d.1 m.d.1
Nagasaki Cotton Spinning and Weaving Co.	Tsingtao	0
Fuji Gasu Cotton Spinning Co.	Tsingtao	0
Manshu Cotton Spinning Co.	Lioyang, Manchuria	n.a.
Nisshin Cotton Spinning Co.	Tsingtao	0
Manshu Fukubo Co.	Dalian	n.a.
Japan & China Cotton Spinning and Weaving Co.	Shanghai	p.1 m.d.1
Shanghai Cotton Spinning and Weaving Co.	Shanghai	c.1. m.d.2
Toyoda Cotton Spinning and Weaving Co.	Shanghai	p.1 s.m.d.1 m.d.1
Tokwa Cotton Spinning Co.	Shanghai	m.d.1
Taian Cotton Spinning Co.	Hankow	m.d.1
Total 15 firms		

Notes
[1] C.: chairman; p.: president; s.m.d.: senior managing director; m.d.: managing director; d.: director.
[2] One of them was a director.
[3] He was a director.
[4] He was a managing director.
[5] The personnel at the mills in Manchuria are not included.

Sources: Kimpusha (ed.), *Zaishi Houjim Jinmes' Roku (The Directory of the Japanese in China)* (Shanghai, February 1931); H.D. Fong, *Cotton Industry and Trade in China*, vol. 2 (August 1932).

Japanese personnel							Chinese workers
Mill manager	Manufacturing	Office work	Purchasing and selling	Medical	Others	Total	
6	197	93	9	0	12	319 } 402	10 350
n.a.	n.a.	n.a.	n.a.	n.a.	n.a.	83	2 500
n.a.	n.a.	n.a.	n.a.	n.a.	n.a.	n.a.	1 960
2[2]	137	46	10	14	0	210 } 264	5 600
1[3]	35	14	1	3	0	54	2 680
1	61		7	0	0	69 } 160	3 963
n.a.	n.a.	n.a.	n.a.	n.a.	n.a.	91	3 440
2	48	21	3	0	0	75	3 713
1[4]	47	18	3	0	0	70	2 300
1	34	10	1	2	0	48	1 350
1	10	12	0	3	0	26	1 400
n.a.	n.a.	n.a.	n.a.	n.a.	n.a.	n.a.	1 692
1	n.a.	n.a.	n.a.	n.a.	n.a.	43	1 371
n.a.	n.a.	n.a.	n.a.	n.a.	n.a.	n.a.	960
3	162	79	6	0	0	252	15 971
0	199	60	8	9	1	280	10 232
1	n.a.	n.a.	n.a.	n.a.	n.a.	61	3 900
0	32	0	9	0	0	42	2 000
1	16	13	1	0	0	32	1 700
						1 755[5]	77 082

Figure 7.1   Organization of Yuhon Cotton Spinning Co., 1931

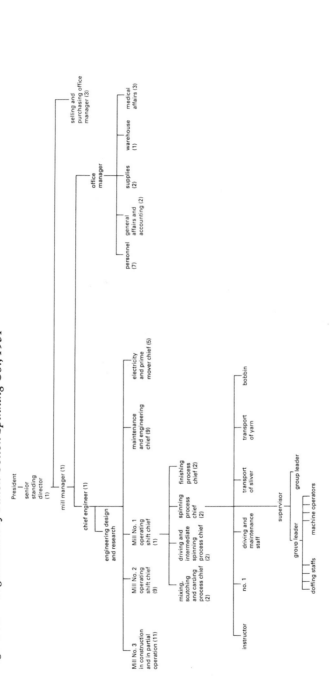

Note: Number in parentheses represents the Japanese employees, including the head of each department.

Source: Kimpusha (ed.), *Zaishi Houjim Jinmes' Roku (The Directory of the Japanese in China)* (Shanghai, Febnary 1931); Toyo Boseki Kaisha, *Shokuin Meibo (Personnel Directory of Toyo Cotton Spinning Co.)* November 1930; organization charts of Yuhon Cotton Spinning Co., drawn by S. Baba, June 1986 and K. Kadono, 12 March 1986.

154

of Dainippon Cotton Spinning Co. prepared a process chart of the mixing ratio of raw cottons appropriate to the projected yarn count, the draft ratio of sliver, setting the gauge span, the speed of spindles and the twisting of sliver and yarn on the basis of the practices at the home mill.[11] Japanese employees were transferred to the local mills through personnel changes every year in Dainippon Cotton Spinning Co. The length of service of dispatched employees at local mills varied from a few to more than ten years.[12] The Japanese employees brought the latest know-how of domestic mills to the local mills. The personnel who were working for local mills returned home on vacation for more than a month every three years. On these occasions they visited the firm's model mill under the direction of the engineering department.[13]

CHINESE AND WESTERN MILL ORGANIZATION

Chinese mill management was distinguished by the contract system and nepotism. There was a variety of problems within each layer of management organization. The operation of each process, such as spinning, roving, drawing and so on, was managed by the masters of the contract system. Direct control of the production process was not common. The master recruited or dismissed workers, provided training, directed and supervised operations, set and paid wage rates, kept machinery adjusted and planned the operation schedule of his section. He was a skilled worker and experienced with machines. But most of the masters did not understand even elementary scientific principles, so that they lacked the talent for improving efficiency.[14] The masters rather resisted rationalization to safeguard their status.[15] Moreover the contract system encouraged exploitation, lowering the morale of subordinate workers and their living standards.

Chinese management failed to control the contract system and to increase mill efficiency. Family members and relatives of owners and managers were appointed as managers and officers.[16] Often they did not have the knowledge or experience required for mill operation and made use of their authority for personal gain. The management duties were delegated by default to holders of lower posts, and were finally left to the master in the contract system. Most Chinese mills lacked bureaucracy. One Japanese professor of engineering who observed a Chinese mill in May–June 1918 reported on the poor conditions in the Chinese mills.[17] At the drawing process the Chinese kept the machines running while slivers were broken and consequently their thickness was irregular. The roller parts were not cleaned; they were covered with cotton and the flutes of the rollers could not be observed. The flutes on many rollers were twisted. Efforts to extend the working time (before cleaning) of the flutes were minimal. The mouth of the trumpet was enlarged by roughly widening to ease the flow of slivers. Afraid of being dismissed because of low production, the millhands speeded up the front roller to 400 to 450 revolutions per minute. They seemed to consider that this was the only means to increase output. Doffing was supposed to be done every time a container became full of sliver, but the millhands waited until several containers became full before they set about doffing. Workers in the Chinese mills were not educated in the function and structure of machines and did not operate them properly. That was the situation of production management under the master system. The management mostly left these difficulties as they were.

Western cotton spinning firms in China, which were divisions of trading firms, did not control the production processes directly either.[18] They employed the compradore system (compradores were originally commercial intermediaries hired for foreign trade) and gave the compradores production contracts. The contract fee was based on output. The company provided the compradores with machines and raw cotton. The compradores employed Chinese engineers and labourers, and organized mill operations. The compradore system worked as a bridge between the Western and the Oriental worlds, but it could not realize in China the advantages developed in the Lancashire cotton industry. Although some engineers from Britain were in charge of engineering affairs as staff managers, the mills only achieved the fruits of technology transfer partially and temporarily. This indirect management system replicated in Western mills the inefficiencies of the Chinese factories.

TECHNOLOGY

The cotton spinning process consists of the production stages of opening, picking, carding, roving and spinning. No spinners had differential advantages over the others in acquiring the machines. Machine markets were open to anybody all over the world; the technology of cotton spinning frames was standardized. The Japanese mills used spinning frames from Platt Brothers and weaving machines from Toyoda. The Chinese mills were less consistent than the Japanese in selecting machine makers, who are listed in Tables 7.3 and 7.4. This equipment consisted entirely of ring frames and the ordinary (non-automatic) power looms. Neither the Japanese nor the Chinese cotton spinning firms operated mule frames.[19] The performance of spinning machines depended on the engineering ability of individual firms. Maintenance, repair and adjustment of machines to a variety of raw cottons, remodelling machines through replacement with the most up-to-date parts and controls of temperature and humidity were major engineering practices in cotton mills. It was difficult for the engineers and experienced workers of other firms to imitate and command expertise accumulated in one company; much know-how, such as the twisting rate of the sliver during the drawing process and preliminary spinning process, was kept secret. This know-how created the differences in quality and productivity of cotton yarn among the firms.

The Japanese mills enforced the regular maintenance of machines. This periodical maintenance had its cost in downtime, supplies such as machine oil, and labour, but it was necessary if machines were to perform well. The Japanese mill engineers also tried to run closer to their maximum theoretical ratings. They tried to rotate the cylinders of the carding machines in an exact circle and to maintain the centre line of top roller and that of bottom roller in parallel.[20]

Table 7.3   Makers of spinning frames

	Japanese mills (1927) %	Chinese mills (1932) %	British mills (1925) %
Platt Brothers	31	12	63
Saco Lowell	15	15	0
Dobson and Barlow	14	12	0
Howard and Bullough	12	14	0
Asa Lees	9	19	25
Whitin	5	n.a.	0
Hetherington	4	9	0
Tweedales & Smalley	3	n.a.	12
Toyoda	2	0	0
Woonsocket	2	n.a.	0
Constructions Mécaniques	1	n.a.	0
Brooks & Doxey	1	9	0
Others	0	n.a.	0
Total	100	100	100
No. of spindles identified	1 320 000	1 552 000	206 000

Note: Spindles and weaving machines in the table covered 56 per cent and 70 per cent in Chinese mills, and 100 per cent each in Japanese and British mills.

Source: Mineo Yoshida, *Zaika Hojim Bosekigyo ni tutte (Japanese Cotton Spinning in China)*; Kobe Hasho (ed.), *Kaigai Ryoko Chosa Hokoku (The Research Report on Overseas Travel of Summer, 1928)* (1929); Wang Tze-chien and Wang Chen-chung, (eds), translated by Fumio Kunimatsu, *Sina Bosekigyo Tokyo*, pp. 87–8, 91–2; Toa Dobunkai (ed.), *Sina Kogyo Soran (General View of Chinese Manufacturing Industry)* (1931), p. 59.

Table 7.4   Makers of weaving machines

	Japanese mills (1927) %	Chinese mills (1932) %	British mills (1925) %
Toyoda	61	10	0
Platt Brothers	21	6	79 (including some Livesey's)
Gregson Monk	5	n.a.	0
William Dickinson	3	7	0
G. Hodgeson	3	n.a.	0
Enshu	3	n.a.	0
Hattersley	2	n.a.	0
Nogami	2	n.a.	0
H. Livesey	0	17	0
Saco Lowell	0	14	0
G. Keighley	0	13	21
Butterworth & Dickinson	0	3	0
Dairyu	0	1	0
Others	0	n.a.	0
Total	100	100	100
Number of looms identified	10 524	13 349	2 102

Note and sources as for Table 7.3.

On the other hand, in the Chinese native mills, managers did not recognize the need for maintenance and constant replacement of parts. They often left machines unrepaired. Consequently machines became inferior as time passed. A Japanese observer, T. Kinukawa, visited native mills in Shanghai in 1918.[21] He found many parts worn out. When he saw that the card clothing of the carding machines had seriously degenerated, and asked where the spare card clothing was, no one could answer him, because they had not checked the stock of spare parts. Actually stocks of card clothing were stored at warehouses. Wang Tze-chien and Wang Chen-chung, who surveyed the native cotton spinning mills in seven provinces, reported that the machinery, once installed in the mills, followed a path of declining function, because the native mills lacked constant maintenance and repair of machines and replacement of parts.[22]

The control of temperature and humidity in spinning mills was essential to stabilize the conditions for spinning, because cotton staples are very sensitive to temperature and humidity. As the air becomes dry and cool, cotton shrinks and distorts. The field managers adjusted the temperature and humidity, while monitoring the conditions of semi-finished products such as web and sliver at the various processing stages of spinning.[23]

Based on high-level engineering practices, the Japanese local mills in China adopted the very sophisticated cotton blending techniques of their parent mills in Japan.[24] The distribution of staple length, elasticity and the mixture of impurities in raw cotton differs according to the type, place of production, soil, weather and crop season. Cotton blending is the technique of mixing inferior and superior kinds of raw cotton, thereby cutting costs and yet spinning yarns of satisfactory quality; this material-saving expertise involved the technique of blending raw cotton and spinning engineering. Spinning firms commanding the cotton blending technique could extend the range of raw cottons used beyond the kinds purchased by their rivals. While Japanese local mills used mostly Chinese cotton, they supplemented it to a much greater extent with Indian cotton than did Chinese and Western manufacturers. Purchasing specialists of raw cotton acquired less expensive raw cotton, considering both the desired yarn count and spinning potential of the staples. The physical quality of raw cotton employed in the spinning process constantly changed according to the price fluctuations of raw cotton markets. The mill manager decided the proportions of raw cottons used in order to achieve the desired yarn count. Engineers and foremen adjusted the machines according to the varying physical nature of the raw cotton and the desired yarn count. They drew up staple diagrams (a chart showing the distribution of length of cotton staple) from which they adjusted the roving frame, the fly frame and the spinning frame to the cotton. The mastery of this blending technique was critical for the local mills in China. As a proportion of total manufacturing cost, raw cotton was as high as 80 per cent in the case of 16 count yarn. Consequently the cotton blending technique provided a major competitive edge for the Japanese local mills.

LABOUR MANAGEMENT PRACTICES

Japanese-owned spinning firms in 1930 had 1.5 million spindles, 11 000 weaving machines and employed 74 000 Chinese workers. Although there was an abundant workforce in China, labourers qualified in terms of health and strength were not always available.[25] The Japanese local mills had to recruit them in several ways. They accepted applicants at the mill on displaying recruitment notices, sent their own recruiters to the villages, and employed the relatives and friends of Chinese labourers. Most popular in Shanghai was contracting outside recruiters to supply labour. The recruiters (called 'mesiya', which literally means 'meal boss') usually hired young girls from their home villages. They rented company-owned houses and let the workers live there, prepared meals, brought lunches to the mill and oversaw the workers' everyday lives. Work was for 12 hours a day, including a meal break of 30 minutes. The company paid workers' wages through the labour contractors.[26]

Once Japanese local subsidiaries hired Chinese workers, they gave them systematic training. Before a Japanese factory was opened in China a number of selected workers was sent to and trained at home mills in Japan.[27] Dong Shing Cotton Spinning & Weaving Co., which was founded by the shareholders of Osaka Godo Cotton Spinning Co., trained 30 Chinese girls in January 1922 at Osaka Godo's Kanzaki Mill close to Osaka, prior to the operation of the Golden Road Mill in China. They were divided into two groups and were trained for a month. The Kanegafuchi Cotton Spinning Co. trained 170 Chinese labourers for its Tsingtao mill at its Hyogo Branch Mill in Kobe and a few other mills in Chugoku and Kyushu districts between September 1922 and February 1923. The workers were divided into four groups and the workers of each group were trained for three to four months. Fukushima Cotton Spinning Co. trained 50 Chinese for their local mill at Shikama Mill in Hyogo in December 1923. When the local mills began full-scale operation, they implemented a training programme,[28] for which Kanegafuchi dispatched 57 instructors. Newly recruited workers were enrolled in the training programme for 30 to 45 days, during which they were educated by Japanese trainers and the Chinese trainers who had been educated in Japan. The trainees practised on machines outside the production line, then practised on the job under the instruction of the experienced workers in the later section of the training period. They mastered the procedures of their appointed job, learned the function and structure of machines and the relationship of their jobs to others, and were taught work discipline. When the workers' skill reached the required level, they were appointed to a specific process. Management encouraged trainees to improve their skills by themselves, and expected them to progress from year to year.

Even after these Chinese labourers were assigned to the machines as regular workers, a few instructors helped to maintain and improve the skill levels on the job. In 1932, Dainippon Cotton Spinning Co. dispatched seven instructors to its Tsingtao mill (two instructors were in drawing and slubbing, three in spinning and two in finishing) and retrained the local workforce under the principles of scientific management.[29] Standard time-and-motion methods had become widely implemented in cotton spinning mills in Japan after the First World War.

The Chinese mills, on the other hand, depended upon masters in the contract system to train workers on the job. The skill level of the masters was low and stagnant. Consequently the workers did not learn good skills. Labourers lacked work discipline.[30] Even if management recognized the importance of systematic training of workers, they could not enforce it. Masters resisted it because they feared the loss of authority and power over subordinate workers. One Chinese researcher reported, in 1932, that some workers were observed sleeping beside machines, chatting and making noise, having meals inside the mills and nursing babies there.[31] The labour management policies of the Japanese-owned cotton spinning mills were not confined to the workplace but were extended to the welfare of labourers. In a mill of Shanghai Silk Manufacturing Co., facilities for sport, music and the practice of religion (Buddhism, Confucianism and Taoism) were provided, along with an elementary school for employees' children, a supplementary education course for employees, a hospital and a discount grocery store, all on mill property.[32] This, together with higher wages and employment security, contributed to high morale in the workplace and low turnover. In 1928, 64 per cent of the girls in the spinning section had served more than one year in the Japanese mill, 52 per cent two years and 43 per cent more than three years, compared with the Chinese mill where the length of service was three to four months, with rare cases of two or three years in 1932 and 1933.[33]

The Japanese mills in China were superior to the native mills in cost control and productivity (see Tables 7.5 and 7.6).

Table 7.5   Production cost of 20 count cotton yarn, 1935

	Native mills yuan	Japanese mills yuan
Wages	10.5	5.8
Labour costs	0.2	0.5
Power and coal	5.5	4.8
Machine repairs	1.8	0.6
Building and repairs	0.4	0.4
Expendable supplies	1.7	0.5
Packing	1.5	1.2
Transportation	0.2	0.2
Salaries	1.2	0.6
Miscellaneous	1.5	0.5
Total	24.5	15.1

Source: T. Okabe, 'Sina Boseki Rodo no Tei-Seisansei,' Toa Sen-i Kogyo, no. 2, (January 1943).

Table 7.6   Efficiency of 20 count cotton yarn, 1929

	Native mills	Japanese mills
Output per spindle per hour	0.025–0.033lb	0.037–0.045lb
Output per worker in charge of spinning process per hour	5.37–5.83lb	8.27–9.09
Spindles per man-hour labour	165–240	200–240

Source: Norio Moriya, *Boseki Seisanhi Bunseki*, (Tokyo, 1948), pp. 400–1.

PURCHASING AND SELLING

The Japanese local mills were provided with abundant working capital with which they could purchase raw cotton in large quantities when the market price was low and so build up stocks. On the Dainippon Cotton Spinning Co.'s balance sheet for the first half of 1923, the accounts of the Shanghai Mill and the Tsingtao Mill count totalled 9.3 million yen, most of which represented the stock of raw cotton. Compared to the fixed assets account of these two mills (16.25 million yen), the working capital was considerable.[34] Kanegafuchi Cotton Spinning Co., which held 99 per cent of the total shares of Shanghai Silk Manufacturing Co., refused to accept any return from its ordinary or preference shares in its subsidiary during the early years of cotton spinning in China, from the first half of 1923 to the first half of 1927.[35] At the same time the Chinese stockholders of Shanghai Silk Manufacturing Co. continued to receive dividends to the full amount. Kanegafuchi's policy allowed the subsidiary to increase its capital surplus. To the contrary, most of the Chinese cotton spinning firms suffered the burdens of heavy debt and interest.[36] They acquired fixed assets, depending on borrowing to form the firm; they lacked working capital; even if they had no profit, they paid the stockholders. In order to make it easy to raise capital the Chinese firms commonly made an agreement with investors that they would make regular payments on the shares as interest. When they had a profit, they frequently paid disproportionately large dividends, while allocating little to depreciation.

When the Japanese cotton spinning firms began operations in China, many Japanese cotton trading firms had established local branches there. They had built these in order to sell imported goods from Japan. The Japanese local mills took advantage of the purchasing and marketing networks of Japanese trading firms. Their business relations had been cultivated in Osaka and their relationship was called 'an association of fish and water'.[37] The Japanese cotton spinning firms reproduced the tight linkages with the Japanese trading firms in China. The Japanese cotton trading firms purchased raw cotton in the producing districts in India and the USA as well as in China. They offered relatively less expensive cotton to spinners, using their knowledge of world markets. The local mills used a wide range of cottons based on a cotton blending technique.

The Japanese trading firms dealing in cotton goods had also established extensive sales networks in the major markets in inland China as well as in the open ports.[38] Their branch offices were located throughout the country: 53 in Shanghai, 17 in Hankow, 15 in Tientsin, 14 in Tsingtao, five in Jinnan, four in Shasi, three in Zhengzhou and Wuhu, two in Beijing, Fancheng, Chongqing, Yichang, Wanhsien, one in Changteh, Wuhsueh, Chiuchiang, Laohokow, Zhangjiakou, Urga, Daye, Yantai, Changsha and Canton in 1919. Mitsui Bussan had branches in Shanghai (with 140 Japanese employees), Tsingtao (64), Tientsin (70), Hankow (81), Canton (16), Yantai (ten), Jinnan (seven), Beijing (six), offices in Wuhu (three), Shantou, Amoi and Fuzhou, and dispatched agents to Changsha (six officers), Chongqing (three), Changteh, Zhangjiakou (two each), Zhengzhou, Wuhsueh, Wanhsien, Urga (one each). In Manchuria it set up branches or offices in Dairen (127 employees), Antung (seven), Niuchuang (11), Liaoyang (ten), Tiehling (11), Changchun (14), Harbin (22) and Vladivostok (eight).

The Japanese-owned cotton spinning mills in China organized a shipping conference *Immen Unka Ren-ekikai* (Association for Transportation of Indian Cotton to China) to reduce the cost of transportation of Indian cotton to China.[39] The Japanese Cotton Spinners Association in China, organized by 13 Japanese spinning firms located in Shanghai and Tsingtao in June 1925, together with three major cotton trading firms (Toyo Menka Co., Nihon Menka Co. and Gosho Co.) concluded an agreement for a discount rate for transportation of cotton with three major shipping companies (Nihon Yusen Co., Osaka Shosen Co. and P. & O. Navigation Co.), which had regular lines between China and India. A total of 18 Chinese firms and 16 Western firms, including spinning firms and trading firms in both cases, joined in the conference. As a result the cotton freight costs between Bombay and Shanghai were cut from 27.5 rupees to 15 rupees per ton. This association for transportation of Indian cotton to China mirrored the shipping conference of Indian cotton (between the shippers of cotton spinners, cotton merchants and a shipping company) organized in Japan in 1893.

CONCLUSION

Incoming foreign firms suffered handicaps in local operation compared to native firms. In order to be successful in local operations, the foreign firms had to have the competitive edge against the native firms, allowing them to overcome the cost of distant operations. The Japanese cotton spinning firms had to become competitive to survive and grow in China.

The Japanese local mills were not given any discriminative advantages over the native mills in access to the capital goods, the latest technology, labour markets and the raw cotton market. Both the Japanese mills and their competitors were equipped with machines made in Britain or the USA, and employed Chinese workers. They consumed Chinese cotton Japanese mills used imported Indian cotton to some extent in addition to the Chinese cotton by mastering the cotton blending technique.

All managerial posts, including the front-line managers, were staffed by Japanese employees who were transferred from home mills in Japan. Much production know-how, which had been developed and sophisticated in Japan, was transferred to and implemented in China under this management organization. Regular maintenance, repair and improvement by replacement of parts, sophisticated adjustment with machine gauges of all processes, and response to varying qualities of cotton and spinning conditions were realized under the direction of the Japanese engineers and technicians through persistent effort. The cotton blending technique was made possible at the local mills because of them. Chinese workers were trained and educated according to a systematic programme. Rigid work discipline was required to be observed inside the mill. Instructors helped workers' skills improve. Through the transfer of this engineering know-how and labour management, the Japanese local mills created productivity and product quality gaps between themselves and the native and Western mills.

Purchasing agents of Japanese mills chose less expensive types among a variety of raw cottons, to suit the yarns and cost schedules they had in mind. Japanese mills, with their strong financial position, purchased raw cotton in large quantities when market prices were low in order to reap the scale economies of stockpiling. They purchased raw cotton from local branches of the Japanese cotton trading firms in China and sold their manufactured goods through the local marketing network of these firms. The reliable ties with cotton merchants, which had been developed in Osaka, revived in China and contributed to purchasing and selling to the benefit of the Japanese local mills.

NOTES

1. On the process of Japanese cotton spinners' investments in China before the Second World War, see the following: Tetsuya Kuwahara, 'Senzen ni okeru Nihon Boseki Kigyo no Kaigai Katudo' ('The Overseas Operations of Japanese Cotton Spinning Firms before the Second World War: Kanegafuchi Cotton Spinning Co.'), *Rokkodai*

Ronshu, **22**, no. 1, (1975); 'The Business Strategies of Japanese Cotton Spinners, 1890–1931: Overseas Operations', in Shinichi Yonekawa and Akio Okochi (eds), *The Textile Industry and Its Business Climate, Proceedings of the Fuji Conference*, **8**, (Tokyo, 1983); 'Japanese Cotton Spinners' Direct Investments into China before WWII', in L. Leboyer, H. Nussbaum and A. Teichova (eds), *Historical Studies in International Corporate Business* (Cambridge, 1989).

2. On this and the next paragraphs, refer to Yen Chungping (translated by Yosi-ie Yoda), *Chugoku Kindai Sangyou Hattatusi (The History of Modern Chinese Industrial Development)* (Tokyo, 1966), pp. 443–70 and Naosuke Takamura, *Kindai Nihon Mengyo to Chugoku (The Modern Japanese Cotton Industry and China)* (Tokyo, 1982), p. 93.

3. T. Kuwahara, 'Senzen ni okeru Nihon Bosekikigyo no Kokusaika Senryaku' ('International Business Strategies of Japanese Cotton Spinners before WWII: Osaka Godo Cotton Spinning Co.'), *Keizai Keiei Ronso*, **21**, no. 4, (1987), p. 209.

4. Dainippon Boseki Rengokai (ed.), *Menshi Boseki Jijo Sankosho (Reference Book of Japanese Cotton Spinning Industry)*, volumes of relevant years.

5. Yen Chungping, *Kindai*, p. 481.

6. Sanji Muto, 'Fukumeisho' ('Mission Report') dated 1899, *Muto Sanji Zansyu (The Complete Works of Sanji Muto)*, **2**, (Tokyo, 1968), pp. 391–8.

7. Kenzo Kadono, personal communication, 12 March 1986, and letters from Suematsu Baba, 13 July 1986.

8. Personal communication from S. Baba, 13 July 1986 and T. Oka, 30 April 1986.

9. Personal communication from Zen-ichi Shirane, 1 and 22 March 1986.

10. Norio Moriya, *Boseki Seisanhi Bunseki (Analysis of Process Cost of Cotton Spinning)* (Tokyo, 1948), p. 317.

11. Personal communication from T. Oka, 30 April 1986.

12. Data prepared by Soumu-bu (the Department of General Affairs), Unitika Kabushiki Kaisha, 1979.

13. Personal communication from T. Oka, September 1989.

14. Toshiyoshi Okabe, 'Chugoku no Kigyo Keiei ni okeru Ningenkankei' ('Human Nexus in Chinese Firms'), *Jinbun Kagaku*, **1**, no. 3, (1946), pp. 169–70; T. Okabe, 'Sina Boseki Rodo no Tei-seisansei' ('Low Productivity of Chinese Labour in Cotton Spinning'), *Toa Sen-i Kogyo*, no. 2, (January 1943), pp. 445–8.

15. Wang Tze-chien and Wang Chen-chung (eds), translated by Fumio Kunimatsu, *Sina Bosekigyo (The Chinese Cotton Spinning Industry: Survey of Cotton Spinning Mills in the Seven Provinces)* (Tokyo, 1940), pp. 201–2.

16. T. Okabe, 'Chugoku no Kigyo', pp. 69–74.

17. Kosuke Moriyama, 'Sina Bosekigyo no Dassenteki Arisama ni Tsuite' ('On the Disordered State of the Chinese Cotton Spinning Mills'), *Dainippon Boseki Rengokai Geppo* (January, 1919), pp. 27–8.

18. Sanji Muto, 'Fukumeisho'. Taichi Kinukawa, *Heiwa to Sina Mengyo (The Chinese Cotton Industry in Peacetime)* (Tokyo, 1919), pp. 191–2. Freda Attley, 'Eijin no mitaru Zaishi Bosekigyo' ('The Chinese Cotton Spinning Industry Observed by an English Woman'), *Toyo Boeki Kenkyu*, **18**, no. 10, pp. 7–8.

19. The Japanese cotton spinning firms used mule frames only during their very early years, when they were learning by trial and error to develop an appropriate cotton spinning technology for mills in Japan. From around 1890, they used ring frames only. The adoption of ring frames is thought to have contributed much to the rapid development of the Japanese cotton spinning industry.
    Automatic weaving machines were installed in mills in Japan for the first time in 1900. The machines were Northrop by Draper. But they could not operate them satisfactorily. They took off the automatic devices and used the machines as ordinary power looms. It was after about 1925 that they began operating automatic looms. Toyo Boseki Kaisha, *Hyakunen Shi Toyobo (One Hundred Years of the Toyo Cotton Spinning Co.)* (Osaka, 1986), pp. 103–4.

20. Personal communication from K. Kadono, March 1984.

21. T. Kinukawa, *Heiwa to Sina Mengyo*, pp. 195–6.

22. Wang and Wang, *Sina Bosekigyo*, pp. 201–2.
23. Personal communication from T. Oka, March, April 1986.
24. For this understanding of cotton blending techniques, see Manji Iijima, *Nihon boseki Shi (The History of the Japanese Cotton Industry)* (Osaka, 1947), pp. 465–6, and Keizo Seki, *The Cotton Industry of Japan* (Tokyo, 1956), pp. 57–9.
25. T. Okabe, 'Sina Boseki Rodo Ukeoi Seido no Hattatu' ('The Development of the Labour Contracting System of Cotton Spinning in China'), *Toa Keizai Ronso*, 1, no. 1, (1941), pp. 141–2, 201–3.
26. These were the practices at the Shanghai Mill of the Yuhon Cotton Spinning Co. around 1938. Toyo Boseki Kaisha (ed.), 'Aoki Yoshio Kaisoroku' ('Memoirs of Yoshio Aoki'), recorded on 14 January 1963, Toyo Boseki Syashi Shiryo (manuscript, 1986).
27. This practice of training Chinese workers was sometimes misunderstood as the recruitment of Chinese for the mills in Japan and caused opposition among the public who felt their jobs were threatened. This and the next paragraphs are based on the following sources: Danzo Tachikawa, *Watashino Ayundamichi (My Footsteps)* (1970), pp. 149–50; Kanegafuchi Boseki Kaisha, 'Shanghai Seizo Kenshi no Keika' ('Course of Shanghai Silk Manufacturing Co.') (manuscript, June 1968), Fukushima Boseki Kaisha, *Fukushima Boseki Goju Nen Ki (The Fifty Years of Fukushima Cotton Spinning Co.)* (Osaka, 1942), p. 161.
28. The procedure of the training programme for female workers in detail is available in Toa Dobunkai (ed.), *Sina Kogyo Soran (General View of Chinese Manufacturing Industry)* (Tokyo, 1931), pp. 93–5.
29. Personal communication from T. Oka, 8 June 1986.
30. Wang and Wang, *Sina Bosekigyo*, p. 202.
31. Ibid., pp. 201–2.
32. Shigeo Imura, *Boseki no Keiei to Seihini (The Management and Products of Cotton Spinning Firms)* (Shanghai, 1926), pp. 353–6.
33. Wang and Wang, *Sina Bosekigyo*, p. 203; Arno Pearse, *The Cotton Industry of Japan and China* (1929), p. 172.
34. T. Kuwahara, 'Zaika bosekigyo no Seisei' ('The Formation of Japanese Cotton Spinning Mills in China'), *Keizai Keiei Ronso*, 16, no. 3, p. 85.
35. T. Kuwahara, 'Senzen' ni okeru Nition Boceki Kigyo no Kaigai Katsudo', p. 15.
36. T. Okabe, 'Kasyo Boseki ni okeru Shihon no Mondai' ('The Problems of Capital of the Chinese Cotton Spinning Firms'), *Sen-i Jukyu Chosei Kyogikai Kaiho*, 3, no. 19, (1942).
37. Yasuzo Horie, 'Bosekigyo Keieishi no Ichisokumen' ('Characteristics of the Business History of the Japanese Cotton Spinning Industry'), *Nihon Boseki Geppo*, 245, (May 1967), pp. 16–18.
38. Kimpusha, *Sina Zairyu Hojin Jinmeiroku (The Directory of Japanese Residents in China)*, 11, (Shanghai, 1920). Mitsubishi Shoji's local branches are not included. As far as it is concerned with Mitsui Bussan's branches in Manchuria see below.
39. Nihon Keieishi Kenkyusho, *Kohon Mitsui Bussan Hyakunen Shi (The Draft of One Hundred Years of Mitsui & Co.)*, 1, (1978), p. 340.
40. Toa Dobunkai (ed.), *Sina Kogyo*, pp. 124–5; Personal communication from Katumi Sato, 14 May 1976. These are preserved as letters, memos and tapes by the present author.

8. Japanese Motor Vehicle Technologies Abroad in the 1980s

Tetsuo Abo

It was during the 1980s that Japanese motor-car manufacturers began in earnest to transplant their production technology abroad, particularly in developed countries, having exported their motor vehicle products on a massive scale since the late 1960s. From the early 1960s, they operated small local plants or had technological assistance contracts with local governments or private firms in developing countries. However the scale of local production and the level of technology brought in were limited to the narrow range that is possible under an import substitution policy in a closed economy. This reluctance to embark on foreign direct investment by the Japanese motor industry, in sharp contrast to its very strong inclination to export, is related to the general nature of Japanese-style production technology itself, which is in turn influenced to a great extent by the sociocultural background in Japan.

In the following study I will first analyse the features of Japanese motor vehicle technologies and outline their international transfers. Then the focus will shift to the activities of Japanese motor firms in the USA, using the materials and data collected and assessed by the joint research team, Japanese Multinational Enterprise Study Group (JMNESG).[1]

FEATURES OF JAPANESE MOTOR VEHICLE TECHNOLOGIES

As Hymer's thesis on multinational enterprise shows,[2] one essential condition for a technology to be transferred abroad is that an industry or a firm have some technological advantage. What kind of advantages are there when Japanese motor-car companies set up their local productions in foreign countries or have licensing contracts with foreign companies? Following Abernathy,[3] it is helpful to divide the question into two aspects – product and process technologies – since a sharp contrast in the different levels of

167

advantage in Japanese industries between these two can be considered as one of the most distinguishing characteristics of Japanese-type technology or know-how. I will take, to begin with, the common features of Japanese industries in terms of product and process technologies and then those of the motor industry.

Advantages of Japanese-type Production Technologies

Generally speaking, Japanese industries have had stronger competitive advantages in process technologies than in product ones. This situation is fundamentally due to the fact that Japan is a latecomer as an industrialized country. Japanese industries and firms have therefore traditionally concentrated their research and development (R&D) efforts on the introduction of theories, ideas and designs related to product innovations invented in more developed, Western countries and on the manufacturing of cost-efficient products by taking advantage of lower wages and a very diligent working people. Since the mid-1960s, especially after the oil crisis of 1973–4, Japanese industries have been greatly concerned with quality of products as well, and with reducing costs of materials and parts by implementing quality circle (QC) activities and just-in-time (JIT) methods (described later), which primarily apply to practices or engineering technologies in manufacturing processes.[4]

What is most significant in the product technologies of Japanese industry is the objective of modifying or improving Western products to suit Japanese market conditions, which are deeply influenced by the natural, economic and sociocultural environment. One typical example of such a product technology is *Kei-Haku-Tan-Sho* (KHTS, light–thin–short–small). The finished goods – from transistor radios, pocket-sized calculators or portable tape recorders, to various kinds of smaller-sized durable goods, such as refrigerators, TVs, vacuum cleaners or motor vehicles – as well as semi-manufactured products, not only parts and components but also materials (such as, typically, steel) have been made lighter, thinner, smaller and so on. These characteristics are profoundly influenced by geographical, social and economic conditions in Japan: small islands, small houses, narrow roads, a traditionally lower level of income, relatively plentiful and high-quality labour, scarce natural resources and so forth. By adeptly responding to such circumstances, Japanese firms have created a modified and even improved product technology as compared with the Western, especially American, models. In this respect it is useful to point out that such a Japanese-type product technology can be an 'interceptor'[5] and transferred to a considerable extent to developing regions or economies, such as many of the Asian countries where the environmental conditions mentioned above are similar to those of Japan. The common feature in this type of product technology or know-how is the steady incremental modifications and improvements of established products to fit changes in market conditions. This produces large product variations and, as also pointed out by Abernathy,[6] is usually seen as a stage of diffusion for a radical product innovation. The main factor in innovation is thus process technology.

In the motor industry, this type of product technology has produced small, sub-compact and even 550 cc mini-cars (called light cars in Japan) as well as many sizes of motor-cycle. In this respect the situation is similar to that of other small countries in Europe. Compared to Japan, Britain has much more road space. In part this is owing to the higher ratio of flat to hilly land, despite the smaller total land area; also the population has been smaller, and the income level of the people has been higher. The Japanese motor industry has therefore had to tailor its product to the needs of each group of customers. It has done so by making the best use of labour-intensive practices, including the subcontract system, and by developing more specific types of motor vehicle, not only smaller in size and lower in price, but also with a larger variety in size, model and cost, on the basis of smaller volume production, than in Britain. It will not be difficult, then, to understand that this traditional background is one of the most important origins in terms of product technology of the earlier and easier development of the recent 'larger variety in smaller volume' production system in Japan.[7]

However it was not until the bombshell of the first oil crisis that these product technologies in the Japanese motor industry acquired a powerful international comparative advantage. Sharp increases in petrol prices and the general atmosphere of resource shortage have made KHTS-type, efficient fuel usage and resource-saving technologies the most favoured internationally, even in US markets. As the air pollution problem is in the same environmental context as the resource shortage one, engine design technology for anti-exhaust emission devices in Japan, such as Honda's CVCC engine and Toyo Kogyo's (Mazda's) rotary engine, have also enjoyed notable superiority over other foreign motor manufacturers. This became apparent after the Clean Air Act (known as the Muskie Act) in the USA (1970) and the standards controlling emissions in Japan (1973) were established. Other Japanese motor manufacturers, Toyota, for example, had to develop comparable anti-pollution engine technology under political pressure from the National Diet and the Environment Agency (created in 1971) against the background of rising public concern about environmental issues.[8] The Japanese situation should be contrasted to that in the USA, where the enforcement of the Muskie Act was postponed and in European countries, where no legislative regulation has been established.

Advantages of Japanese-type Process Technologies

It has been very significant in process technology that, since the 1970s, the Japanese-type production system achieved its comparative advantage over those of other industrialized countries. The level of product quality and efficiency in production at Japanese automotive firms has been far ahead of foreign rivals working to produce a greater variety of cars in smaller volumes with less defects and more resource- and cost-saving methods. Here flexibility emerges as the essential element, but, to put it more strictly, a compatible combination of flexibility and cost-minimizing practices in process technology has become the most decisive and necessary condition for car makers to survive.

A flexible manufacture (or production) system (FMS) has been essential for any manufacturers wishing to adapt to changing market needs in this period. For car makers it is particularly necessary to be able to respond to new tastes for diversification in car models and options in a mature market with limited growth. Two types of FMS are seen among world motor vehicle manufacturers: the Western and the Japanese. Generally speaking, most European and American firms have tried to adapt to this situation primarily by introducing machine- and computer-oriented methods, typically represented by CAD (computer-aided designing), CAM (computer-aided manufacturing), CIM (computer-integrated manufacturing) and so forth.[9] Such methods, mainly supported by numerically controlled (NC) machine tools and robots based on microelectronics (ME) technologies, are of course effective in manufacturing a large variety of models, types and options in smaller or even variable volumes on the same line. This system, however, has soon come up against serious problems in its operation. First of all, it has encountered the problem of 'qualification'; that is, inadaptability of skilled workers. Especially in European countries there are long historical traditions of the apprenticeship which trains skilled workers and gives them qualifications according to their jobs. The system is so firmly established that it is not easy to adapt to the changes of skills reflecting the new FMS. In the USA there has also been a rigid job classification system based on American-style mass-production techniques (Fordism or Taylorism). It is interesting to note that both of these job classification systems have been supported and strengthened by trade unions. The systems therefore cannot adjust to the new process technologies. Often they become one of the major obstacles to introduction of FMS owing to union resistance. A second problem for Western-type FMS is the enormous cost of capital investment. Methods principally relying on capital equipment in order to create flexibility in production processes need huge amounts of money if they are to operate successfully, causing a heavy burden of depreciation costs long after settlement terms.[10]

The Japanese-type FMS, by contrast, essentially relies on the human element. It goes without saying that Japanese car makers have been much ahead of American and European makers in introducing robots and microelectronic-controlled machine tools, though original R&D and the pioneering introduction of robots, CAD and CAM systems and so on were led by American companies.[11] However in Japanese car plants people are still playing key roles at many levels. The plant-level people in the automated FMS are expected, first of all, to be 'multifunctional' or 'intellectual'[12]; that is, having the ability to understand more of the linked processes before and after their own jobs and to be involved in attending the machines as well as the products handled by them. The critical role of shop-floor managers and workers here is to check and respond to usual and unusual changes in the operation of numerically controlled equipment and robots as well as to spot product defects. In the processes of LVSV (large variety in smaller volume) production, various levels of 'usual' changes, such as of models, types and options according to market conditions, would induce more frequent unusual changes, such as missed supply of parts and components, problems or missed adjustment of robots and other ME-controlled machines. In order to cope with these situations, it would be much more costly to bring in more sophisticated machines and more machine coordinators, maintenance specialists and 'checkmen' (quality inspectors) on the shop floor. In Japanese motor plants ordinary workers, besides doing their own regular work, also monitor the proper functioning of the machines they attend and respond to defects in products. As they are more or less 'multiskilled' many of them can be transferred to other work groups or shops as 'temporary helpers' for unusual changes and even to a different plant when their current plant is shut down. As the result of such combinations of machines and shop-floor workers, Japanese plants are being operated very flexibly and incur much lower costs, both for capital equipment and employees, compared to Western car companies.

This raises the question, how can Japanese motor firms train such unique multifunctional workers and managers? An answer is connected to the 'universality–particularity' issue of Japanese-type skill formation. To begin with, this type of skill should be distinguished from a traditional one – the ability to do a specific job, such as shaping, drilling, welding and painting, with the skill of a craftsman–artist. These new types of multiple or versatile skills need not be as intensive as traditional skills because many complex tasks can now be performed by NC machine tools or robots. A less intensive but broader range of skills is required here.

What should be emphasized, in my opinion, is that the Japanese-style workplace-oriented team concept is the basic background for skill formation. It is true, indeed, as K. Koike stresses,[13] that skill formation is a matter of techniques for training workers, but, at the same time, the extent to which the technique is effective largely depends on the various conditions surrounding plants. According to Koike, 'intellectual skills' require shop-floor workers to handle flexibly various kinds of unusual situations during the production process; these skills result from both horizontal and vertical 'career' extension, primarily through 'on-the-job training' (OJT) at the workplace. He also emphasizes that, though developed in Japan, such methods can be generalized as objective and universally applicable production management techniques. It is doubtless useful to see these techniques as the core of Japanese-style skill formation, but I also believe that we should take into consideration the limitations and costs of the international application of such methods. This is closely related to the problem of team concept.

It is my principal understanding that the multifunctional sense and behaviour of employees in Japanese companies cannot be sufficiently acquired through technical training alone because they are deep-rooted in the 'my company' consciousness of almost all Japanese employees. Such behaviour is thought to be, to a considerable extent, the function of employees' loyalty and expectations of the improving performance of their company or shop. Such a strong sense of participation in their company leads employees to pay closer attention to their workplace. And, as is often pointed out, since the 'my company' consciousness in Japan is greatly influenced by the 'high context' of society's group orientation, with people good at communication informally as well as through the more formal structures of companies, we have to take into account here the sociocultural factors.[14] If we neglect these dimensions, we would be unable to explain (a) why Japan alone has diffused such management practices, without being definitely aware of their real meaning,[15] into almost all large firms; and (b) why such a strong spirit of involvement can be easily created at almost every level of staff in a company, as well as in a broad range of subcontractors.

It is well known that the team-oriented centripetal force in Japanese firms is also critical in achieving the incremental accumulation of cost-saving measures, such as bit-by-bit avoidance of waste and defects, or improvements (*Kaizen*) in production know-how.[16] Needless to say, these measures are supplemented by 'voluntary' small group activities with 100 per cent participation, such as QCC (quality control circles) or suggestion systems. The JIT (just-in-time) system,[17] for instance, is one of the typical information-sharing measures, both inside a plant and between an assembler and materials or components vendors, made possible by group orientation. This system was developed mainly for assemblers to minimize inventory stock at the cost of parts suppliers, but now, in the era of LVSV, it has been playing a more important role, not to mention its flexible adjustment of inventory stock, in order to control all the production processes from the vendors to the final assembly lines.

INTERNATIONAL TRANSFER OF JAPANESE MOTOR VEHICLE TECHNOLOGIES

Considering these salient features of Japanese-type culture-embodied production technologies, it is easy to understand why Japanese firms, when applying their technological advantages to foreign countries, would have to face problems in adapting to local environments. Japanese motor technology is heavily culture-specific. We in the JMNESG have therefore created a working model, called the 'application-adaptation dilemma model', which indicates the difficult or even trade-off relationship between both aspects, and have also developed a hybrid ratio (HR, to be mentioned later) to test the correlation between the degrees of application of Japanese management techniques at the plants abroad and of adaptation to the local climates. Hereafter, in accordance with the above point of view, I will draw first an overview on the overseas production activities including licensing agreements of Japanese motor firms and their impact on the technological transfer to local motor industry. Then I will focus on the findings and analysis regarding the degree and situation of application-adaptation of Japanese production and management methods in the USA.

An Overview on the Overseas Production Activities of Japanese Motor Firms

One of the fundamental historical features in the overseas business of Japanese firms is, as mentioned earlier, that leading large manufacturing firms traditionally tried to expand abroad mainly through the export of their products. Further, they were rather reluctant to opt for offshore production through foreign direct investment, opposing both base and host positions. By sharp contrast, Western, and especially American, enterprises were very active in transplanting their production and management methods almost immediately after establishing their US businesses.[18] Recently Japanese firms have begun to change this pattern under the threat of trade friction and the drastic appreciation of the yen. This is also the case with the Japanese motor industry. It is clear that the uniqueness of Japanese-style production technology described above is the principal reason why Japanese motor manufacturers were so reluctant to manufacture abroad. And this situation is closely connected to the manner, degree and regional distribution of technological transfer by Japanese car makers.

Historically, although the start-up of Honda's passenger car production in 1982 in Marysville, Ohio, was so epoch-making, 'grass-roots' small-scale local manufacturing by other Japanese makers had begun in the mid-1960s. Figure 8.1 shows the distribution of the manufacturing and KD (knock down) plants of the Japanese motor vehicle industry, by company and by country, as of the end of March 1989. Many of those plants which were set up before the 1970s are very small-scale assembly facilities in developing countries, mainly in Asia, Oceania and Africa. As KD export-related plants, which range from 'semi-knock down' (bolt and nut completing) to 'complete knock down' (the value of export is less than 60 per cent of a complete car), are major forms, these are classified as export rather than local manufacturing. Indeed, in the regions of Asia, Oceania and Africa, about one-third of total assembly facilities are among 'manufacturing', but most of them are operating under a far lower level of normal economies of scale, which have been imposed by the import substitution policies of the nationalistic local governments. Therefore we cannot simply see them from the usual economical or efficiency point of view; still they should be considered as one limited route of technological transfer from the developed countries to the latecomers.

In these developing regions, the second or third ranking group motor companies are distinguished in local production. Mitsubishi Motor Co. is the most outstanding, in that its number of local manufacturing plants (eight), as well as its total (11), is remarkably large. The company, ranked third to fifth in domestic production, has apparently sought comparative advantage over big competitors in those countries where a combination of minute techniques and know-how in manufacturing, marketing and even political negotiation is required in the tiny markets protected by local regulations policies.

Mitsubishi has taken advantage of its special management resources as a division of the leading corporate group (pre-war *zaibatsu*) by making the best use of its related *sogo shosha* (general trading company), such as Mitsubishi Shoji and Nisho Iwai, and the political influence of Mitsubishi Heavy Industry. The national car project in Malaysia is representative of Mitsubishi Motor's activities. The Proton Corporation, a joint venture of the Malaysia Heavy Industry Development Corporation (70 per cent), Mitsubishi Motor (15 per cent) and Mitsubishi Shoji (15 per cent), started in 1985 to produce two models of passenger cars (1.3–1.5 litre) and jumped up from number four to number one in 1986, producing around 66 000 units in 1989, followed by Nissan (KD plant, 100 per cent local ownership), Toyota (KD plants, 15 per cent) and so on. Mitsubishi Motor also has two joint venture (JV) plants in Thailand which are for KD and engine assembly. And it is interesting to note that these two or three Mitsubishi plants in the South East Asian region have been trying between them to implement an international division of labour in their press parts, engine and so on, though it has been very limited. Judging from the fact that in these markets an 80 to 90 per cent share is occupied by Japanese cars and trucks, we can safely say that the Japanese-type KHTS product technology and human-oriented flexible management and production methods, with Mitsubishi as a typical example, are more applicable there than the Western type. The extent to which the production technology has really been transferred to the local industry and people, however, is not easy to report definitely because there are few and limited field researches on this,[19] and there is another problem – how to evaluate international competitiveness in this kind of closed economy.

In this respect, however, Mitsubishi Motor has also provided good evidence in Korea. Although the Korean motor market has been closed to foreign competitors the sharp increase in production in the Korean motor industry since around 1983 has been supported primarily by export to developed markets, particularly to Canada and the USA. Mitsubishi Motor had an agreement with the Hyundai Motor Co. regarding technology licensing (since 1974) and Joint Venture (JV) (since 1982) in order to produce the Pony. It is clear that these agreements and the related technological cooperation between the two companies must have played a critical role in production areas. Hyundai Motor started to manufacture cars in 1967, as a very late entrant in the motor manufacturing industry, with the assistance of Ford. The technological tie with Ford was abandoned in 1985, when Mitsubishi Motor and Mitsubishi Shoji raised their ownership interests in Hyundai Motor from 10 per cent to 15 per cent (7.5 per cent each). Hyundai has since become an exporter of small cars to the US market. This indicates that Japanese product and process technologies have been substituted for American ones.

In terms of process technology, Mitsubishi must have helped Hyundai learn the fundamental engineering methods and know-how for small-car production which Japanese companies had accumulated. For that purpose Mitsubishi has retained several dozen expatriates from its Japanese operations at the Hyundai plant. This is important, especially for Japanese-style manufacturing practices, since the training system is principally OJT, based on workplace-oriented human relations. It is also interesting to learn that a retired high-level Mitsubishi engineer has been working as a production advisor at the Hyundai plant in Korea. Needless to say, Hyundai, on the other hand, has made the best use of the strong support of the nationalistic government, its organizing power as a newly developed *zaibatsu*, as well as the cheaper labour costs, longer working hours and the undervalued won. Judging from the short plant tour observations made by myself in the spring of 1989,[20] however, Hyundai is now at a turning-point. It will have to improve its techniques at the plant level: for example by mastering the ability to manufacture a larger variety of cars with a lower defect ratio; a smaller volume of inventory stock; a lesser number of workers; and so forth, in order to meet the standards of quality and efficiency in the US market and also in the domestic market where the rapid progress of Kia Motors Corporation is remarkable.

Kia, ranked third, just below Daewoo Motor Co. in 1988 production, was allowed by the Korean government to reopen the production of passenger

Figure 8.1   Distribution of overseas production plants of Japanese motor firms, by country and company, 1989

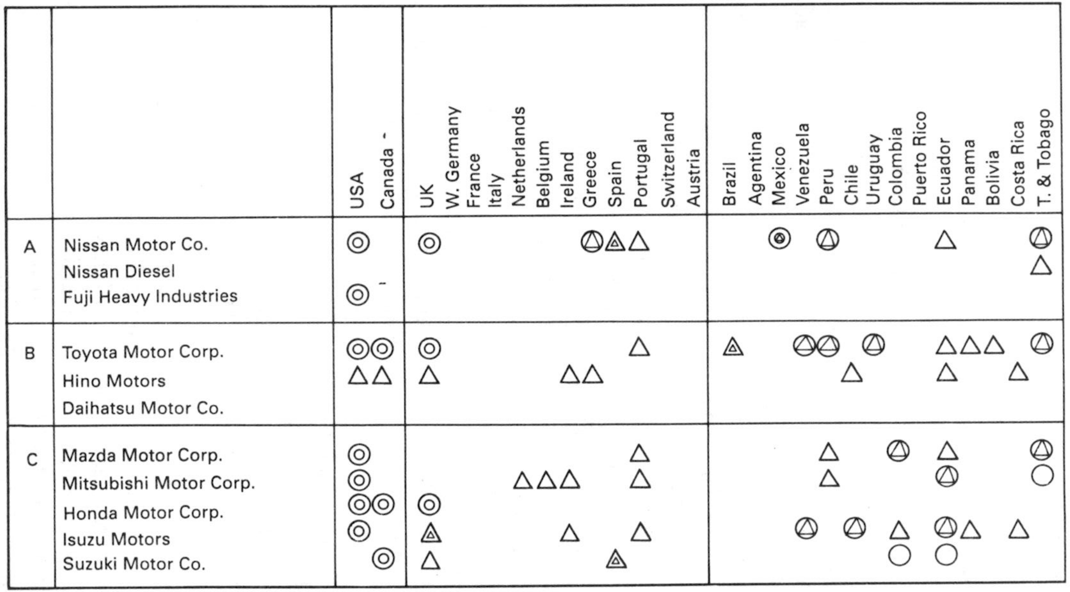

Country columns (reading across the table):
Zaire, Morocco, S. Africa, Algeria, Liberia, Nigeria, Ivory Coast, Congo, Tunisia, Togo, Cameroon, Kenya, Sierra Leone, Egypt, Malawi, Zimbabwe, Turkey, Iran, Iraq, U.A. Emerates, Saudi Arabia, Taiwan, Korea, China, Hong Kong, India, Malaysia, Philippines, Indonesia, Thailand, Singapore, Burma, Bangladesh, Pakistan, Australasia, New Zealand, Micronesia

A — Nissan group
- Nissan Motor Co.
- Nissan Diesel
- Fuji Heavy Industries

B — Toyota group
- Toyota Motor Corp.
- Hino Motors
- Daihatsu Motor Co.

C — Others
- Mazda Motor Corp.
- Mitsubishi Motor Corp.
- Honda Motor Corp.
- Isuzu Motors
- Suzuki Motor Co.

Notes
1. Planned plants are partially included.
2. A: Nissan group B: Toyota group C: Others
3. ⊚ Passenger car manufacturing; ◯ Passenger car KD; ▲ Truck manufacturing; △ Truck KD

Sources: Nissan Motor Co. (ed.), *Jidosha Sangyo Handobukko (Automobile Industry Handbook); Kinokuniya shoten* (1988) (in Japanese) and others.

cars in 1987, with the technological assistance of Mazda Motor Corporation, which in 1983 participated in the capital ownership (8 per cent) of Kia with Itoh Chu (2 per cent), a Japanese general trading company. Kia has been quick to introduce Japanese-style flexible management and production methods, from a sort of LVSV and JIT practices at the plant to organizing a cooperative association of affiliated suppliers. There is only space here to mention the well-known problems which the Korean motor industry has recently faced: from bottlenecks due to insufficient development of the technology, to a lack of key components in sufficient quantities, such as engines and transmission, and of parts suppliers, and the shortage of workers (especially skilled workers), to the drastically appreciated won. It would be tempting to examine the extent to which Korean firms or society are similar to the Japanese in terms of multifunctional flexibility (or individualistic demarcation), team or group orientation and so on, compared with Western countries. However owing to the limitation of data and space, I can only suggest here that there seem to be important similarities between Japanese and Korean societies. At the same time we should not overlook certain differences, a delicate divergence of implications arising from family orientation in Korea and group orientation in Japan, for example.

In Asia, and to a considerable degree in other developing areas as well, as is seen in Figure 8.1, Isuzu Motors Ltd and Hino Motors Ltd are distinguished in their overseas production activities, though both are mainly concentrated in trucks and buses. Isuzu, the world's leading small–medium-sized truck maker, is especially noticeable in that the company has taken advantage of its special connection with GM (General Motors), which has a 40.2 per cent ownership interest in Isuzu. Consequently it has exploited the huge international network of GM management assets. The Isuzu–GM JV truck and commercial car plants in Egypt, the Philippines and the UK are among former GM facilities in which the actual responsibilities of production have been taken over by Isuzu. IBC Vehicles Ltd (former Bedford Motors facility, the UK commercial car maker) is a similar case in a developed country. Isuzu is also an OEM (Original Equipment Manufacturer) supplier for the US market for small-sized passenger cars as well as trucks and transaxles to GM.

Suzuki, the leading mini-car maker in the Japanese domestic market, has a very similar relationship to Isuzu in terms of a business alliance with GM, which owns a 4.95 per cent equity share of Suzuki. At the Toronto plant in Canada, a 50–50 JV with GM, Suzuki started in the spring of 1989 to produce small cars both for GM (OEM) and itself for Canadian and US markets. On the other hand, Suzuki is also characterized as one of the 'grass-root'-type multinational producers in many developing countries. Its activities as a leading car maker in India are of especial interest. Toyota, the overwhelming market leader in Japan, has had relatively wide and deep commitments, particularly in Asia and Oceania, although it has been generally slow in direct foreign investment. In Thailand the company has, since 1962, been eagerly stamping major parts, such as body presses, assembling engines and transmissions and producing finished cars under the closed economy.

In comparison with the above Japanese motor companies, Nissan has been the most internationalized all-round player in terms of the regional distribution of offshore production.[21] It has started up several important foreign manufacturing plants since the mid-1960s, both in developing and developed countries. In developing regions Nissan's salient feature has been the setting up of production facilities, not only in Asian and Oceanian countries, such as Taiwan, Thailand and Australia, but also in Mexico and Spain, where no other Japanese car maker (apart from Suzuki's jeep plant in Spain) operates. Most Japanese makers have been particularly reluctant to manufacture motor-cars in these developing Latin countries, since sociocultural and economic environments there are extremely different from those of Japan. Nissan has somehow managed to develop its manufacturing plants against extremely different cultural backgrounds in these Latin countries for a long period without making substantial profits. In several recent years, however, both these Latin subsidiaries have been making money and are looking forward to better performance.

Nissan Mexico, in particular, is outstanding in that, since it began to assemble motor-cars in 1966, it has been competing in the closed domestic market against the subsidiary plants of major world car makers such as Chrysler, Ford, GM and Volkswagen (VW), all of which were set up before or just after the First World War. Nissan at last took the place of number one producer (market share of 29 per cent, 1988) from VW in 1987. Nissan Mexico has two contrasting plants as well as a small engine casting plant. One is the oldest in Cuauhnabuac, and has been assembling small cars and trucks including some for export (20 per cent of product units) by actively adapting to the various aspects of local environment. It is procuring locally a large variety of parts and components, employing relatively larger numbers of employees (4 860 in 1989) in order to respond to much less flexibility of job rotation (partly because of the policy of traditional unions), a lower level of product quality and so on. It has developed a special engine which is suited to low atmospheric pressure and steep gradients on roads at high altitudes, and it imports a small number of key parts (a company's imports cannot exceed its exports in a given year). Another new plant in Aguascalientes (1 865 employees in 1989) was built in 1983 to manufacture the functional components (engine, transaxle and so on) both for Cuauhnabuac plant and the Smyrna plant in the USA (mentioned later). At this plant, Nissan Mexico took advantage of its location where the influence of unions is weaker. Here Nissan has tried to introduce more aggressively Japanese-style management practices such as a smaller number of job classifications and an individual merit system based on more innovative hardware production technology. Also it has decided to build, in the near future, a new and very advanced assembly facility for small-car manufacture for export to the US market. The combination of these two types of Nissan Mexico plants is one of the most suggestive models of a Japanese motor manufacturer that applies its managerial advantages to developing countries, simultaneously making considerable efforts to adapt to local conditions.

The main overseas production activities of Nissan, however, have been pursued in developed countries. Nissan Motor Manufacturing (UK) Ltd (NMUK) is one example, along with Nissan US, which will be described later. The NMUK plant at Sunderland started to produce cars in mid-1986, far earlier than other Japanese motor manufacturers in the UK (Isuzu at West Bromwich, West Midlands in 1987, mentioned above; the Honda engine plant at Swindon in 1989; the Toyota plant at Derby will be opened in 1992). The NMUK plant seemed, judging from my own observation at the end of 1986, to be eagerly pursuing the transplantation of Japan-style practices at the shop-floor level, as compared with other Nissan plants abroad. The training of multifunctional workers must be among its top priorities because I saw every production worker or 'technician' (with no job classification and covering a very wide range of job elements on a station of the assembly line – a range comparable to that found at its parent plant in Japan) working at an extremely slow speed, at least during the initial phase. Most of the workers trained as technicians would be candidates for team leader and maintenance people in the next phase of plant expansion. The 'single union agreement' is of special importance for these practices in the UK where traditionally a company has to have many contracts with many unions at its plants, resulting in solid walls of demarcation between jobs. NMUK has been able to introduce a sort of individual merit system which evaluates the performance of each worker: consequently the amount of wages paid can be different, from worker to worker, within a small margin, even in the same job classification. This individual evaluation is taken into account in promotion, which obviously affects the work attitude of workers.[22] Notably there is a relatively larger number and a higher level of Japanese expatriates in the UK: as of mid-1989, the ratio of Japanese to total employees (2.6 per cent) is higher than in the US plant (0.6 per cent) and those in Mexico (Aguascalientes, 2.5 per cent and Cuauhnabuac plant, 1.2 per cent respectively). The NMUK has thus learned from experiences derived from Nissan's many plants abroad.

It is interesting that such group-oriented types of production methods have been accepted by NMUK's blue-collar workers (though not necessarily by white-collar ones) in Britain, which is regarded as the mother country of individualism. At the same time, however, we have to take into account the performance of time-consuming and costly practices, productivity and profitability as well as quality, which largely depend on the scale of production. With fewer than 30 000 units produced in 1986 (77 000 in 1989) it is not easy to assess such a level of performance.

Application and Adaptation of Japanese Motor Vehicle Technologies in the USA

Here I will introduce the outline of the interim report of the joint field research project of JMNESG (mentioned at the beginning of the chapter) carried out in 1986 on Japanese motor and electronics plants in the USA, and add to it some new information which was derived from a second plant tour by the same project team during the summer and autumn of 1989.[23] In Table 8.1, we see profiles of major Japanese motor plants in the USA and Canada, as of autumn 1989. Our project team visited the plants in 1986 (plants A–E) and 1989 (plants A–K). It is our policy not to publish the names of the companies which own them. Eight assembly plants of eight makers (three plants for one company and one JV plant for two Japanese companies) and two plants of parts suppliers are included.

The plants A–E in the table are the earliest of these plants. We tried to apply a working model called the 'application and adaptation model' to their local production activities in order to illuminate the level and features of transfer of Japanese-style production systems in the motor industry to the USA. 'Application' is the aspect of an MNE's (multinational enterprise) activities which retain the comparative advantages by introducing its methods to local production facilities. In MNE theory it is referred to as a 'firm-specific factor'. 'Adaptation' is the other aspect of the MNE's activities which involves modifying or adjusting parent practices to the various kinds of local environment. In MNE theory it is described as the 'location-specific factor'.[24] It will be clear, judging from the characteristic features of Japanese-style management described in the first section of the chapter, that it is not easy for Japanese car makers to balance these two types of activity. We thus regard these two aspects as presenting a trade-off relationship or dilemma. What interests us most is, therefore, the degree of the mixture or 'hybrid ratio', in other words the extent to which the system of the Japanese motor industry is either applied or adapted in the USA. In assessing this hybrid ratio we identified over 20 characteristics of Japanese management practices and grouped them into six categories, as shown in Table 8.2. Data were gathered from plant observations and interviews at the above Japanese motor plants in Japan (ten) and the USA (five), and at one other US plant. In order to quantify and illustrate major findings from this study, we then created a five-point grading technique for each category. Within this ranking

Table 8.1 Profile of Japanese motor plants in the USA, autumn 1989

Company	Opening year	Main products	Production capacity (000 units)	Number of employees	Location	Mode of entry
A	1982[1]	passenger cars, motor-cycles	510(360)[2]	6 000(3 900)[2]	Mid-west	wholly owned
B	1983	passenger cars, pickup trucks	265(240)[2]	3 300(3 200)[2]	Mid-south	wholly owned
C	1984	passenger cars	250(250)[2]	2 500(2 500)[2]	West coast	JV(US maker)
D	1984	air conditioners, radiators, etc.		670(420)[2]	Mid-south	wholly owned
E	1985	plastic parts, instruments		410(130)[2]	Mid-south	wholly owned
F	1987	passenger cars	240	3 500	Mid-west	wholly owned
G	1988	passenger cars	200	2 950(3 500)[3]	Mid-south	wholly owned
H	1988	passenger cars	240(100)[4]	2 800(2 900)[3]	Mid-west	JV(US maker)
I	1988	passenger cars	50(25)[4]	710	Canada	wholly owned
J	1989	passenger cars, pickup trucks	60	550(1 700)[3]	Mid-west	JV(JPN makers)
K	1989	passenger cars	200(40)[4]	1 000	Canada	JV(US maker)

Notes
[1] Production of motor-cycles started in this plant in 1979.
[2] Numbers in parentheses are those as of autumn 1986.
[3] Numbers in parentheses are those planned for employees in full production.
[4] Numbers in parentheses are the actual ones produced in 1989.

a five-point score indicates the highest possible degree of 'application' (and, consequently, the lowest level of 'adaptation' – such a score would be given to a Japanese plant operating in Japan). A one-point ranking indicates the highest possible degree of 'adaptation' (and would be given to an American plant operating in the USA). Although these rankings are by no means exact,[25] with these we can easily estimate 'application–adaptation' levels. In Table 8.2, the main findings are as follows.

1. Regarding the meanings of the interrelationships between the six groups, first of all, I (job organization and operation) and II (production control) are the core parts of the Japanese production system at the shop-floor level. III (sense of togetherness) and IV (employment situation) are human-related factors supporting the core parts. V (procurement) involves material factors which have a great influence on efficiency and quality in the operation of the core parts. VI (parent–subsidiary relations) is the upper framework of administrative organization which decides and controls the methods and directions of the core parts.

2. Group I (GI), the organizational framework of the flexible production system, is assessed, on average, as the next highest (3.7) to GIV (4.1). Japanese car makers show a strong inclination to transfer the integral aspects of Japanese production techniques in GI to their plants in the USA in terms of 'method', compared with GII, which reveals, on the other hand, a clear inclination to bring in the Japanese techniques in terms of 'outcome' or 'result'. 'Method' means ideas or know-how about practices regarding process technology which can be transferred only when such practices are actually perceived and realized by local employees. Job classification (JC) will necessarily provide the basis for the implementation of other practices, especially within those in GI. JC is assessed very highly (4.0) because all the Japanese car plants in the USA (and also the Nissan plant in the UK) have adopted an extremely simplified JC system, with essentially only one classification, as contrasted with more than 200 JCs at a normal US motor plant. Even 40 JCs at the US plant which we visited at the same time is exceptional by American standards (this plant was shut down in the summer of 1988).[26] It is interesting to note that such a simplification is not to be seen even in Japan! This is a modification, indeed, but in which direction? I will come back to this point later. As was explained in the second section of this chapter, with such a simplified JC system an equally high score of job rotation (JR, 4.0), training (4.0) and role of supervisor (3.8) were made possible. On-the-job training (OJT) through JR was being tried in order to widen the employee's workplace horizons and his or her multifunctional skills. However the range of JR was primarily limited to a team and wage system (3.0), so was rigidly connected to a simple JC system. A Japanese-style promotion system based on seniority and individual merit evaluation

Table 8.2   Hybrid ratio of Japanese motor plants in the USA, 1986

I		Work organ. & its operation	3.7
	1	Job classification	4.0
	2	Wage system	3.0
	3	Job rotation	4.0
	4	Training	4.0
	5	Promotion	3.5
	6	Role of supervisor	3.8
II		Production control	3.5
	7	Process technology	4.6
	8	Quality control	3.2
	9	Maintenance	2.6
III		Sense of togetherness	3.6
	10	Employment security	4.0
	11	Small-group activity	2.8
	12	Open-style office & dining hall	3.4
	13	Uniform	4.0
	14	Socializing	4.0
	15	Company meeting	3.5
IV		Employment situation	4.1
	16	Homogeneity of employees	3.4
	17	Turnover rate	4.6
	18	Union & labour relations	4.4
V		Procurement	3.3
	19	Local contents	3.2
	20	Suppliers	3.4
VI		Parent–subsidiary relations	3.5
	21	Ratio of JPN expatriates	2.8
	22	Decision making	3.8
	23	Status of American managers	3.8
		Average	3.6

Note: 5=the highest degree of application (the lowest degree of adaptation); 1=the lowest degree of application (the highest adaptation).

Source: Japanese Multinational Enterprise Study Group.

was working only to a certain extent (so 'promotion' is assessed as 3.5). On the other hand, the wage system among production workers who belong to a JC is similar to the American one (so the score is 3.0). This restricts the scope for working a Japanese seniority-related system linked to a correspondingly increasing wage level, which helps to accumulate broader skills based on long-term experience. (In Japan it is an institutional condition that supervisors and technicians, including even maintenance people, should be trained inside the plants by production workers.) Also this wage system makes it difficult to introduce individual merit awards, which motivate workers to increase their income and, even more importantly, acts as a system to evaluate workers for promotion. In this sense, the scores for promotion (3.5) and supervisors (3.8) are not very high at these plants in the USA. In short, Japanese car plants in the USA were especially eager to transfer the 'method' of human-related production techniques, but with some limitations.

3.   The extremely high score of process technology (4.6) in GII meant, by contrast with the above, that the visible 'outcome' of Japanese techniques such as machine, equipment and layout of manufacturing lines, was directly transferred into the Japanese plants in the USA, along with imported parts and components, ensuring the principal competitive advantage of these plants against US makers. On the other hand, quality control (QC, 3.2) and maintenance (2.6) in GII were assessed as among the lowest because the 'method' of QC and maintenance used there was rather similar to the American one: specialist engineers or technicians in the QC and maintenance sections, trained in colleges or vocational schools, were primarily responsible for this work. Although Japanese car plants in the USA emphasize high quality of product and well-maintained automation processes, the ways of implementing the same goal as in Japan have to be much more 'adaptation'-oriented, and therefore are more costly and less flexible.

4.   Among various kinds of human-related elements in GIII and IV, which support GI and II, higher scores of employment security (4.0), turn-over rate (4.6) and union and labour relations (4.4) and the low score of small-group activity (2.8) are particularly noticeable. All Japanese car plants in the USA emphasized a policy (written or unwritten) of avoiding lay-offs for as long as possible. Turnover rate was assessed as very high in terms of 'hybrid ratio' since the actual turnover rates at these plants (around 4 per cent per year) were much lower than those (10 per cent) at the plants of US car makers, though higher than at the Japanese parent plants. These kinds of long-term employment practices, needless to say, are the crucial conditions for the Japanese-style training–promotion system. Four of the five Japanese plants are non-union and the remaining one has accepted UAW (Union of Automobile Workers) under an exceptionally modified agreement in which the drastic reduction of the number of JCs and flexible operation of JR and so on, mentioned above, are possible. With a distinctive difference between the functions of the UAW (United Auto Workers) and the Japanese Federation of Auto Workers in terms of flexibility concerning GI, II and III, it is no wonder that all the Japanese

motor companies prefer non-union plant in the USA. QC (quality circle) activity, one of the typical small-group activities, is among the most difficult of practices for Japanese firms to introduce into the USA. Of course most Japanese plants there, except for one parts maker, were trying to implement some sort of QC but differences from Japanese-style QC were quite clear in many respects: (a) the main goal in the Japanese plants in the USA was just to enhance team and quality consciousness as far as possible. By contrast, in Japan, QC is a team activity for all the production members, intended to improve quality and efficiency (*Kaizen*) in production processes; (b) 'voluntary' participation rates in the USA were 20–30 per cent, compared with the 100 per cent (!) usual in Japan; (c) as a rule, QC activities in the USA were held during company time and paid, while in Japan there is no payment and they are pursued during the workers' own time.

5.   The local contents of three Japanese assembly plants were around 50 per cent and those of two parts plants were 60–70 per cent (score 3.2). In other words, almost half of the parts and components used in major plants, which consisted of key components such as engines, transmissions and axles, were imported mainly from Japan. These were the critical material condition, the 'outcome' of Japanese techniques, which compensated for the insufficient transplant of the core elements. The important difference between this and the above process technology (introduction of machine and equipment produced in Japan) is that imported parts by themselves do not effect technology transfer, whilst the machine and equipment can be a part of it if combined with 'method'.

6.   The ratio of Japanese expatriates in GVI is the key human element which expresses the most significant characteristic of Japanese manufacturing plants in foreign countries. Expatriates play the decisive role in the overall performance of the plants. This is not a problem of system or 'method' but, here also, one of 'outcome' in the form of human beings – although Japanese expatriates can either train or substitute for local employees. The very low score of this ratio (2.8) is a little misleading, because two extreme groups of plants were mixed here. One is a group where the ratios were higher than 5 per cent (score of 4.0) and the ratios in another group were around 1 per cent (1.0–2.0). Either way these ratios must be much higher than in the case of Western MNEs. My special emphasis is that it would be difficult for local Japanese plants to survive (as of autumn 1989) without a considerable number of lower- to middle-level Japanese managers (section managers or managers), called 'coordinators' or 'advisors', who, like the shadows of American or Japanese general managers, take charge of almost all practices, particularly at the shop-floor level. This means that the role of these 'coordinator'-type Japanese expatriates may be even more crucial than that of top managers.

CONCLUSION

Historically, Japanese motor companies have been very reluctant to transplant their production technologies to foreign countries because of the culture-embodied nature of their process technologies which are their main comparative advantage compared with their product technologies. Japanese-type product technologies such as KHTS, however, found their advantage and began to be transferred, first to developing countries and, after the oil shocks, even to developed countries. In Asian countries, Japanese motor vehicle production technologies began to be transferred as an import-substitution measure in closed economies. Later they were transferred to support the export-oriented developments of local motor industries. Here the socio-cultural similarity seems to be one of the important factors for successful transfer. It is also interesting to note that Japanese motor companies in the second and third ranking group have been more aggressive in local production (direct foreign investment) in developing regions and have had various kinds of tie-up relations with local governments or private firms, including US car makers.

In developed countries, according to our joint researches, we can offer the following conclusions regarding the present stage in the transfer of Japanese motor vehicle technologies, particularly to the USA. We have found a strong orientation towards the application of Japanese management practices. In order to apply the human aspect of Japanese 'methods' at the shop-floor level of plants in the USA, Japanese companies, to a considerable extent, have been introducing the core part of practices such as simplified JC, OJT, and JR and the supporting subsystem or conditions such as socializing activities, longer-term employment and cooperative labour relations. At the same time there is particular emphasis on the introduction of hardware or 'outcome' of technologies, such as process technology and key parts, from Japan, which play critical roles in achieving high product quality and efficiency in the production processes. On the other hand, however, Japanese plants in the USA have had to adapt to local conditions and to modify to a greater or lesser extent the original methods, such as, in particular, QC, maintenance and promotion, which should be closely connected with the above core part and subsystem, and are integral aspects of the Japanese production system. As a whole, it should be expressly noted that all the above transplanting processes of Japanese methods are actually enabled to materialize by a considerable number of Japanese expatriates, particularly those called 'coordinators'. In relation to this, one of the most impressive findings during our second-round 1989 plant tour in the USA was that many Japanese coordinators were actively trying to develop the ideas of modifications that cannot yet be seen, either in plants in Japan or in the US plants of

American companies. A good example, as well as the simplified JC, is the 'Skilled Trade Training Program', which has just been tried at plant G. In this programme to select and train maintenance technicians, qualified employees who have passed a certain screening test take a series of training courses that would enable them to learn the essence of multifunctional maintenance skills. At the Japanese parent plants, instead, OJT methods play the primary role in this process, as described earlier. Japanese 'coordinators' in the USA are also energetically contributing to analyse the parent system and to translate it into a 'third form' adaptable to American conditions. Of course, so far, the result is not certain.

To sum up, the overall level of technology transfer of Japanese motor vehicle firms to the USA, maintaining the same level of product quality as in Japan and reducing the productivity gap (productivity is usually said to be 10–20 per cent less than in Japan) entails a sizeable cost both in terms of manpower expense and hardware technologies. The transfer of 'outcomes' of technologies is by no means an actual transplanting of technologies, although Japanese 'coordinators' could train local people to perform Japanese 'methods' so as to reduce costs. At any rate, as the cost performance of the Japanese car plants in the USA has been somewhat better than that of the plants of US motor manufacturers, almost all of those Japanese plants will still be able to survive, so long as 'market discrimination', such as voluntary restraint agreements, tariffs and appreciation of the yen, remain fairly effective in preventing import competition from Japan.

NOTES

1. Japanese Multinational Enterprise Study Group, directed by Professor Tetsuo Abo, University of Tokyo, has been organized since 1983 by Japanese and American researchers and awarded grants from the Toyota Foundation in 1985 and 1987–88 for the researches under the title of 'Japan–US Joint Research on Problems with Local Production by Japanese Manufacturing Firms in the United States: An Assessment of Japanese-Style Management Transferability in the Automobile, Consumer Electronics and Semiconductor Industries'. We undertook field studies in the summer/autumn of 1986 and 1989 in the USA and have published in 1990 the English version of the interim paper for the preliminary research submitted to the Toyota Foundation and published by the Japanese in 1988: The Institute of Social Science, University of Tokyo, *Local Production of Japanese Automobile and Electronics Firms in the United States: The 'Application' and 'Adaptation' of Japanese Style Management* (Research Report No. 23, 1990).
2. S.H. Hymer, 'The International Operations of National Firms: A Study of Direct Foreign Investment', MIT, PhD thesis, 1960.
3. W.J. Abernathy, *The Productivity Dilemma: Roadblock to Innovation in the Automobile Industry* (Baltimore, 1978), chs 1–4.
4. The emphasis of Japanese manufacturing firms on process or engineering technologies can be shown, for example, in the international comparison of the number of graduates of BEng and BSc in the following table:

	Japan		USA		UK		W. Germany	
	1975	1987	1975	1983	1974	1985	1975	1985
B Eng	65 422	75 843	53 520	128 195	10 374	16 600	4 344	7 869
BSc	9 504	13 389	88 990	75 522	15 479	25 100	4 656	8 184

Source: Japan Ministry of Education, *International Comparison of Indicators on Education* (Tokyo, 1988) (in Japanese).

5. T. Ozawa, *Multinationalism, Japanese Style* (Princeton, 1979), pp. 206–11.
6. Abernathy, *Productivity Dilemma*, especially ch. 2.
7. T. Ohno, *Toyota Seisan Hoshiki (Toyota Production System)* (Daiyamondo Sha, 1978), ch. 1, *passim*; M. Cusumano, *The Japanese Automobile Industry* (Cambridge, Mass., 1986), ch. 5.
8. Toyota Motor Corporation, *Toyota: A History of the First 50 Years* (Toyota City, 1988), pp. 203–9.
9. US Dept. of Commerce, *The US Automobile Industry, 1984* (Washington, DC, 1985); *Ward's Automotive Yearbook* (Detroit, various issues, especially 1984–7).
10. 'Make-or-Break Time', *Fortune*, 15 February 1988; T. Abo, 'The Capital Expenditures of US Manufacturing Industries in the 1980s', *Sekai Keizai Hyoron* (*World Economic Survey*) (November 1988).
11. See T. Abo, 'New Technology and Manpower Utilization in Japanese Automobile Firms in Japan and Their Plants in the United States', in Sung-Jo Park (ed.), *Technology and Labor in the Automotive Industry* (Frankfurt/New York, 1991). Papers of the Seoul International Symposium sponsored by the Korean Automobile Manufacturers Association.
12. K. Koike, *Understanding Industrial Relations in Modern Japan* (London, 1988), pp. xiii–xv and 266 ff.
13. Ibid.
14. E.T. Hall, *Beyond Culture* (New York, 1976), p. 39 and chs 6–8; also see T. Abo, 'The Emergence of Japanese Multinational Enterprise and the Theory of Foreign Direct Investment', in T. Shibagaki, M. Trevor and T. Abo (eds), *Japanese and European Management: Their International Adaptability* (Tokyo, 1989), pp. 11–12.
15. It is interesting to learn the following stories regarding this. One of the members of the board of directors in the Japanese headquarters of plant B, who had been an advisor to the first American president at that plant, told us that Japanese people could not answer immediately after they were asked by the American president staying at a Japanese plant how Japanese practices were created, because they had not necessarily developed all such practices on purpose. The active Japanese coordinators at plant G told us that, when they tried to develop modified training methods for the American plant of the Japanese parent plant, described on page 87–8, they had to reinterpret for themselves the real meaning or 'logic' of what they are practising at their Japanese plants, which is now a world-famous production system.
16. *Kaizen* essentially means, said a Japanese vice-president at plant H, 'that people do more than what is decided to do'.
17. Regarding JIT, see Y. Monden, *Toyota Production System* (Atlanta, 1983), chs 2–3.
18. Regarding the reluctant nature of Japanese multinationals, see M. Trevor, *Japan's Reluctant Multinationals* (London, 1983); M. Yoshino, *Japan's Multinational Enterprises* (Cambridge, Mass., 1976). As for some examples of the active American multinationals, see T. Abo, 'American Automobile Enterprises Abroad during the Interwar Period Case Studies on Ford and General Motors with Emphasis on the Process of Their Multinational Adaptation to Local Climates', *Annals of the Institute of Social Science* (University of Tokyo) no. 22, (1981); also Mira Wilkins, *The Maturing of Multinational Enterprise: American Business Abroad from 1914 to 1970* (Cambridge, Mass., Harvard University Press, 1974).
19. International joint research directed by Professor Shoichi Yamashita, Hiroshima Uni-

versity, (University of Tokyo Press, 1990), is among the most useful regarding this, but not specifically for the motor industry. Professor Hiroshi Itagaki, Saitama University and a member of our JMNESG, made several on-site researches on Japanese car plants in ASEAN countries in the autumn of 1989 and kindly provided me with some recent information about those plants. Also Nissan Motor Corporation, *The Handbook of Motor Vehicle Industry* (1988) and *Overseas Productions of Nissan Motor* various issues (both in Japanese), are very useful sources and have data for other motor companies besides Nissan.

20. The major Korean motor manufacturers invited foreign researchers including myself to their plants when they sponsored an international workshop in the spring of 1989 (see note 11).

21. People at Nissan Motor have been very cooperative in arranging my plant tours and interviews in many countries, such as the USA (1986, 1989), the UK (1990), Spain (1987), Mexico (1989) and Japan, which has been a great help for the present chapter.

22. P. Wickens, *The Road to Nissan* (London, 1987), ch. 8 is also very useful. (The author accepted me as one of the interviewees at the UK plant in 1986.)

23. Regarding the joint field researches of JMNESG, besides the forthcoming interim report and my papers (see notes 11, 26), see the several outcomes in English by its members: D. Kujawa and M. Yoshida, 'Cross-Cultural Transfers of Management Practices: Japanese Manufacturing Plants in the United States', paper presented at the 1987 Annual Meeting of the Academy of International Business in Chicago; H. Itagaki, 'Application–Adaptation Problems in Japanese Automobile and Electronics Plants in the USA', in Shibagaki *et al.*, *Japanese and European Management*; R. Grosse and D. Kujawa, *International Business* (Irwin, 1988), pp. 322–7.

24. J.H. Dunning, *International Production and Multinational Enterprise* (George Allen & Unwin, 1981) Part One. N. Hood and S. Young, *The Economics of Multinational Enterprise* (London, 1979), ch.2.

25. We decided an evaluation criterion for each item in Table 8.2 according to Japanese model (5) and American model (1). But for the items for which we could not find any quantitative index we had to judge the scores from qualitative information through very intensive discussion.

26. For this American plant, also see T. Abo, 'The Application of Japanese-Style Management Concepts in Japanese Automobile Plants in the United States', in B. Dankbaar, U. Jurgens and T. Malsch (eds), *Die Zukunft der Arbeit in der Automobilindustrie* (Berlin, 1988), pp. 333–5.

PART III

Transfers of Management

9. Diffusion of Management Thought and Practice, 1880–1970

Jennifer Tann

Management, as John Child has observed,[1] can be considered from three major perspectives. It can be regarded as an economic resource performing a series of technical functions concerned with the organizing and administering of other resources; alternatively, management can be viewed as a system of authority by which policy is translated into the execution of tasks; thirdly, management can be regarded as a social elite which acts as an economic resource and maintains the associated system of authority. It is the first two perspectives which inform the following discussion of the origins and development of management thought and practice. In addition, three major themes underpin the discussion: first, the lag between theory and practice; second, the penetration of the diffusion of new management practices and the representativeness of the adopters; and third, the extent to which the managers of adopting firms were capable of disaggregating the bundle of features constituting a management innovation and selecting those aspects best suited to their business situation.

Some of the most significant and robust features of twentieth-century industrial management can be demonstrated to have derived from the environment under which the genesis of management in the late eighteenth and early nineteenth centuries took place. Nevertheless, although the managerial methods adopted were generally, although not always, adequate to the demands of the time, they were rarely 'very brilliant or very central'.[2] Management was not a cause of Britain's Industrial Revolution, but it was an instrument of the forces which shaped ownership and control, functional specialization and the emergence of methods of record keeping.

Before the new developments in management thought and practice in the twentieth century are explored it is appropriate to consider the broader context from which these developments grew. By the beginning of the

nineteenth century, entrepreneurs and managers of firms at the leading edge
in manufacturing industry and mining were encountering new demands for
organizing and controlling resources. Technological innovation entailed
managerial choice and the evaluation of one technique or process against
another; vertically integrated factories demanded effective production planning and a growing sophistication in the design of flow production systems;
production cycles were required in batch production facilities such as iron
smelting; and a logical sub-division of labour characterized many of the
larger manufacturing organizations. These newly emerging forms of work
organization entailed the identification of specific skills and the negotiation
of contracts in which functional specialization and hierarchy were reflected
in wages.[3] Managerial control became a necessary function in the organizing
of production; the human resource, referred to by Ure and Babbage as the
'human machine',[4] required recruiting, training, disciplining and retaining.
Intricate forms of subcontract emerged, acting as a bridge between practices
that were characteristic of proto-industry and those of the corporate economy.

As the task of the manager became more complicated and the difficulty of
knowing whether or not a firm was in profit increased, demands for increased financial information in order to facilitate decision making emerged.
The widely held orthodox view,[5] reiterated in the 1980s,[6] was that, in the
absence of known evidence of the fairly general employment of cost accounting, it must be deduced that there had been little demand for information on costs in the Industrial Revolution. Two explanations have been
proffered. Solomons draws attention to an absence of keen competition,
together with pricing levels which gave generous profit margins.[7] Johnson puts
down the survival of old systems of financial accounting and the apparent
non-appearance of cost accounting to the fact that the typical company was a
'single activity organization' with a single product or a narrow range of
related products.[8]

It has been shown,[9] however, that some leading eighteenth-century entrepreneurs recognized the need for cost accounting, and Edwards and Newell,[10]
in challenging the established orthodoxy, have made the significant point
that cost accounting records were kept by managers, not by the bookkeepers
who kept the financial accounts. Historians have not been looking for evidence of cost accounting in the appropriate places. In drawing together new
evidence of cost accounting, Edwards and Newell claim that a 'growing
body of evidence shows that *ad hoc* costing data was much more widely used
as the basis for management decisions than has previously been believed the
case'.[11] Having made the distinction between cost accounting and management accounting, the former being concerned with the identification and
accumulation of costs, the latter with the provision of statistical information
for planning, decision making and control, Edwards and Newell conclude

that 'many of the tools of modern management accounting were, therefore, in use by 1850'.[12]

By the early 1800s, there was a clear notion of managerial hierarchy in the larger organizations and a managerial class of paid managers had emerged. In organizations with several partners, management functions were sometimes divided amongst the partners as well as devolved to deputies. Where there was a single owner-manager, administration of resources and managerial control had, of necessity, to be devolved in part to a range of deputies. Where production was carried out at more than one site, greater autonomy prevailed, either by conscious devolution or by assumption.[13]

While leaders in different sectors of manufacturing industry shared experience with their counterparts in other sectors,[14] and keen observation promoted the diffusion of best practice in management, there was no body of management theory on which to draw. There was the assumption, amongst those who sought to describe management practice in their own works,[15] that the practices they were describing were largely sector- or site-specific. Management, as evidenced by the surviving manuscript examples, was closely concerned with the management of technical functions and of labour, in so far as the efficient use of machinery was concerned. None of these innovators in management practice sought to publish their thoughts. This may have been largely owing to a desire to protect their competitive edge in a period of rapid technological change.

In the 1820s and 1830s, a number of studies covering the important large-scale industries of the period began to be published. The works of Ure and Montgomery on the cotton industry, Thompson on coal mining, Griffiths on iron making and Evans in engineering are examples.[16] While they were mainly concerned with the technology of their respective industries and the associated production planning, they incorporated the codification of managerial experience too. There were, in addition, encyclopaedias and, most important of all, Babbage's study, *On the Economy of Machinery and Manufactures*, published in 1832 and running to four editions in as many years.

Charles Babbage spent many years visiting workshops and factories both in Britain and on the Continent and it was observations arising out of his interest in calculating machines which led to the writing of his book.[17] In this he tried to apply 'those principles of generalization to which my other pursuits had naturally given rise'. This excursion took him into economics and also into an analysis of the amount of labour needed for different parts of the production process. In this Babbage was many years ahead of his time and a notable predecessor of Frederick Taylor, whose published pronouncements on scientific management first appeared 71 years later, in 1903.

The question as to why there was such a long lead in management practice before a theory of management began to develop can have no single answer. The Industrial Revolution and its aftermath and indeed the great Victorian boom were periods of successive structural changes in technology during which it was difficult to isolate a managerial function from that of technical supervision and commercial control and it was to these aspects of management that the first British theorizers addressed themselves. Furthermore many of the issues of greatest concern to entrepreneurs of the eighteenth and nineteenth centuries were to do with external context, the business environment. The infrastructure of business was required to be developed in order to enable firms to grow; thus we find manufacturers of the day engrossed in the problems of transport, banking, housing and education.[18] It is a point echoed by contemporary writers on the subjects of industry and individual firms and their founders, who focused on heroic individualism rather than seeking to identify areas of commonality in entrepreneurship. As Pollard has said, 'Each firm (much more so than today) was a law unto itself.'[19]

A further issue is that of managerial attitudes to the labour process. There was, on the one hand, the belief that labour was hostile to the factory system and that cultural norms needed to be broken in order that a new time work discipline could be imposed.[20] From this perspective labour was subservient to the clock and to the factory machine. By contrast there were those philanthropic employers who believed that the human resource, the 'human machine', needed to be well cared for to optimize efficiency.[21] These two strands provide a thread of continuity, albeit fractured and diffuse, to the twentieth century.

The first major text addressing issues of central concern to management was Schloss's work, published in 1892.[22] While being a landmark for this reason, the book has, nevertheless, more in common with the earlier nineteenth-century industrial treatises than with the emerging theory of management of the early twentieth century. Schloss introduces his book with a statement which emphatically places the labour process on the agenda: 'Of all the questions which press for an answer at the present moment, none is fraught with weightier issues than the Labour Problem.' The central issue 'has two branches, the one of which relates to the amount, the other to the method of industrial remuneration'. Schloss was sensitive to what he believed to be well-founded allegations concerning 'harsh and exacting task-masters' and the lack of representation and was aware that changes were needed in both supervision and subcontracting.

The bridge between the two centuries was provided by Frederick W. Taylor (1856–1915), and it is with Taylor that the locus of management theory shifted to the USA. Taylor became foreman in the machine shop of the Midvale Steel Works in Philadelphia in the early 1880s and turned his attention to the question of labour productivity. His first approach was from the engineering perspective, in which he considered the question of the improvement of machinery. After a series of experiments he succeeded in developing high-speed cutting steel, and improved machine tool design as well as setting out methodologies for the most efficient use of the improved tools. It was this latter aspect which bridged the nineteenth and twentieth centuries: the manner in which tools were used by employees having been addressed, it was but a short step to the analysis of work methods, an aspect of production which had, until then, been little considered by engineers.[23]

Taylor brought his work to the attention of a wider public in the USA in three publications: *Shop Management*, a paper presented to the American Society of Mechanical Engineers in 1903; *The Principles of Scientific Management*, written in 1909 but not published until 1911; and his 1912 testimony to the Special House Committee, in which he presented a justification of his views following public criticism of his approach. The essence of Taylor's work is that, through detailed research involving the measurement of time and job design, together with the analysis of raw materials, equipment, work flows and reward systems, management would be able to determine the optimal levels of output, as well as changes in the specifications for tools and materials, the selection and training of workmen and the supervision of work. Only when this foundation had been laid would it be possible to gear reward systems to individual output. Taylor maintained that it was through this combination of methods – and he visualized this as a tightly linked package[24] – would it be possible to obtain the dramatic increases in efficiency sought by management. Although Taylor recognized that it would be important to obtain workpeople's cooperation, it would have to be 'enforced co-operation'. In Taylor's words:

> It is only through enforced standardization of methods, enforced adaptation of the best implements and working conditions and enforced co-operation that this faster work can be assured. And the duty of enforcing the adaptation of standards and of enforcing this co-operation rests with the management alone.[25]

Many commentators have emphasized Taylor's contribution to the development of work study through the translation of the observation techniques employed in studying metal cutting machines to the movements of workers' bodies in the prosecution of work tasks.[26] Operations were broken down into their smallest components and carefully timed. It became possible to construct an ideal method for various tasks and to 'eliminate all false movements, slow movements and useless movements'. Allowances of time for fatigue could also be mathematically computed and in this way Taylor strove to discover 'the one best method' for accomplishing work in the shortest possible time.[27] This system arose, as Braverman notes,[28] from Taylor's observations of output regulation employed by workers. The practice had been adopted by workers as a defence against piece-rate cutting and the possibility of job loss resulting from productivity increases. Management had been compelled to respond, as predicted, by piece-rate cutting since it lacked the kind of detailed knowledge of production which would have enabled productivity to be raised. It was, as Wood and Kelly point out,[29] this knowledge which Taylor set out to acquire through work study. He soon came to realize, however, that, if labour productivity was to be raised, improvements had to be achieved simultaneously in machine maintenance, materials and tools supply, work flow and detailed supervision.

A contribution to increased productivity was to be made by the standardization of tools in the context of the needs of specific tasks. Taylor conducted an experiment at the Bethlehem Steel Works on the shovelling of coal, finding that the average shovel load varied by about 22 lb. He experimented with different types of shovels for different materials, with the consequence that, after some time, workers received written instructions concerning what kind of shovel to use for what material. Taylor was concerned that tasks be allocated to the most appropriate worker in each case: 'There is work for each type of man ... there is no type of work, however, that suits all types of man.'[30] Individual workers required formal training and specific instructions on the performance of prescribed motions with standardized tools and materials.

Taylor's conception of control emerged in the course of his observations and writing. In his publication, *A Piece Rate System*, there was little emphasis on control, for Taylor was still working within a classical economics conception of the employment relationship as an economic exchange.[31] Work study would, he believed, be accepted because workers would realize that increased productivity would lead to increased wages. It was his own work experience at both Midvale and Bethlehem Steel that led him to believe that it was important to apply knowledge gathered through the scientific study of production to the control of the labour process. This wresting of control from labour has been, as Wood and Kelly observe,[32] much misunderstood. They point out that knowledge is not a commodity that can be lost by labour and that Braverman and others have conflated the acquisition of knowledge with its monopoly by management. Workers continued to possess their knowledge, but they lost 'the advantage of management ignorance'.[33]

Associated with time measurement, job design and the analysis of raw material, equipment and work flows, was the notion of payment in accordance with output. Having identified how the methods and the rate of production could be planned, Taylor developed systems of differential payment, the essence of which was the payment of bonuses to workers who met or exceeded the defined 'task'. The 'task' constituted the agreed output achieved within a stated period of time. The essential feature of this was that each worker should be paid in accordance with his individual output, rather than in respect of the group, for 'each man in the gang becomes far less efficient than when his personal ambition is stimulated'.[34]

Opposition to Taylor's ideas and practices was manifested not only on the shop floor amongst workpeople and foremen but also amongst managers. In his evidence to the House Committee Taylor emphasized the necessity of a 'mental revolution' amongst both workers and managers.[35] By 1903, Taylor had recognized that a new system of supervision would be required and proposed, following the division of work into its component parts, the division of the task of foremanship into eight separate functions, only four of which would be represented on the shop floor. This suggests that Taylor was recognizing that certain preconditions were necessary for the implementation of his techniques. In Taylor's view the introduction of scientific management could be achieved without union cooperation and would, in time, make unions unnecessary. The system should be introduced by an autocratic but paternalistic management which would itself be subject to the principles of Taylorism. His associates, Cooke and Valentine, however, came to the opposite conclusion, namely that Taylorism could only be implemented successfully with the cooperation of trade unions in the context of industrial democracy.[36]

For Taylor, scientific management was a tightly bound package to be applied as a totality.[37] The distinction must be made, however, between the theory and its implementation. Taylorism was implemented in the USA within varied strategic frameworks and it was rejected by some leading entrepreneurs. Some users selected certain elements and rejected others, while others such as Henry Ford adopted quite different approaches to the analysis of work.[38] The international diffusion of elements of Taylorism can be seen to have taken distinctive trajectories. In Japan, Taylor's approach to managerial control was one that matched the cultures of large industrial organizations and Taylor's writings were rapidly translated into Japanese and sold very widely. The Japanese Taylor Society was one of the earliest to be formed. Taylorism in Japan was, however, implemented alongside the welfare strategies which are now regarded as core features of Japanese management – those of lifelong employment.

The nature of Taylorism was subjected to a full debate in the Soviet Union. Lenin emphasized the importance of the scientific components of Taylorism, such as work study and planned work flow, while opposing the ideological elements associated with the bourgeoisie, notably the intensification of labour. Taylorism found support in fascist Italy, although it was often implemented in an authoritarian manner; instead of leading to the raising of wages and reduction of working hours, Taylorism was employed to achieve the opposite of its originator's intentions.

The diffusion of Taylorism to Britain was achieved by two routes: the operation of the pull mechanism by British industrialists seeking to abstract principles of best practice management from the USA, usually after visiting America; and the push mechanism of American consultants informed by Taylor's work taking the innovation to British firms. From the early twentieth century, leading British manufacturers looked to the USA for new perspectives on management. Laurence Cadbury, for instance, visited the USA in 1913 to study business methods there;[39] and William Stuckey Piercy sought information on management issues while visiting the USA during the First World War.[40] He was a founder member, as was Seebohm Rowntree, of the Management Research Groups, the first of which was established in 1927. By 1935, eight were established.[41] The Group consisted of senior members of many of the leading firms of the period who met to discuss matters of mutual interest, particularly methods of payment and American management practices. Members found difficulty in identifying the core differences between British and American methods, partly because of differences in terminology – a problem that had been experienced in the reverse direction with the transfer of British technologies to America in the early nineteenth century.[42] In 1931, a visiting French speaker addressed Management Research Group No. 1 on Taylor's approach to management. He observed, 'I think the essential part of "Taylorism" is the substitution of measurement for guessing.'[43] He commented on the extent to which he had been impressed by the practical approach that Americans took to the reorganizing of production consequent upon experiment and observation and the use of statistics. Although the speaker sought to interest his audience in work study, they were more eager to learn about the American system of payment.

After Frederick Taylor's death in 1915, the torch of Taylorism was taken up by management consultants who offered 'new' managerial systems within the Systematic Management Movement. One of the most influential of these, in the context of Taylorism, was Charles E. Bedaux.[44] Bedaux was born in Paris, emigrating in 1906 to the USA, where he took a variety of jobs, from selling life insurance to promoting a toothpaste which also removed inkspots. Eventually he came to work for a furniture company and developed the system which made his fortune. In 1918, the first Bedaux consultancy firm was established in Cleveland and such was the success of the system that the business was split into two divisions, one based in the USA and the other the International Branch with a number of overseas offices.

Bedaux returned to France in 1927 to live in a luxury chateau, and during the 1930s his politics became more and more fascist. After the fall of France in 1940, he became industrial advisor to both the Nazi and Vichy governments. He was captured by the Allies in 1942 and, as a naturalized American, was taken back to the USA to face trial for treason. Rather than stand trial he committed suicide in February 1944. Bedaux's espousing of fascism and the linkage this made between Taylorism and fascism explains why he was excised from texts on management published in the post-war period. This has served to obscure the very considerable influence that Bedaux had on the diffusion of Tayloristic principles. While Taylor had been concerned principally with gaining intellectual acceptance, Bedaux set out to establish himself as a practitioner. Littler establishes the linkages between the Bedaux system and Taylorism, showing that Bedaux's only book owes much to Taylor and is clearly set within the mainstream of Systematic Management.[45] It was this book which was the training manual for the Bedaux consultants in Britain recruited between 1926 and 1932. The early British recruits to the Bedaux Company were selected on the basis of their knowledge of Taylor's works. An analysis of the Bedaux system demonstrates that job analysis, job simplification, work study and the promotion of minimum interaction industrial relations were all based on Taylorian principles. It becomes clear from Littler's work that Bedaux was one of the most important figures in the international diffusion of scientific management in the inter-war period and a leading actor in the diffusion of Taylorian workshop practices to Britain.

The Bedaux system was fundamentally a structure of control over the labour process. Bedaux claimed to have solved the problem which had plagued Frederick Taylor, 'namely that of discovering the precise scientific relationship between work and fatigue'.[46] Taylor wrote almost nothing on the question of fatigue and what Bedaux did was to combine emerging studies of fatigue with Taylorism. He established so-called laws of work to build up a 'relaxation curve' which showed the rest times which were necessary to offset working time, dependent on the specific effort required in a job. Unlike Taylor, there is no evidence to suggest that Bedaux engaged in any experimental investigation and he was not called to account for his results. The Bedaux system incorporated a universal measurement known as the Bedaux Unit or the B. The B was a fraction of a minute of work plus a fraction of a minute of rest which varied in proportion to the nature of strain. The essence was a unit of labour measurement, which made it possible to undertake comparisons of the relative efficiency of workers, departments and factories, even when the type of work was different. A basic element of the system was the Factory Posting Sheet, on which the performance of each operative was posted. All workers whose output fell below 60B were recorded in coloured ink, a practice which harkens back to Robert Owen's practice of displaying colours equivalent to effort by each machine at New

Lanark.[47] It was not easy for a worker to understand how his pay packet had been calculated and this complexity, when combined with the pseudo-scientific underpinning of the system, meant that the Bedaux system was less accessible to collective bargaining than other, simpler, payment systems.

A British-based Bedaux consultancy was established in 1926 and, after a relatively slow start, the system diffused rapidly during the 1930s. Littler attributes this partly to the fact that the firms which adopted the Bedaux system were in the new and expanding industries of the 1930s – food processing, light engineering, chemicals, motor components (although not motor vehicles). But the Bedaux system was also adopted in the iron and steel industries and textiles. A further reason why the Bedaux system was so rapidly implemented was that it did not require, as Taylor's system did, a total management restructuring. The Bedaux system could be tacked onto the existing management structure. By 1939, something like 250 firms, including ICI, Lucas, Lyons and Wolsey had adopted Bedaux techniques. Since many of the adopting firms were industry leaders, their actions were emulated by follower firms in the same sector, with the result that the Bedaux system became the most widely used system of managerial control in British industry.

Taylorism, as has already been noted, encountered considerable opposition in the USA. Amongst those who rejected it was Henry Ford. Ford's production system innovations for the Model T consisted of interrelated strands involving flowline production, the conveyance of parts along an assembly line and, of particular significance, the use of the even pacing of the technology to set the work rhythms of employees.[48] It was Ford's use of machine pacing that led Braverman to believe that Fordism was an advance over the control system implied by Taylorism.[49] At the Detroit plant, car assembly time was markedly reduced, a fact which should not, however, be attributed entirely to the moving assembly line. Ford introduced an eight-hour day and doubled wages. Piece work was replaced by a day rate which contributed to a sharp reduction in labour turnover. Fordism, like Taylorism, has been regarded as a sealed package, the most important element of which was direct control, which became the means by which management wrested ownership of the production process and control of the level of effort out of the hands of labour: 'Machinery offers to management the opportunity to do by wholly mechanical means that which it had previously attempted to do by organizational and disciplinary means.'[50]

Two studies of the diffusion of Fordism to Britain address aspects of the innovation package but neither considers the package in its entirety. Fridenson addresses the question of the adoption of the assembly line without considering pacing or wage rates and their calculation.[51] Lewchuk considers the question of wages rather than technology.[52] In examining the diffusion of

Fordism to Britain, the essential differences between the British and American car markets must be considered. The British market was clearly smaller and British car manufacturers had not developed a design capacity to meet the needs of working-class consumption in the way that Ford had done for the American worker with the Model T. British manufacturers had aimed at the middle- and upper-class car market. The British market was, moreover, characterized by a seasonality of demand.[53]

As with Taylorism, Fordism was introduced to Britain by several routes which can be characterized as operating push and pull mechanisms. Pull mechanisms included the acquisition of ideas by British managers and engineers who visited the USA or who employed American technicians and engineers, or who had read of American ideas in the British technical press. The push mechanism operated through US managers, engineers and consultants selling their services and, more directly, through the Ford-owned plant in Manchester and later at the General Motors-owned Vauxhall plant. Herbert Austin visited Detroit in 1924, reports of his impressions being published in the trade press. The general manager and chief engineer at Morris visited the USA after Austin, but acquired much of their knowledge of Fordism through the technical press. The factory manager of the new Rover plant built at Southall in 1926 was said to be 'suffering from Forditis' and in 1930 the Engineering Employers Federation criticized Rover for being over-sympathetic to Fordism. The building of Ford's own works at Manchester and General Motors' acquisition of Vauxhall in 1925 provided Fordist models on British soil.[54]

Not only were the routes by which Fordism reached the British motor industry varied, but the elements of Fordism adopted by British car manufacturers varied too. No motor manufacturer replicated the plant at Detroit. There was considerable variety in the wage strategy element of Fordism. Morris paid on piece work with high bonus rates, the general manager arguing that this system provided more incentive, while the chief engineer strongly favoured day rates. Both, however, were in favour of a high wages strategy. Austin believed that methods of payment promoted attitude change and a new 'bonus on time' system was introduced in which prices were set in time rather than cash. Rover introduced day rates at their Southall factory, as did Ford at Manchester. Rolls Royce, on the other hand, did not follow a high wage policy, although it introduced a plan by which workers could purchase company shares, thereby seeking a perceived linkage between profitability and work effort. Day rates were not fully absorbed into British corporate culture, however, and managers largely favoured incentive payments. By the late 1920s, payment by results was considered to be such an integral part of British management that the Engineering Employers Federation considered expelling any members who adopted Fordist day work.

The extent to which British motor manufacturers adopted centralized financial control on the Ford model is less clear. Rolls-Royce did, however, introduce a system as a check both on productivity and inventory levels.

The adoption of flow production and its manifestation in the assembly line, core features of Fordism, demonstrate the greatest variety both between British motor manufacturers and as between Britain and the USA.[55] Rolls-Royce, for instance, offered their employees responsible autonomy rather than imposing managerial control through technology. Vauxhall intended to erect an assembly line and purchased a large amount of machinery from the USA. The precipitating event was the collapse of the car market in 1921, when the factory was closed.[56] During this period the production facility was redesigned for the production of high-volume repetitive work. Each task was studied, timed, graded and costed. But even then the line was semi-automatic rather than being on the fully automatic Ford principle. Only later, when the firm was taken over by General Motors in 1925, was a full Fordist assembly line installed under the supervision of American advisors, with 23 self-contained departments, each of which worked on a specialized aspect of sub-assembly. The machine pacing of work was introduced in 1928. It would appear, however, that much of the specialized machinery was sub-optimal, the justification for its use being quality of the end product rather than quantity. As would be expected, Ford designed their Manchester plant on flow principles, installing a mechanical assembly line in 1920.

Morris appears to have gone the furthest towards the indirect control of work, including machine pacing. A manually operated flow system was employed in the production of engines at the Coventry factory, a chassis assembly line was introduced in 1919, but this was not mechanized until 1934. Automatic transfer machines were installed in some departments in the early 1920s, using techniques which appear to have been in advance of those to be found in car factories in either the USA or elsewhere in Britain. The justification for machine pacing was a moral one, Morris arguing that this prevented overwork by some and underwork by others. Austin initially rejected the flowline principle for assembly, although after a 1924 reorganization a system of flows for components was introduced. It was team spirit rather than technology which impressed the managers who visited Detroit, Herbert Austin arguing that a change in labour's attitude was more important than machine pacing in the British context. Manually operated assembly lines were installed between 1920 and 1924, mechanization coming in 1928. The Sunbeam factory in Wolverhampton was the earliest British car factory in which chassis were moved mechanically from one group of fitters to another (from 1913) but the Associated Equipment Company (AEC) was the first vehicle producer to install an assembly line, one being erected in 1917. The mechanized moving platform, 265 ft long, cost £3 500. But management's agenda for achieving control through technology was less successful there than anticipated; workers managed to protect customs which kept earnings high, whilst workload was reduced. In 1926, when AEC established a new factory at Southall, the work was designed on flow principles, component assembly lines feeding into the main assembly area.

From the foregoing discussion it will be clear that Fordism neither succeeded nor failed in the British context. The concept of Fordism as a sealed package is relatively meaningless. This is not to argue that Fordist principles could have been more fully implemented in practice than they were, but to emphasize the exercising of managerial choice in the selection of features of Fordism perceived to be relevant in the specific manufacturing context. Fordism was not 'rejected by British management', for it meant different things to different managers.[57]

Lewchuk discusses an unintended consequence of the introduction of Fordist principles to Britain, namely the fact that workers and their representatives were, in some cases, stronger advocates of Fordist wage principles than their managers. Representatives of the National Union of Vehicle Builders suggested that Fordism was an acceptable system to their members. In reply to the question, 'Do you think for one moment your men would submit themselves to the principles of Henry Ford?', the reply was 'They do it ... our people seem quite well satisfied. It is true for a period they did not take to it, but today they are quite satisfied with their employment.'[58] This situation at Ford's plant at Manchester should not, however, be regarded as one that characterized other car plants.

Rather than implement Ford's day rates, Rolls-Royce sought to legitimize managerial control by a form of profit sharing. Profit sharing had first come to prominence in Britain in the 1860s, at a time of increasing labour unrest and trade union activity, after the passage of the 1862 Companies Act, which legalized industrial partnerships. One of the earliest attempts to introduce profit sharing, that at the Whitwood and Methley Junction Collieries, provides clear evidence of a policy to wean men away from union membership and undermine the influence of the unions at the collieries. The fact that the scheme was introduced after a strike, which became a lock-out leading to the employment of blackleg labour, firmly places the introduction of profit sharing in the purview of managerial control. Indeed, in this particular example, the profit-sharing experiment was abandoned in a period of trade boom. The failure of the scheme after extensive favourable publicity appears to have been effective in deterring further experimentation until what R. A. Church refers to as the second phase in the history of profit sharing in Britain, which began in the 1880s.[59] While there are clear instances of profit sharing being introduced by paternalistic manufacturers such as Joseph Rowntree and James Alexander Bowie,[60] the pattern of profit-sharing schemes between the

1880s and the outbreak of the First World War suggests a direct relationship between the introduction of profit sharing or co-partnership schemes and high levels of employment and labour unrest, the peaks for new schemes occurring in 1889–92, 1908–9 and 1912–14. Reports produced by the Ministry of Labour in 1912 and 1920 provide evidence of the level of participation in British industry up to the First World War.[61] The high rate of abandonment, together with the fluctuations in the formation of schemes, suggests that the underlying motives were self-interested attempts to improve industrial relations while undermining the power and influence of trade unions implicitly or explicitly. It is also clear that workers were less interested in such schemes in periods of low employment and low profits, when the prospects for bonuses were poor.

In 1912, 163 schemes known to have existed had ceased and only 14 schemes then existing had lasted for more than 30 years. In 1912, 133 firms were involved in profit sharing but the number of employees participating numbered a mere 106 000. Over 28 000 of these were workers in the gas industry, over 17 000 in engineering and shipbuilding and over 15 000 in the chemical, glass and pottery trades. Advocates of profit sharing asserted that labour productivity was enhanced, strikes were less likely to occur, workers would be offered a means of saving, the scheme thereby encouraging thrift, and closer links were forged between managers and workers. Trade unionists drew attention to what they perceived as the essential weakness in profit sharing, namely that it was a device for breaking up unions and for tying employees to a single firm, thereby increasing dependence on an employer. The views of many trade unionists was that, if employers could afford to share profits, they could afford to pay higher wages.

The First World War hastened the spread of new thinking on participation, with a belief in the need for new methods of managing labour. The Garton Foundation recommended the establishment of joint employer–worker committees in a report of 1916. The Whitley Committee, established by the government in 1917, came to the same conclusion in its interim report, recommending the establishment of Joint Standing Industrial Councils, which rapidly became known as Whitley Councils. Towards the close of the war a number of prominent employers, including a number belonging to Committee Number One, advocated a new start in industry in the hope that greater unity of purpose would evolve. Three elements to this movement can be identified: the willingness of employers to acknowledge their wider public responsibility; a renouncing of autocratic methods of management; and a belief that labour should be treated on human criteria rather than as a commodity.[62]

Whitley Councils were established in a number of factories owned and managed by Quakers. It was believed that experience on Whitley Councils would provide an opportunity for training shop-floor members for a greater participative role in industry. In practice, however, it was comparatively rare for employees to take such steps as the selection of foremen. In this regard Renolds and Rowntree were exceptions. There was a paradox, in practice, in that the more evolving management thought emphasized specialized administrative/managerial expertise, the more problematical was any notion of sharing in the commercial and financial administration of the organization. In practice many works councils were reduced rapidly to vehicles for the communication of information rather than joint decision making.[63]

The post-First World War slump and the rising level of unemployment led to a fall in the number of Whitley Councils, from 73 in 1921 to 47 in 1926, and the parallel collapse of a number of other works committees. The breakdown could usually be attributed to the employers, many of which reverted to earlier forms of managerial control. Amongst the employers who retained Whitley Councils, it has been suggested that the emphasis was on a form of control which was manipulative under a participative guise.[64]

In the period of reconstruction during the inter-war years a reaction against the idea of shared worker control in management is noticeable, the rejection being apparent even amongst the Quaker industrialists. There was, however, a renewed interest in works committees in, for example, ICI, Renolds and Rowntree, although they were viewed as communication channels and consultative bodies, rather than a means of affording workers a share in control.

Quaker manufacturers, including George, Edward and Laurence Cadbury, Seebohm and Joseph Rowntree as well as others such as Arthur Chamberlain,[65] were greatly interested in the Human Relations school of management emerging out of the Hawthorne Studies conducted by Elton Mayo and Fritz Roethlisberger of Harvard University. What had begun as a study to measure the effect of improved lighting on workers' output emerged as a classic study of human behaviour in organizations. The experiments at the Hawthorne plant were conducted with just as scientific an approach as Frederick Taylor's experiments, but, at Hawthorne, the human relations between workers and their supervisors and among the workers themselves were found to be at least as important in influencing workers' behaviour as physical and monetary incentives.[66] Many years later Roethlisberger suggested that the Hawthorne Studies merely represented 'the systematic exploitation of the simple and the obvious',[67] yet this was not the only instance of a major advance in management theory being the explicit formulation of what, from the practitioner's point of view, seemed to be intuitive wisdom.

The Human Relations Movement occupied a pre-eminent position in British management thought until the mid-1950s. Productivity was deemed to be influenced primarily by social satisfaction in the workplace rather than by physical working conditions and the responsibility for achieving this was placed on foremen. Managers, therefore, were urged to incorporate foremen as an integral part of management. Nevertheless communication, while regarded as essential, continued to be a top-downward activity rather than one which could be both bottom-up and lateral as well. John Child sees a deep irony in management 'having to make known to employees what was supposed to be a shared purpose, and having, in effect, to create a co-operation which was supposed to be spontaneous and eagerly desired', indicating 'the manipulative features in what was put forward as a democratic and participative system of industrial control'.[68]

Linkages can be made in the British context between the Human Relations Movement and Organizational Development (OD) but the direct antecedents are different. OD is a non-structural approach to organizing the management of change by identifying conflicts, emotions and attachments of individual members of the organization. It has been applied far more widely within areas of management and to white-collar workers than to vertical relationships within organizations. The approach of OD is experiential with little direct attention being given to knowledge bases in organizations, or to the content of decisions. Most users of OD in North America are clearly aware of the distinction between what Clark refers to as systemic and experiential, and systemic and cognitive, the cognitive aspects being the focus of other established approaches and procedures.[69]

The origins of OD are in social psychology, leading, on the one hand, to T (experiential development) groups and the direct experience of interpersonal learning, and on the other to individual and collective survey feedback as a trigger to behavioural modification. In the 1950s, a number of major firms in the food, drink and tobacco sectors, as well as petrochemicals, incorporated OD into their portfolio of management learning. The potential for OD came to be realized through experiments in major companies, on the one hand, and articulate championing of the practice, on the other. During the 1960s, OD was diffused through several prestigious texts and consultancy practices, but it never became tightly bound into a single package as was Taylorism, initially, in the USA.

OD was developed in Britain during the 1940s and 1950s by members of the Tavistock Institute of Human Relations in London, who applied group experiences to the rehabilitation of returning prisoners of war. A clinical theory was developed which, after 1948, was used in industrial contexts, most significantly in the newly nationalized coal industry. In a well-known study using what came to be known as sociotechnical analysis, Trist and colleagues demonstrated that self-organized work groups were more effective than hierarchical control.[70] This group autonomy was itself a survival of the form of internal contract within coal mining known as the Butty System. This rediscovered form of work organization was later labelled 'responsible autonomy' and, in the British context, transferred the former control of internal contractors to the group as a whole.

The sociotechnical approach to work organization did not gain a firm foothold in Britain. Esso pioneered the employment of full-time social science consultants but, more typically, British firms employed US consultants or sent their senior managers to American business centres. In the 1960s, for instance, ICI sent senior personnel managers to America and also imported Americans, but OD did not become institutionalized in ICI as had work study.

A major exception was the National Health Service, in which a system of structured action learning was devised in the early 1970s, based on a modification of the American practice of survey feedback.[71] There was, also, one British attempt to combine the organization design approach of the sociotechnical school with the use of OD in the design of new factories.[72] But neither of these attempts survived for long.

The innovations considered thus far have been behavioural. There were, however, structural innovations in management in the twentieth century which had as great an impact. Two will be considered here – developments in accountancy and new organizational structures developed in response to strategic change.

The last two decades of the nineteenth century saw the publication of text books on accountancy aimed at articled clerks of the new Institute of Chartered Accountants and of its rival bodies, such as the Society of Incorporated Accountants and Auditors. Lawrence R. Dicksee's *Auditing* (1892) shows that the idiosyncratic methods of financial accounting in the eighteenth century had been left behind and that, in many respects, the computation of annual profit in the accounts of limited liability companies anticipated requirements in the early to mid-twentieth century. Revenues were calculated on an 'accruals' basis and matched with their associated costs. The opening and closing inventories of industrial and commercial firms were normally priced at cost or lower market value but selling prices were used for the unsold output of a mine or quarry as well as for agricultural produce. In regard to capital expenditure, commercial companies registered under the Limited Liability Act of 1862 had no obligation to retain any particular assets for any length of time and used the single account system with an undivided balance sheet. Fixed assets were usually valued initially at historical cost, with depreciation being written off to revenue over the estimated economic life of the property. Depreciation rates varied, Dicksee suggesting 1.25 per cent to 3 per cent per annum. The accounts of unincorporated businesses were similar, except that, with every change of partner or of profit-sharing ratios, their assets were subjected to a revaluation. There was resistance to the introduction of the compulsory publication of accounts by many directors, especially those of family firms. The belief that a businessman's accounts were his private concern was one that was widely shared. It was believed that, as long as shareholders received their dividends, they had no concern with the manner in which the figure had been arrived at.

A 'Costing Renaissance' occurred in the late nineteenth century,[73] the leading English contribution to which was the book by John Fells and Emile Garcke, entitled *Factory Accounts*. This was first published in 1887 and had gone through seven editions by 1922. Fells was the son of a tailor and woollen draper, becoming accountant and assistant secretary of the Brush Electrical Engineering Co. In 1889 he joined the Salt Union Ltd, first as superintendent accountant and later as general manager. His co-author was an electrical engineer. The book provided 'a systematized statement of the principles regulating Factory Accounts; and of the methods by which those principles can be put into practice and made to serve important purposes in the economy of manufacture',[74] thus highlighting the management information available from a broader range of accounts. While there was no mention of standard costing for scientific management, the discussion of piece work showed an appreciation of behavioural aspects of management.

A significant contribution to the practice of accountancy was made by Gilbert Francis Garnsey.[75] Having been placed first in order of merit in both the intermediate and final examinations of the Institute of Chartered Accountants in England and Wales, he joined the London office of Price Waterhouse and Co. and, being rejected for active service on the outbreak of the First World War on grounds of ill health, he set about streamlining the administrative machinery in Whitehall as his contribution to the war effort. He was severely critical of the accounting procedures which operated at the Ministry of Munitions; investigation showed that undue concentration on cash accounting, to the exclusion of accruals accounting, resulted in a large loss of money due. The recommendations of Garnsey and J. H. Guy, with whom he worked, led to far-reaching changes, both in the internal accounting system and, ultimately, in the form of public accounts submitted to Parliament. Double entry accounting replaced single entry and there was the preparation of a production (income and expenditure) account and balance sheet which were little used in government accounting until that time. At the end of the First World War, Sir Josiah Stamp joined Explosives Trading Services (later Nobel Industries), where he set out to improve the accounting within the company.[76] With his assistant he produced the first consolidated balance sheet of Nobel Industries, covering 40 wholly-owned and 35 majority-owned companies, together with some investment companies. His objective was to present more information than was legally required at the time, although the level of disclosure was lower than that of standard US practice. Stamp became known as a leading critic of contemporary accounting practices, delivering a swingeing attack on the accountancy profession in a lecture to the Society of Incorporated Accountants and Auditors in 1921.

Stamp's level of expertise in accounting was exceptional amongst businessmen of his day. Accounting was developing a specialized language which became a serious obstacle to communication between accountants and managers, a situation that was only mediated by the growing number of accountants working in industry. By 1939, over half of the accountants in England were directly employed by business.[77] Accountants became directors of companies, Francis D'Arcy Cooper of Unilever being largely responsible for consolidating the industrial empire built by William Lever.

By the late nineteenth century there had already been clear economic inducements for the development of larger-scale businesses. Amalgamations and cartels had led to the emergence of holding companies as a structural solution to the administration of these organizations. During the First World War, and in the years that followed, these ideas, which came to be known as rationalization, gained 'wide currency and ... the status of the conventional wisdom in leading business circles'.[78] As L.F. Urwick said in his address to the Economic Section of the Association for the Advancement of Science in 1930, 'The rapid development of the idea of rationalization has given rise to amalgamations at a speed and to a degree which are altogether novel.'[79] The term 'rationalization' meant different things to different observers. To some it implied horizontal amalgamation, while to others it had more to do with the extent to which business should be encouraged or required to reorganize itself by amalgamation. While between 1880 and 1918 only 8 per cent of mergers concerned diversification or vertical integration, by 1919–39 the proportion had risen to 37 per cent.

Companies in the USA, prevented by anti-trust legislation from setting up holding companies, sought a different solution to the structural problems posed by growth. Chandler,[80] in his insightful historical analysis of the strategy and structure of American companies in the early twentieth century, concluded that a number of major manufacturing companies had encountered organizational problems as a consequence of their policies of corporate diversification. These firms discovered that the most appropriate management solution to diversification was to restructure into separate divisions, a structure commonly known as M-Form. M-Form, in Chandler's terms, was not merely a structural gloss but should be reserved as a descriptive form for 'those firms that combine the appropriate structural control and internal operating attributes'.[81] Chandler's thesis was that M-Form, once discovered, was recognized as a generic solution to a common problem and rapidly diffused to other firms which had diversified. Chandler sought to demonstrate that M-Form was diffused from the USA to the rest of the industrial world, where it was adopted through a process of imitation.

The expansion of British manufacturing industry by merger and acquisition in the early part of the twentieth century was largely along the lines of horizontal integration leading to centralization. Strategic diversification was relatively uncommon. Hannah has shown the infrequency of diversifying mergers.[82] Of the 50 largest companies of 1930, few had grown by a programme of diversification, Vickers and ICI being relative exceptions at this period. The Nobel Industries and Brunner Mond merger which brought about the formation of ICI produced a diversified manufacturing base applied to a wide range of products which included paints, metals, leather cloth, plastics, solvents, dye stuffs, fertilizers and high-pressure engineering, and ICI was one of the first British companies to adopt a variant of M-Form. The germ of a decentralized divisional management structure can be identified in Nobel Industries, where it had been instituted by Sir Josiah Stamp on a model in which the centralization of staff functions (accounts, R & D, for example) preceded divisionalization on a manufacturing product-based logic.[83] This cycle was repeated with the ICI merger when full centralization of ICI preceded the programme of decentralization into manufacturing units.[84]

The diffusion of M-Form to Britain occurred in four main ways:[85]

1. British directors and managers visited multidivisionalized firms in the USA, sometimes specifically to investigate M-Form, sometimes observing the effects of structural change while discussing other agendas.
2. The number of American-owned firms in the UK increased and many of these were divisionalized.
3. American technology was marketed to Britain through licences and machinery exports.
4. US consultants, such as McKinsey, were employed by British firms to assist in structural change.

Chandler's *Strategy and Structure* initially received little attention in Britain, but over the next decade a replication study was undertaken of British industry,[86] and a conference brought together empirical studies on the theme.[87] Channon conducted a longitudinal study of the hundred largest manufacturing companies which had undergone strategic and structural change over the period 1950–69/70.[88] In his analysis, Channon found that 94 of the 100 companies were diversified to some extent, the largest category being companies which had diversified into related products. Diversification into non-related products was a strategy chosen by only 6 per cent of the companies. By 1970, 71 per cent of the companies had adopted some form of divisional structure, 28 companies being multidivisional by product; nine companies had divisionalized by area and 21 by product, with the addition of an international division. When divisionalized companies are analysed by sector it can be seen that approximately two-thirds of the food/drink/tobacco companies were divisionalized, as were just over half the metals/machinery companies and more than three-quarters of the engineering/car companies.

British firms seeking consultants' help for reorganization in the 1950s seem to have been likely to have employed a local firm or a nationally known British firm, such as Urwick Orr. By the 1960s, however, the American influence was in the ascendant, with McKinsey and Co. being called in to advise on the restructuring of a number of large companies, including ICI (1962), Plessey (1964), Cadbury (1966), Unigate (1968) and Unilever (1971). Channon's aim was to explore similarities between Britain and the USA and he allows little space for the identification and discussion of differences. There are, however, fundamental differences between M-Form in Britain and in the USA, both in the form itself and in the process by which that form emerged. M-Form was not a relatively sealed package, the evidence suggesting only a surface similarity between the American format and its British counterparts. Imitation of American M-Form was difficult in the British context, where divisionalization was preceded by a holding company. Many UK holding companies adopting M-Form did little more than insert another layer of management between the operating units/subsidiaries and the central functions. In this context M-Form becomes little more than a cosmetic change conditioned by inherited options. Moreover as Williamson points out,[89] for M-Form to be effective it is essential that all divisions adopt a uniform set of accounting conventions in order to generate comparable cost and revenue data. By this criterion, multidivisionalization in Britain was, with some major exceptions, certainly different from that in the USA in the 1960s and early 1970s and only marginally effective. Moreover there are further differences. Alford comments on the fact that structural change sometimes preceded strategic change in the British context.[90] It is clear that such change was not entered into unknowingly but was seen as an enabling device for strategic change.

The knowledge bases from which the theory of management has evolved are located firmly in the social sciences and engineering. While engineering provided the principles from which a technically oriented 'science' of administration developed, the social sciences provided the base from which evolved theories of organizations and human resource management. Much of the literature of public administration derives from the field of political science; theories of the firm, studies of industrial fatigue, managerial economics and theories of pricing developed out of mainstream economics. Psychology provided a key to understanding the operation of an industrial enterprise: morale, motivation, fatigue, organizational learning and planned change; whilst the contribution of sociology includes the study of the division of labour, conflict and power, elites, bureaucracy and control, stratification, and leadership. Anthropologists have contributed to the study of organizational culture, while ethics in business and an underpinning to the value systems of organizations derive from philosophy and theology.[91]

The translation from theory to practice has proved problematical. While Simon attacked the proverbs of managers[92] – the simplistic templates which managers fall prey to when seeking a safe route through a partly conflicting theory – it becomes clear that, within the field of practice, those organizations which could be identified as best practice ones may be far from typical. The study of business history prompts the question of the typicality of best practice.

The routes by which innovations in management have diffused through British organizations have been shown to be varied. One route, however, has appeared consistently from the 1930s onwards – the consultant. Management consultancy developed in Britain more slowly than in the USA and some of the most innovative consultancy firms in Britain were branches of American firms. James Alexander Bowie effectively bridged practical business management with management education and management consultancy[93] – a model more frequently to be found in the USA than in Britain. He became Director of the Department of Industrial Administration in the Manchester College of Technology, which became part of Manchester University, where he founded a full-time course in industrial administration. He based the design of the course on the case-study method which he had observed in his visit to Harvard in 1931. In 1943, Bowie joined the staff of PA Ltd, the management consultants, before returning to academe at the University of Dundee three years later. Lyndall Urwick regarded Bowie as 'the first British writer of importance on education for management'.[94] In his *Education for Business Management* (Oxford, 1930), Bowie argued that an effective means of creating responsible and legitimate managerial power was through the professionalization of management.

Lyndall Urwick was the founder of a pioneering and successful management consultancy, in 1934, becoming a leader in consultancy to large organizations. Urwick's writings on management were amongst the most influential for British management. He was well acquainted with American theory and practice and his own theoretical perspective was informed by his experience in the Armed Forces. His views on the role of chief executives, leadership, delegation and span of control were clearly influenced by his military service, as was his use of the terms 'staff' and 'line management'.[95] He was the first Honorary Secretary to the Management Research Groups, he became leader of the British Management Consultants Association, and was a founder member and, later, chairman of the British Institute of Management (1947–52). His book, *The Making of Scientific Management* (3 vols, New York, 1945–8) was probably the most widely read book on management in Britain in the immediate post-war years. He was the first British person to be awarded the Gantt Memorial Gold Medal for services to management.

Another pioneer of management theory and practice in Britain was Sir Walter Charles Puckey.[96] After a formative period at Hoover Ltd, during which time his professional practice was influenced by a wide reading of American management practice, Puckey became co-founder, with Harry Roff, of Management Selection Ltd in 1955. Aware of the growth of head-hunting in America, Puckey and Roff saw the need for a consultancy service which would advise companies on management selection. The partners were aware that head-hunting would be unacceptable in Britain and that a broader consultancy service would be more appropriate.

Linkages between management consultancy and business schools in the USA have been and still are many. Faculty members have traditionally had personal consultancies, many of them being partners in consultancy firms, while management consultants in major consulting companies have often had visiting faculty status in the major business schools. In Britain, on the other hand, the linkages have been much more tenuous. Fewer theoreticians have engaged in consultancy, while links between major firms of management consultants and the business schools have been fragile.

Until the founding of the first two British business schools (London and Manchester) in the mid-1960s, British universities had made relatively little contribution to management education. By 1960, only five universities were running full-time postgraduate courses in business administration and few of the students received employer sponsorship. Post-experience courses of a non-academic kind appeared to fit managers' perceptions of their education and training needs rather better. While industry showed little interest in the more academic offerings in management education, the universities, for their part, reinforced perceptions of ivory towerism by evincing a reluctance to admit that management was a fit subject for university study at all.

British productivity teams reporting on visits to the USA in the early 1950s linked American business success to the quality of management. The USA was identified both as a model for future developments in Britain and as a yardstick against which to measure British productivity failings. By the late 1950s, a number of young British managers, identifying the benefits of post-graduate management education, studied at Harvard Business School. In 1960, they established a ginger group, the Foundation for Management Education (FME), which raised funds to establish a set of management teaching experiments at three universities (Bristol, Cambridge and Leeds). In 1963 a further five universities were involved.[97] These actions prompted resistance from both the academic and business worlds on the question of the legitimacy of university involvement in management education and the whole subject became a matter for public debate after the publication of the Robbins Report in 1963.

A second group was established, consisting of senior industrialists including Lord Nelson and Sir Anthony Bowlby. This 'Savoy Group', while critical of FME's work, was convinced of the need to establish a 'British Harvard', but was pessimistic about the possibility of grafting such an institution upon an existing university.[98] The group was guided by the underlying belief that 'America had business schools and was successful; Britain had no business schools and was not.'[99] The Savoy Group recommended that a business school be established alongside the new University of Warwick and the Chancellor-elect, Lord Rootes, asked the new Vice-Chancellor to visit the USA to study business schools there.[100]

Both university- and industry-promoted action was overtaken by government intervention, however, for the National Economic Development Council (NEDC) issued a report in 1963, indicating that there was 'a need for at least one very high-level new school or institute somewhat on the lines of the Harvard Business School or the School of Industrial Management at the Massachusetts Institute of Technology'.[101] After further discussion the FME, the Savoy Group, the British Institute of Managers, the Federation of British Industry and NEDC commissioned Lord Franks to produce a set of proposals which would lead to the establishment of the means of delivering high-level management education. The Franks Report (1963) proposed that 'two major Postgraduate Schools should be built in addition to other developments already possible in universities and other institutions'. It was recommended that both business schools be part of a university but should have considerable autonomy as a partnership between the world of business and academe. Lord Nelson headed a major appeal and, in 1965, London and Manchester Business Schools were opened.

Lord Franks had recognized the importance of selecting features from American models for the British context:

> We have a great deal to learn from the successful practices of the leading American Business Schools ... But ... it is impossible to select any one American Business School and transplant it, its way of life, purposes, methods and curricula holus bolus into British soil, and expect the result to be successful ... we cannot successfully borrow Harvard or any of the others whole.[102]

In the event both London and Manchester Business Schools modelled the structure and format of their courses strongly on the American precedent, arguing for two-year masters programmes. However, within a few years, it became clear that industry, commerce and the service sectors were not happy with developments at the two business schools. Criticism was voiced of the 'academic' nature of the jewel in the crowns of the schools, the postgraduate courses. Employers asserted that business school graduates lacked skill, calibre and potential and they favoured a one-year rather than two-year course. Participants on the courses criticized American teaching methods, in particular the Harvard model of study analysis and the practice of public disclosure for peer evaluation. The presidents of the Confederation of British Industry acknowledged that 'there is now a very wide gulf between what the British business schools want to do and what industry thinks they ought to do'.[103]

Both business schools established liaison committees to improve relations with the business world. New university schools of management, established in the 1970s and 1980s, sought to learn from the experience of London and Manchester; they launched one-year MBA programmes, consisting of taught modules in functional management areas and emphasized the syndicate method in case-study analysis, in which small groups discussed a case in private, group inputs being depersonalized at the report-back stage. Had London and Manchester Universities heeded Lord Franks' recommendation to select from and modify American practice, rather than to replicate it, a tighter initial fit between the needs of British managers and the universities' provision might have been attained and the subsequent process of modification less painful.

In the foregoing discussion of the diffusion of innovations in management theory and practice in Britain, a unifying principle emerges. Where an innovation was regarded as a sealed or tightly bound package, its adoption in different cultural settings and business contexts was problematical. The totality has often been misinterpreted by adopting agencies and misapplied as a result. On the other hand, in those situations where the innovation was unpacked and selectively implemented, the ownership of the innovation was transferred and appropriation took place.

In the diffusion of management theory and practice Britain lagged behind the USA in timescale. But the reluctance, inability or refusal of British managers to adopt an American innovation in totality should not necessarily be interpreted as either ignorance or failure. Those British managers and their advisors who understood that by unpacking an innovation they could alter the locus of the innovation through a transfer of ownership were often the ones who could embed new practices successfully.

NOTES

1.   John Child, *British Management Thought* (London, 1969), p. 13.
2.   Sidney Pollard, *The Genesis of Modern Management* (London, 1965), p. 251.
3.   Ibid., pp. 251–3; Jennifer Tann, *The Development of the Factory* (London, 1970).
4.   Andrew Ure, *Philosophy of Manufactures* (London, 1835); Charles Babbage, *On the Economy of Machinery and Manufactures* (London, 1832).
5.   Sidney Pollard, *Genesis*, p. 248.

6. E. Jones, *Accountancy and the British Economy, 1840–1980: The Evolution of Ernst and Whinney* (London, 1981); R.S. Kaplan, 'The Evolution of Management Accounting', *Accounting Review*, **LIX**, (1984).

7. D. Solomons, 'The Historical Development of Costing', in D. Solomons (ed.), *Studies in Cost Analysis*, second edition. (1968).

8. H.T. Johnson, 'Towards a New Understanding of 19th Century Cost Accounting', *Accounting Review*, **LVI**, (1981).

9. N. McKendrick, 'Josiah Wedgwood and Cost Accounting in the Industrial Revolution', *Economic History Review*, **23**, (1970); Jennifer Tann, *Development*, p. 39.

10. John Richard Edwards and Edmund Newell, 'Development of Industrial Cost and Management Accounting', *Business History*, **33**, (1991).

11. Ibid., p. 48.

12. Ibid., p. 54.

13. See S.D. Chapman, *The Early Factory Masters* (Newton Abbot, 1967); Peter Mathias, *The Brewing Industry* (Cambridge, 1959).

14. For example, see evidence in the Boulton and Watt Papers, Birmingham Reference Library; Jennifer Tann, 'Richard Arkwright and Technology', *History*, **58**, (1973).

15. Dennis Chapman, 'William Brown of Dundee, 1791–1864: Management in a Scottish Flax Mill', *Explorations in Entrepreneurial History*, **IV**, no. 3, (1952).

16. Andrew Ure, *The Cotton Manufacture of Great Britain*, 2 vols,(London, 1836); James Montgomery, *The Cotton Spinner's Manual* (Glasgow, 1835); Benjamin Thompson, *Inventions, Improvements and Practice of B.T.* (Newcastle, 1847); S. Griffiths, *A Guide to the Iron Trade of Great Britain* (London, 1873); Oliver Evans, *The Young Millwright and Millers Guide* (Philadelphia, 1834).

17. Charles Babbage, *Machinery and Manufactures*.

18. Sidney Pollard, *Genesis*, p. 255.

19. Ibid.

20. E.P. Thompson, 'Time, Work Discipline and Industrial Capitalism', *Past and Present*, **38**, (1967).

21. For example, Robert Owen.

22. David F. Schloss, *Methods of Industrial Remuneration* (London, 1892).

23. Frederick W. Taylor, *The Principles of Scientific Management* (New York, 1911).

24. Peter Clark, *Anglo-American Innovation* (Berlin and New York, 1987), pp. 282–6.

25. Frederick W. Taylor, *Principles*, p. 53.

26. Peter Clark, *Anglo-American Innovation*; A. Friedman, *Industry and Labour: Class Struggle at Work and Monopoly Capitalism* (London, 1977); Stephen Wood and John Kelly, 'Taylorism, Responsible Autonomy and Management Strategy', in Stephen Wood (ed.), *The Degradation of Work?* (London, 1982).

27. Craig R. Littler, *The Development of the Labour Process in Capitalist Societies* (London, 1982), pp. 48–63.

28. H. Braverman, *Labour and Monopoly Capital* (New York, 1974).

29. Stephen Wood and John Kelly, 'Taylorism', p. 78.

30. Frederick W. Taylor, *Principles*, pp. 59, 175.

31. Peter Clark, *Anglo-American Innovation*, pp. 329–32.

32. Stephen Wood and John Kelly, 'Taylorism', p. 79.

33. Ibid.

34. Quoted in Bertram M. Gross, *The Managing of Organizations: The Administrative Struggle*, 2 vols (New York, 1964), p. 125.

35. Ibid.

36. Craig R. Littler, *Labour Process*, p. 182; Stephen Wood and John Kelly, 'Taylorism', p. 79.

37. Peter Clark, *Anglo-American Innovation*, pp. 329–32.

38. Peter Clark and Jennifer Tann, 'The Transatlantic Diffusion of the Assembly Line: The Case of the Automobile Industry', (Aston/UMIST, Labour Process Conference, 1980).

39. Basil G. Murray, 'Laurence Cadbury', in David J. Jeremy (ed.), *Dictionary of Business Biography* (London, 1984–6). Hereafter *DBB*.

40. Martin Chick, 'William Stuckey Piercy', ibid.
41. Shirley Keeble, 'Benjamin Seebohm Rowntree', ibid. The Ward Papers are preserved at the Business History Unit, London School of Economics.
42. David J. Jeremy, *Transatlantic Industrial Revolution* (Oxford, 1981).
43. Ward Papers, Minutes, 20 March 1930.
44. Craig R. Littler, *Labour Process*, pp. 99–116.
45. Ibid.; C.E. Bedaux, *The Bedaux Efficiency Course for Industrial Application* (Grand Rapids, Mich., 1917) quoted in Littler, *Labour Process*.
46. Craig R. Littler, *Labour Process*, pp. 108–9.
47. O. Podmore, *Robert Owen* (London, 1923).
48. Wayne Lewchuk, 'Fordism and the British Motor Car Employers, 1896–1932', in H.F. Gospel and Craig R. Littler (eds), *Managerial Strategies and Industrial Relations* (London, 1983), pp. 82–110.
49. H. Braverman, *Monopoly Capital*, pp. 56–7.
50. Ibid.
51. P. Fridenson, 'The Coming of the Assembly Line to Europe', in Krohn, Layton and Weingart (eds), *The Dynamics of Science and Technology in Sociology of the Sciences*, vol. 2 (Dordrecht, 1978), pp. 159–74.
52. Wayne Lewchuk, 'Fordism'.
53. Clark and Tann, 'The Transatlantic Diffusion of the Assembly Line'.
54. Ibid.
55. Ibid.
56. The phrase, 'precipitating event', is M.J. Kirton's – see M.J. Kirton, 'Adaptors and Innovators: A Description and a Measure', *Journal of Applied Psychology*, (1976).
57. Clark and Tann, 'The Transatlantic Diffusion of the Assembly Line'.
58. Wayne Lewchuk, 'Fordism', p. 105.
59. R. A. Church, 'Profit Sharing and Labour Relations in England in the Nineteenth Century', *International Review of Social History*, XVI, (1971).
60. Martin Higham, 'Joseph Rowntree', in *DBB*; Catherine E. Meakin and Shirley Keeble, 'James Alexander Bowie', ibid.
61. *Report on Profit-Sharing and Labour Co-Partnership in the UK*, Cd 6496 (London, 1912); *Report on Profit-Sharing and Labour Co-Partnership* (London, 1920).
62. *Interim Report on Joint Standing Industrial Councils*, Cd 8606 (London, 1917); John Child, *British Management Thought*.
63. Ibid., p. 51.
64. J. Lee, *Management: A Study of Industrial Organization* (London, 1921), p. 61.
65. Basil G. Murray, 'George Cadbury', in *DBB*; Basil G. Murray, 'Laurence John Cadbury', ibid.; Martin Higham, 'Joseph Rowntree', ibid.; Barbara M.D. Smith, 'Arthur Chamberlain', ibid.
66. Bertram M. Gross, *Managing*, pp. 160–5.
67. F. Roethlisberger, *Management and Morale* (Cambridge, Mass., 1941) quoted in Gross, *Managing*.
68. John Child, *British Management Thought*, p. 119.
69. Peter Clark, *Anglo-American Innovation*, pp. 332–8.
70. E.L. Trist et al., *Organizational Choice: The Loss, Rediscovery and Transformation of a Work Tradition* (London, 1963) cited in Clark, *Anglo-American Innovation*, p. 335.
71. R.W. Revans, *Hospitals: Communication, Choice and Change* (London, 1972).
72. Peter Clark, *Anglo-American Innovation*, p. 337.
73. The phrase is D. Solomons'. See D. Solomons, 'The Historical Development of Costing'.
74. R.H. Parker, 'John Manger Fells', in *DBB*.
75. J.R. Edwards, 'Gilbert Francis Garnsey', ibid.
76. Michael Bywater, 'Josiah Charles Stamp', ibid.
77. Leslie Hannah, *The Rise of the Corporate Economy* (London, 1976), p. 90.
78. Ibid., pp. 29–44.
79. L.F. Urwick, quoted ibid., p. 29.

80. A.D. Chandler, *Strategy and Structure* (Boston, 1962).
81. A.D. Chandler, *The Visible Hand: The Managerial Revolution in America* (Cambridge, Mass., 1977), p. 1.
82. Leslie Hannah, *Corporate Economy*, pp. 120–1.
83. W.J. Reader, *Imperial Chemical Industries: A History* (London, 1970–5).
84. Leslie Hannah, *Corporate Economy*, pp. 92–3.
85. Peter Clark and Jennifer Tann, 'Cultures and Corporations: The M-Form in the USA and Britain', paper presented to the International Academy of Business, 1986.
86. D.F. Channon, *The Strategy and Structure of British Enterprises* (London, 1973).
87. Leslie Hannah (ed.), *Management Strategy and Business Development* (London, 1976).
88. D.F. Channon, *Strategy and Structure*.
89. O.E. Williamson, *Markets and Hierarchy: Analysis and Antitrust Implications* (New York, 1975).
90. B.W.E. Alford, 'Strategy and Structure in the UK Tobacco Industry', in Leslie Hannah (ed.), *Management Strategy and Business Development* (London, 1976).
91. See Bertram M. Gross, *Managing*, pp. 182, 191–225; D.J. Jeremy, *Capitalists and Christians* (Oxford, 1990).
92. Herbert Simon, *Administrative Behavior: A Study of Decision-making Processes* (New York, 1947).
93. Catherine E. Meakin and Shirley Keeble, 'James Alexander Bowie', in *DBB*.
94. Ibid.
95. Bertram M. Gross, *Managing*, pp. 143–8; Rosamund M. Thomas, 'Lyndall Fownes Urwick', in *DBB*.
96. Martin Davis, 'Sir Walter Charles Puckey', in *DBB*.
97. M. Wheatcroft, *The Revolution in British Management Education* (London, 1970).
98. Ibid.
99. T. Lupton, 'Business Education', *Newsletter, Centre for Business Research* (Manchester Business School, 1972).
100. M. Wheatcroft, *Revolution*.
101. NEDC, *Conditions Favourable to Foster Growth* (London, 1963).
102. Franks Report (1963) quoted in Wheatcroft, *Revolution*.
103. Sir J. Partridge, *What's Wrong with Business Education?* (London, 1970).

Index